IMAGES
of America

GROVELAND

Groveland, Florida ★ 1941

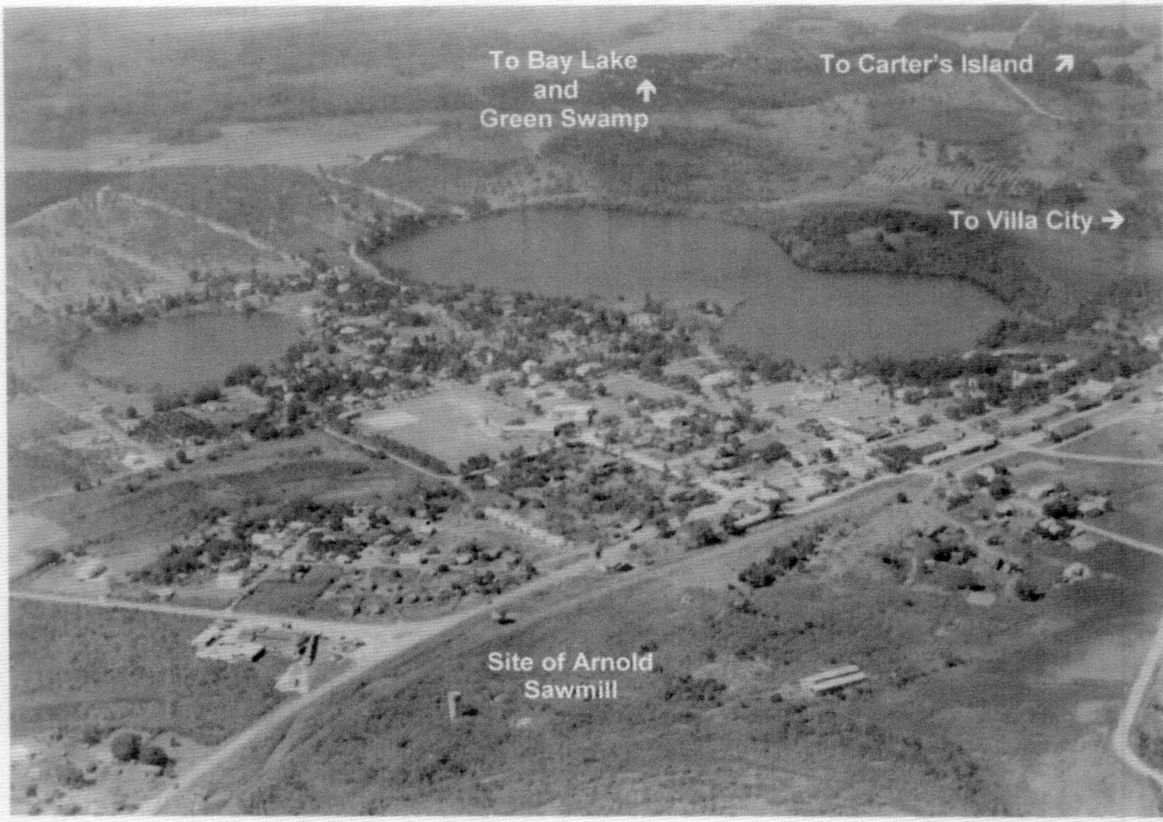

This 1941 aerial view shows the city of Groveland, 19 years after the community had officially changed its name from Taylorville to its present name and 16 years after a fire destroyed the Arnold Sawmill, the largest mill in the Southeast United States and the county's largest employer. (Courtesy of the Lake County Historical Society.)

ON THE COVER: Settlers of Carter's Island are shown in front of their family home in this c. 1890 photograph. From left to right are Joseph Carter, Ollie Carter, Bessie Carter, James Carter, Curtis Carter, father Stephen Carter, and mother Matilda Carter. At the rear is hired hand Pete Sheffield. Stephen Carter was a pioneer Lake County commissioner. (Courtesy of Cyleta Lee Austin.)

IMAGES
of America

GROVELAND

Doris Bloodsworth

ARCADIA
PUBLISHING

ISBN 978-0-7385-6751-8

Published by Arcadia Publishing
Charleston, South Carolina

Printed in the United States of America

Library of Congress Control Number: 2008943070

For all general information contact Arcadia Publishing at:
Telephone 843-853-2070
Fax 843-853-0044
E-mail sales@arcadiapublishing.com
For customer service and orders:
Toll-Free 1-888-313-2665

Visit us on the Internet at www.arcadiapublishing.com

To my family, schoolmates, and members of the Groveland Historical Society who inspire me to treasure our shared history.

Contents

ACKNOWLEDGMENTS

Like an heirloom quilt, the following pages stitch together a colorful portrait of a community shaped by hardworking, caring individuals, including those who unselfishly shared their photographs and memories for this book. Although it is impossible to tell Groveland's entire history in these few pages, it is the hope of the author and the Groveland Historical Society that these images, mined from hundreds of sources, will encourage people to start their own quests to learn more about the charmed place we call our hometown.

Special thanks go to those who shared their treasure trove of photographs and memorabilia or helped in other significant ways. They include Charlie Arnold, Mary Nell McFadden Arnold, Cyleta Lee Austin, Ric Baysinger, Cookie Stewart Beard, Jerry Beard, Teresa Begley, Rebecca Winn Best, Jeff Boswell, Dennis and Valerie Bronson, Shirley Cashwell, Carol Willard Clark, Carl Chambers, Linda Stephens Davis, Mike Dinkins, Debby Eisinger, June Fairchild, Connie Woolum Fleetwood, John Griffin, Kathryn "Kitty" Arnold Herzog, Jenifer Bloodsworth Hunt, Ward Hunt, Eloise Tomlinson Johns, Lindsay Keegan, Howard King, Kendall Koehne, Mandy McKinney, Gail Morris, Alison Mullany, Mary Helen Myers, Susan Pegram, Kristie Willard Ponsell, Herb Pilgrim, Ann Herzog Probst, Rev. Wallace Register, Austin "Red" Robbins, Charlie Rowe, Julian Rowe, Donald Richard Sloan, Peggy Parrish Sloan, Kemp and Marilyn Gammon Smith, Billy Speer, Jewell Murray Stansell, Emma Sullivan, Imogene Weir Tallant, Ellen Langenbach Thompson, Carol Murray Tomlinson, Dolores Gano Walker, Dale Watson, Jimmy Watson, and Rex Winn.

Also, I am grateful for access to the photograph archives of the City of Groveland, the Groveland Historical Museum, the Lake County Historical Society, the Marion Baysinger Memorial Library, the State Archives of Florida, the Tampa-Hillsborough Public Library, the Florida National Guard, the Oakland Raiders, and the Federal Bureau of Investigation.

And finally, there is a special appreciation for the support I received from my husband, John, my children, and my editors at Arcadia Publishing, Lindsay Harris and the production team.

INTRODUCTION

In the heart of Florida, halfway between the Atlantic Ocean and the Gulf of Mexico, lies the city of Groveland. Blessed with bass-filled lakes, bountiful pine forests, wild game, and a near-perfect climate, the land has long beckoned to settlers, including the Timacua tribe and Civil War veterans.

The Homesteading Act after the war drew several families from Georgia and South Carolina, including Daniel Sloan, a former Confederate soldier who was a farmer and preacher. Other early settlers included the Carter, Slone, Stewart, Tomlinson, Daniels, Duke, Brown, Lee, and King families.

In the late 1890s, brothers B. M. and C. C. Taylor started a turpentine still near the northern edge of Lake David. The brothers called the settlement Taylorville.

In 1899, Elliott "E. E." Edge from South Carolina bought the Taylors' turpentine still and home. Along with Edge came numerous African American workers and their families, including the Gadsens, Blues, and Harts.

Around 1907, Edge built a sawmill to salvage the pine timber that was ravaged by a severe drought. Five years later, he sold an interest to timber baron Robert Dowling. Dowling's son-in-law, J. Ray Arnold, took over the mill, renaming it the J. Ray Arnold Lumber Company in 1920.

A few miles north, George T. King and a group of wealthy Northerners founded Villa City, a lakeside community of upscale homes and exotic gardens that flourished until "the Great Freeze" of 1894–1895 turned the settlement into a virtual ghost town.

Meanwhile, farming, cattle ranching, and the business empires of Edge and Arnold thrived as the town became an important stop on the *Orange Blossom Special* rail line that connected Sanford to St. Petersburg.

In 1911, John W. Beach, from Rockford, Illinois, bought more than 30,000 acres from Edge and formed the Groveland Development Corporation. Beach aggressively promoted "Groveland Farms" to Northerners. "Lots purchased in this rapidly growing, progressive little city, will treble and quadruple in value in a short time," promised a Groveland Farms brochure.

In 1922, residents voted to change the city's name from Taylorville to Groveland during a meeting presided over by the town's first mayor, L. Day Edge, E. E. Edge's son.

The following year, the Edges built a large, brick department store that became the shopping destination for several counties. The expanding empire would grow to include a hardware store, gas station, feed store, heating oil company, and funeral home in addition to acres of citrus groves. To communicate with this vast enterprise, E. E. Edge created a telephone network that grew into Lake Telephone Company and eventually Florida Telephone Company.

Arnold, joined by his brothers Luther and Baker, grew the sawmill into a phenomenal success. At its peak, the mill stretched along the entire northern edge of the town. The mill ran nearly nonstop, employed about 500 workers, and had a payroll of $70,000 a month, making it the largest employer in Lake County.

Even in the heady boom era, not every enterprise succeeded. A perfume factory and silk plant failed. But the town's people and leadership were resilient.

L. Day Edge became a rising star in politics, representing Lake County as a state legislator for several terms, beginning in 1915. He became the youngest-ever state Speaker of the House and also served in the Florida Senate. Edge is sometimes referred to as the "Father of the Department of Transportation." He influenced the building of Highway 50 through the center of Groveland. After his political career, he spent the remainder of his life running the Edge businesses.

Women also played an active role in the town's history. In 1928, the Groveland Women's Club organized and started the city's first library.

On the evening of May 9, 1925, the city's fate changed overnight when the Arnold sawmill and lumber company burned to the ground. Flames shot into the air more than 100 feet and could be seen as far away as Leesburg, 20 miles away. Although the Arnolds spent millions rebuilding a state-of-the-art mill, it never fully recovered as the nation's economy slid into the Great Depression.

During the 1930s, Groveland's unemployment rate soared and two banks failed. Edge and Arnold issued their own currencies, nicknamed "babbitt" and "lumies" by the townspeople, who used the money at local stores.

Hopes rose when J. Ray Arnold drilled for oil a few miles south of town. Although the drillers found oil more than 6,000 feet below the surface, it was not in sufficient quantities to make the drilling worthwhile. Arnold lost a fortune in the process.

World War II and government work programs played important roles in the city's history. Many young Groveland High graduates served their country with distinction. The entire community waited anxiously for the return of Abner "Butch" Rowe Jr., who was held prisoner by the Japanese. Rowe's letters home ran on the front page of the *Groveland Graphic* newspaper published by A. W. Newett. The Works Progress Administration, or WPA, brought significant improvements, including a new high school, city auditorium, community building, and tennis courts.

Eventually citrus brought prosperity back to Groveland. The B and W Canning Plant, and groves laden with orange blossoms, made the air smell like sweet perfume.

The city's population grew, and so did the local high school's reputation, where Hall of Fame coach Shaw Buck led football and baseball teams to unparalleled victories while stressing the importance of character and sportsmanship. The 1957–1958 football team went undefeated. No opponent even scored that year.

Church pews filled, and a visionary man named Joe Fairchild established People's State Bank, bringing financial stability back to the town. Fairchild was active in church and civic groups and helped bring many improvements to Groveland, including residential mail delivery and streetlights.

There have been other notable people throughout the city's history, including Edmond Darrell Cashwell, a brilliant mathematician and physicist who was one of the team of scientists that created the atomic bomb; two professional athletes, Austin "Red" Robbins and Derrick Graham; and the Watson brothers—Dale Watson, who rose to the No. 2 position in the FBI during the September 11, 2001, attacks; and Brig. Gen. Jimmy Watson, who was over the Florida National Guard during its largest ever deployment to Iraq.

Today Groveland is the second-fastest growing city in Lake County. After catastrophic freezes in the late 1980s, the area no longer depends on citrus and has turned to other employment, such as a large distribution center, tree farms, and one of the country's biggest biodiesel facilities.

Groveland residents have seen many changes. But some things remain constant, such as the community's appreciation for history, neighbors who care about each other, and a fierce sense of community pride. At no time is this more evident than every March, when hundreds of Groveland High School alumni gather to renew friendships, and on the Fourth of July, when fireworks light up the sky over Lake David.

May this pictorial history touch the hearts and minds of those who read it.

One

Taylorville
Pioneers and Pine Trees
1860s–1911

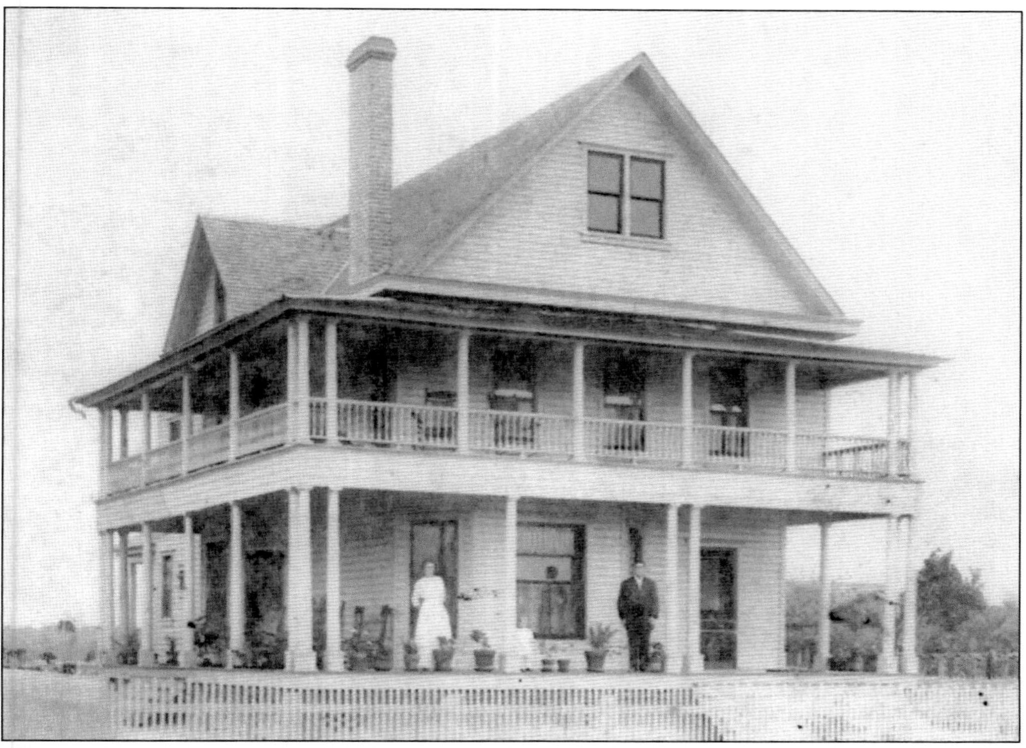

Elliott Erastus "E. E." Edge (right) and his wife, Cornelia, stand on the porch of their home built in 1902. The house, listed on the National Register of Historic Places, was built on Broad Street a block west of Highway 19. In 1988, the home was moved one mile west to make way for a restaurant. (Courtesy of Alison Mullany, Kendall Koehne, and the Winn family.)

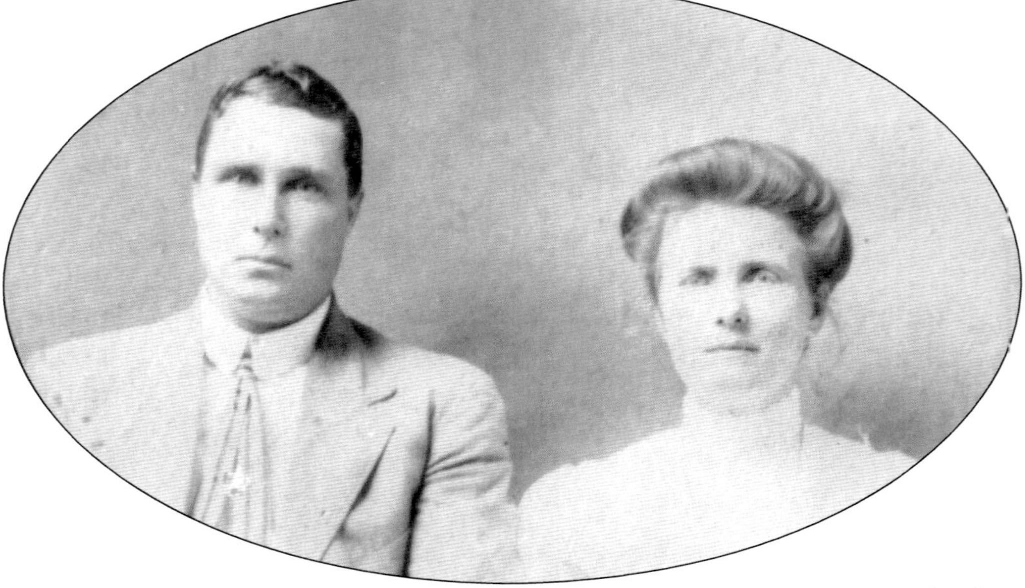

Elliott (left) and Cornelia Edge left North Carolina to run a naval store in Georgia for about 10 years. Around 1899, they moved to Taylorville and bought the home and turpentine business of the Taylor brothers, for whom the settlement that would later become Groveland was named. The Edges' nicknames were "Ras" and "Nelie." (Courtesy of Alison Mullany, Kendall Koehne, and the Winn family.)

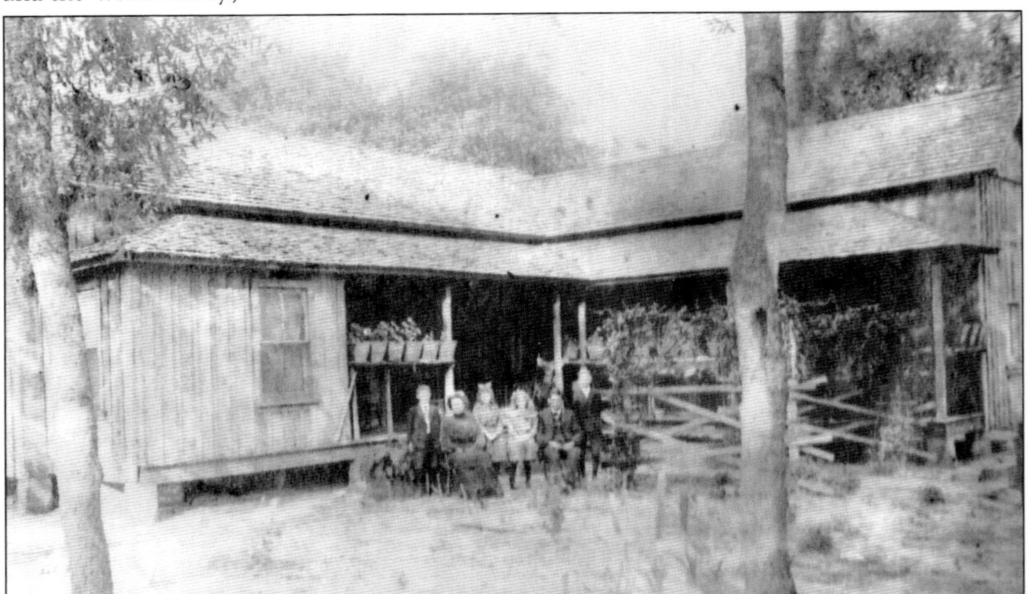

The pioneering Edge family is pictured shortly after they arrived in Taylorville. While father E. E. Edge, born in 1870, ran businesses that included turpentining, lumber, farming, a commissary, citrus, and the county's largest department store, his wife, Cornelia, took care of the couple's children. From left to right are Lacy Day, Cornelia, Bertha, Kate, Elliott, and Freddie, who died young. (Courtesy of Alison Mullany, Kendall Koehne, and the Winn family.)

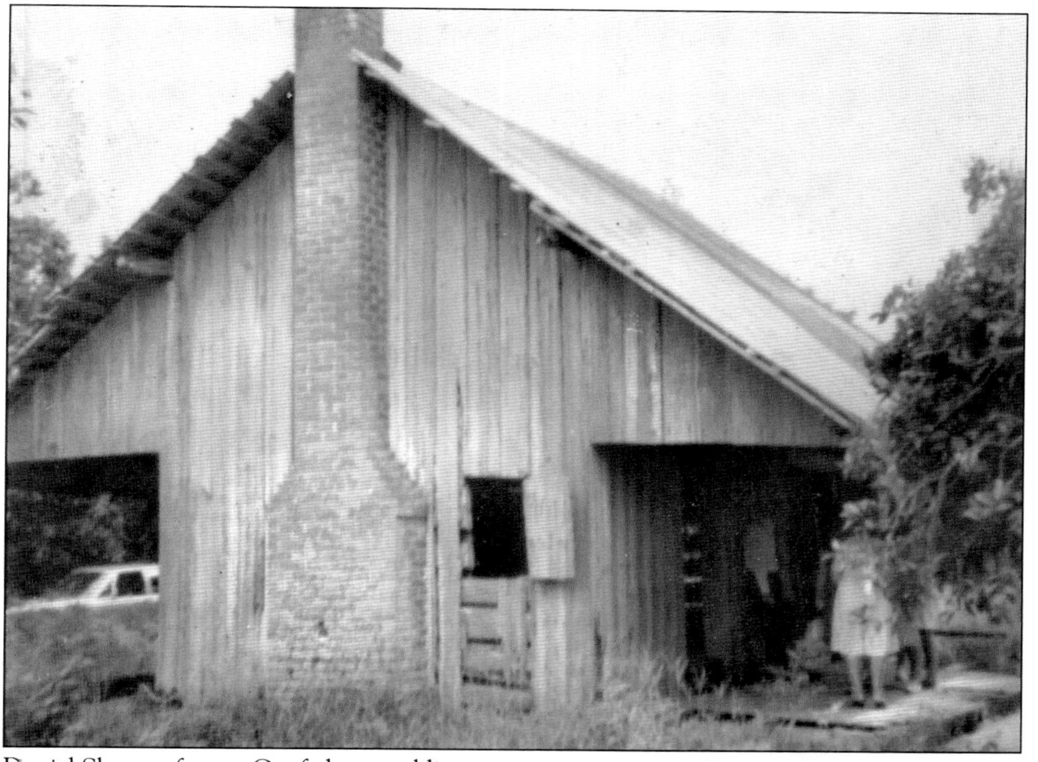

Daniel Sloan, a former Confederate soldier who was a farmer and Baptist preacher born in 1811 in North Carolina, built this log cabin on Edge's Island about 1866. Sloan, one of Groveland's first permanent white settlers, and his wife, Nancy, had 13 children. The Sloans lived here until their deaths. He died in 1888, and she died in 1914. The high ceiling of this log cabin, and the overhanging roof, helped keep the family cool. The fireplace kept them warm in the winters and was used for cooking the family meals, which likely included hominy, sweet potato pone, venison, turkey, and fish. Sloan, who is buried in nearby Dukes Cemetery, served in the Cow Cavalry, 1st Battalion Florida, of the Confederate army. A few years ago, descendants reassembled this cabin in nearby Pasco County. (Both courtesy of Jewell Sloan Stansell.)

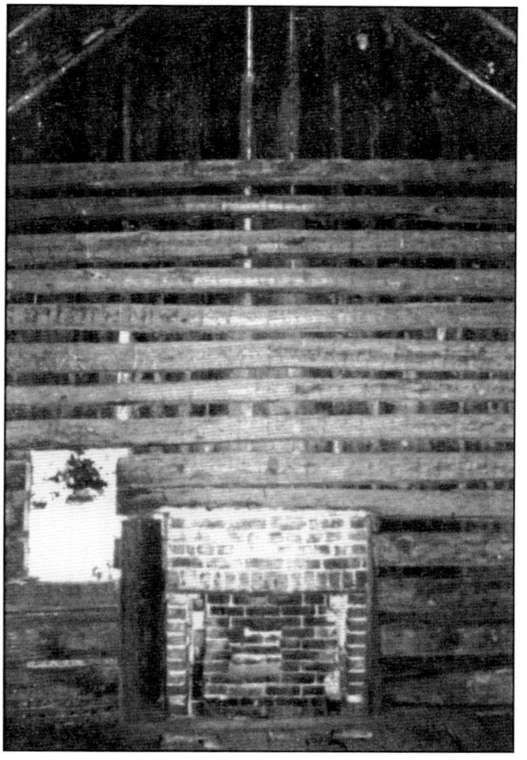

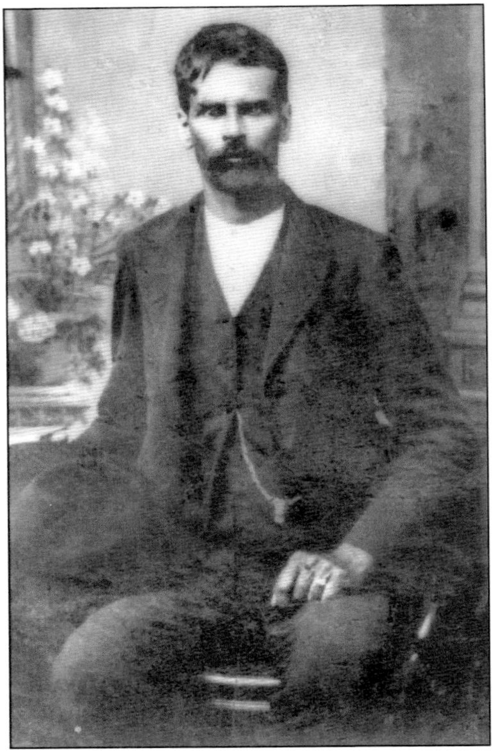

Simon Thomas Brown, born in 1845 in Columbia County, Florida, married his wife Polly in 1867. The couple settled in the early 1870s several miles north of Groveland at Indian House Lake near the present-day intersection of Highways 19 and 27. Later the couple and their eight children built a log cabin a short distance south near a place in the Palatlakaha River where it was shallow enough for wagons and livestock to cross. The pass became known as Brown's Ford. One of the area's first schools was built nearby and was named Brown's Ford School. Brown grew sugarcane among other crops. In 1886, he reportedly left after work one day without notice. Family members discovered some time later that he had married a woman named Sallie Cinderella Carpenter. He lived the rest of his life in Hardee County. The pass that still bears his name is a popular boat ramp and fishing destination. (Courtesy of Peggy Parrish Sloan.)

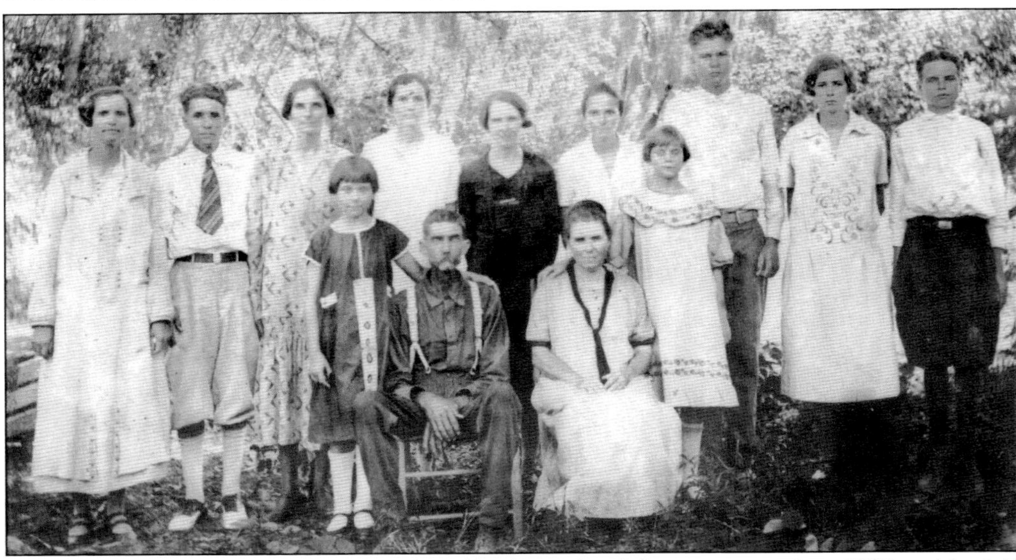

William Jesse Brown (seated left) and Mollie (seated right) were married in 1889 and had 12 children. The son of pioneer Simon Thomas Brown, William Jesse Brown was a farmer and grove owner. His son, also called Simon Brown, was a well-known Groveland barber for decades. From left to right are (first row) Doris Brown, William Jesse Brown, Mollie Brown, and Ovedia Brown; (second row) Lucy Brown, Delmar "Earl" Brown, Carrie Brown, Bertie Brown, Bessie Brown, Annie Mae Brown, Alfred Brown, Edna Brown, and Simon Brown. (Courtesy of Peggy Parrish Sloan.)

Lorem Brown, another son of Simon Thomas Brown's, was one of South Lake's most colorful pioneers. He was considered an experienced outdoorsman. Northern visitors hired him as a hunting guide. He is shown in this c. 1900 photograph after bagging two wild turkeys, which were plentiful in the Taylorville area and were a main source of food. (Courtesy of Peggy Parrish Sloan.)

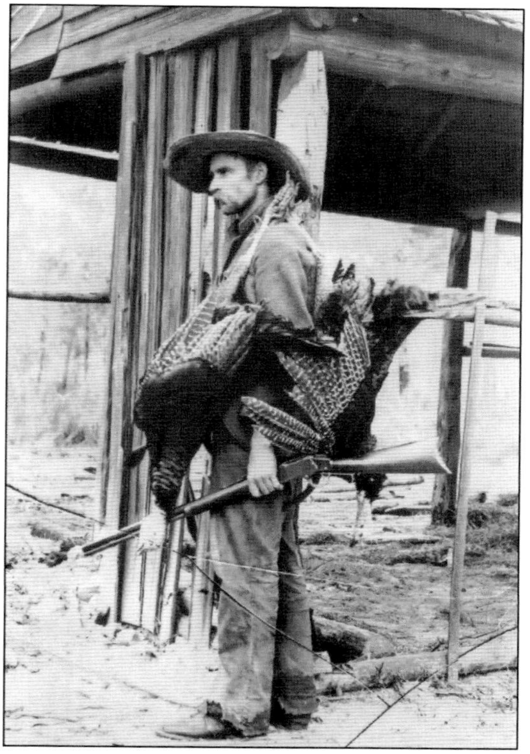

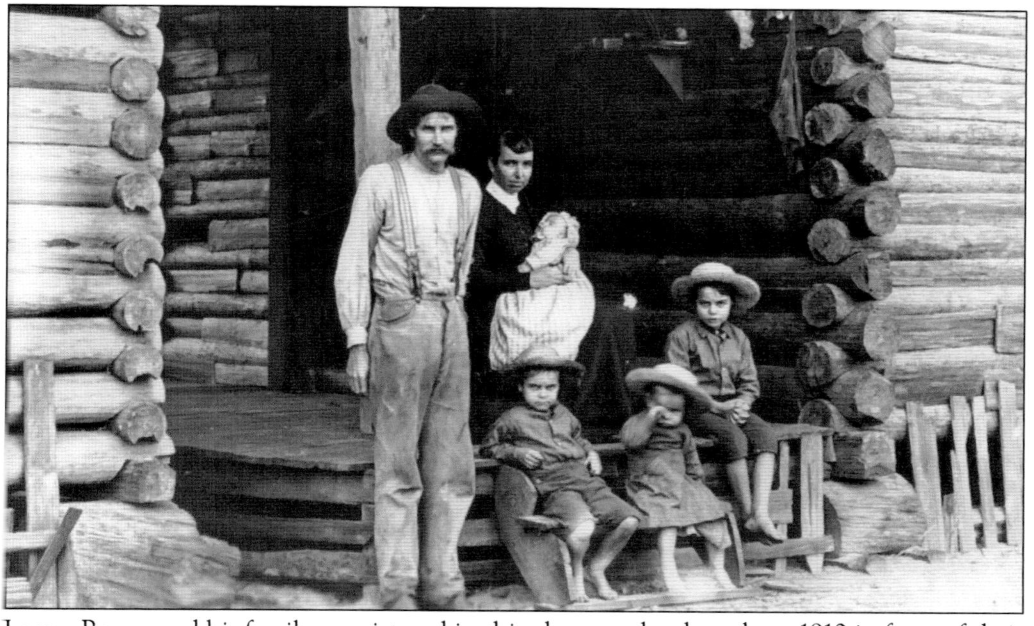

Lorem Brown and his family are pictured in this photograph taken about 1910 in front of their Green Swamp log cabin. Brown, an expert hunting guide, loved wilderness life. During Prohibition, he became known as the Moonshiner of Green Swamp. Brown (standing left) and his wife, Flora Parrish (seated right), are shown here with four of their seven children: Perry, E. K., Dewitte, Fanny, Emory, Arnold, and Mary Ellen. (Courtesy of Peggy Parrish Sloan.)

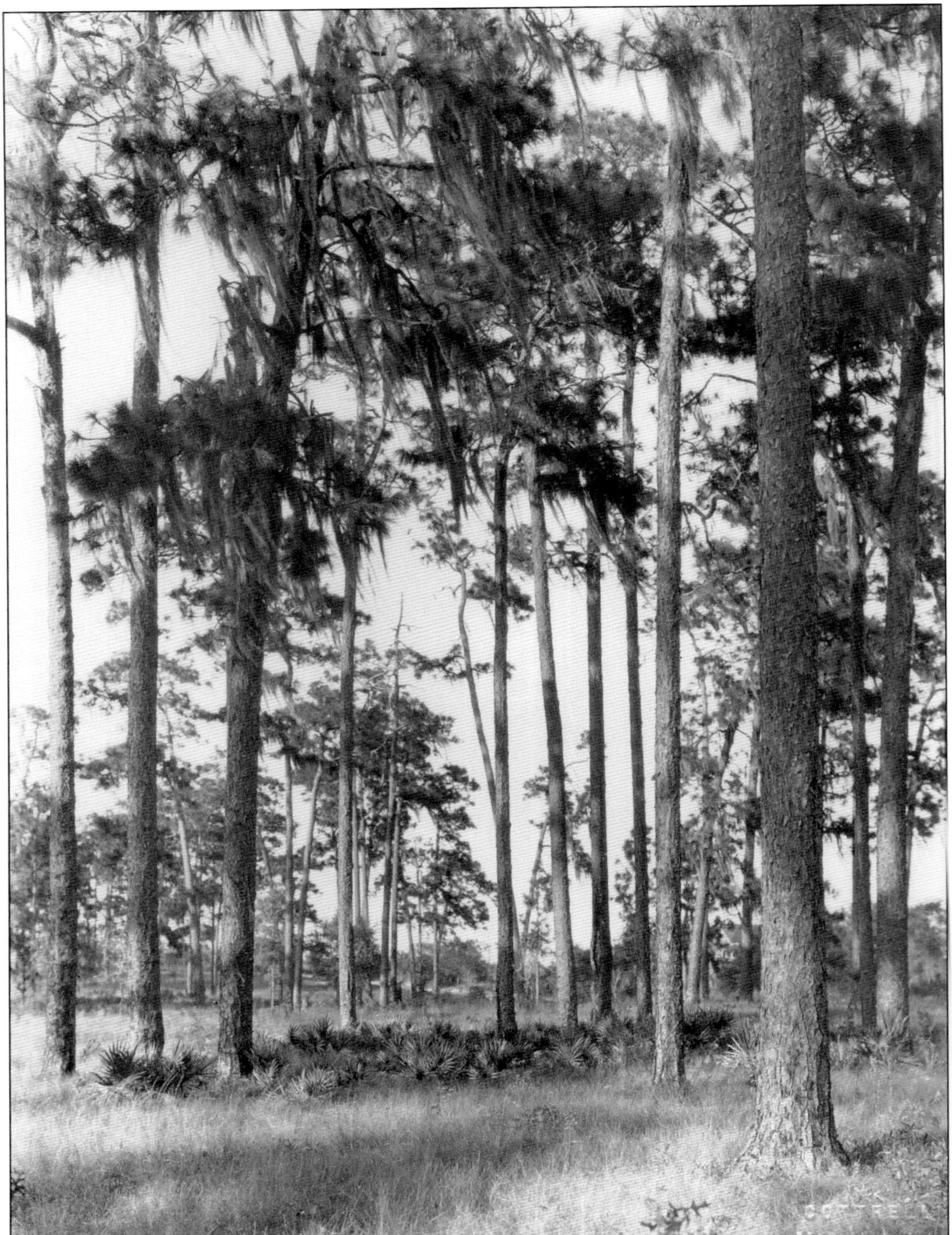

Early South Lake settlers were greeted by majestic, longleaf pine forests that had remained basically undisturbed for centuries. Longleaf pines take about 100 years to fully mature and can live to 300 years old. They reached heights of more than 100 feet with diameters of 47 inches. They were harvested first for their turpentine and later for lumber. (Courtesy of the Lake County Historical Society.)

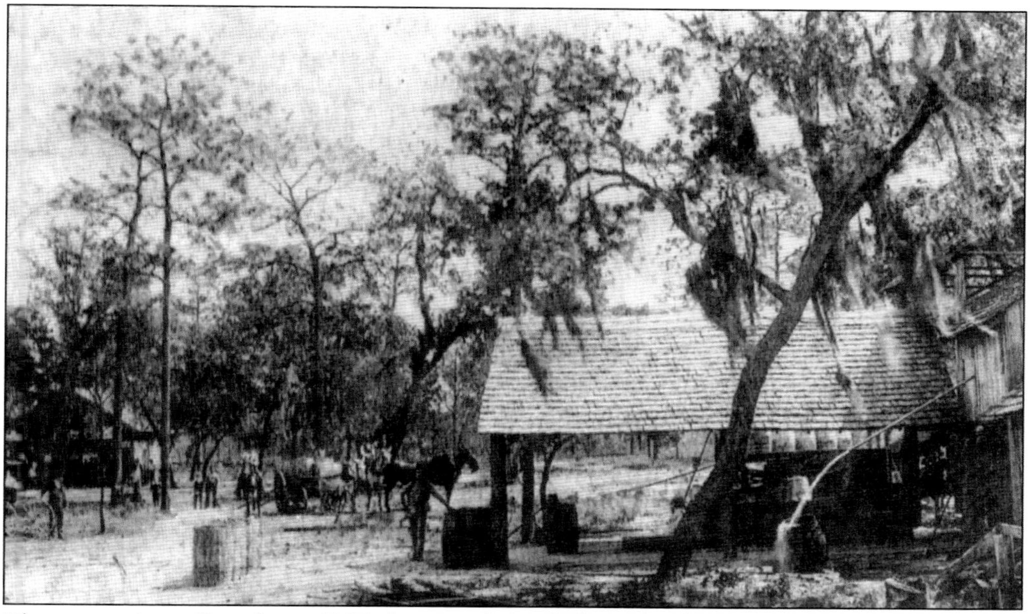

The turpentine still in this *c.* 1900 photograph first belonged to brothers C. C. and B. M. Taylor. The still, near present-day Broad Street, was sold to E. E. Edge, who built another beside Lake Emma in Villa City. Sap from longleaf pines was distilled to produce turpentine for paint thinning and varnishes. Edge brought workers from Georgia, including Albert Blue and Israel Gadsen. (Courtesy of Alison Mullany, Kendall Koehne, and the Winn family.)

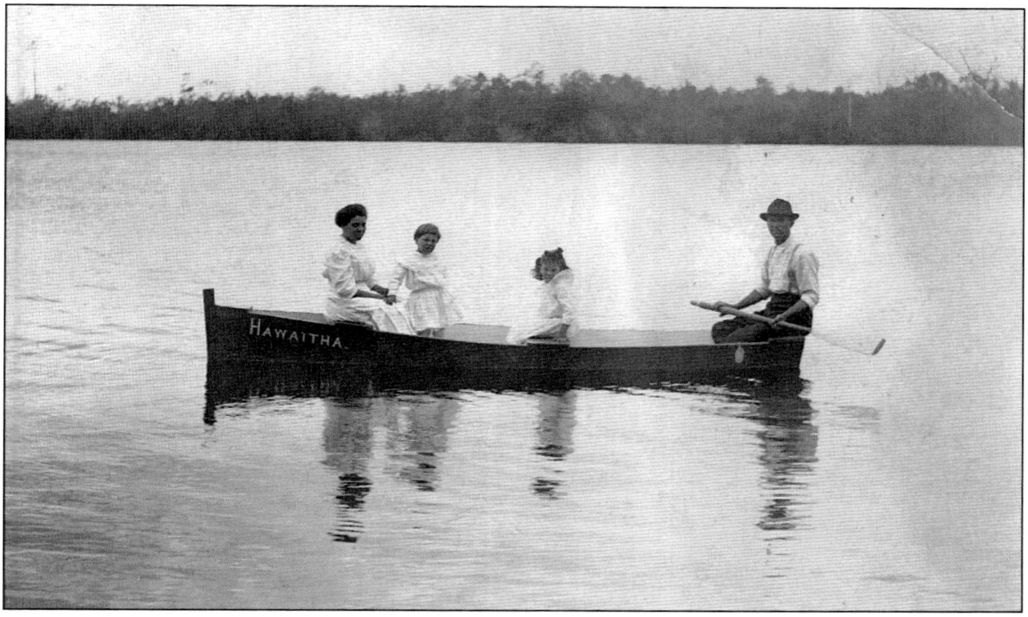

Settlers worked hard but also enjoyed spending leisure time fishing or boating. In this early-1900s photograph, the Pate family is enjoying a boat ride on tranquil Lake David, which was named for David Crum after he killed a large black bear near the shore. From left to right are Quinnie Watson Pate (mother), Gladys Pate, Eva Mae Pate, and James Allen Pate (father). (Courtesy of Imogene Weir Tallant.)

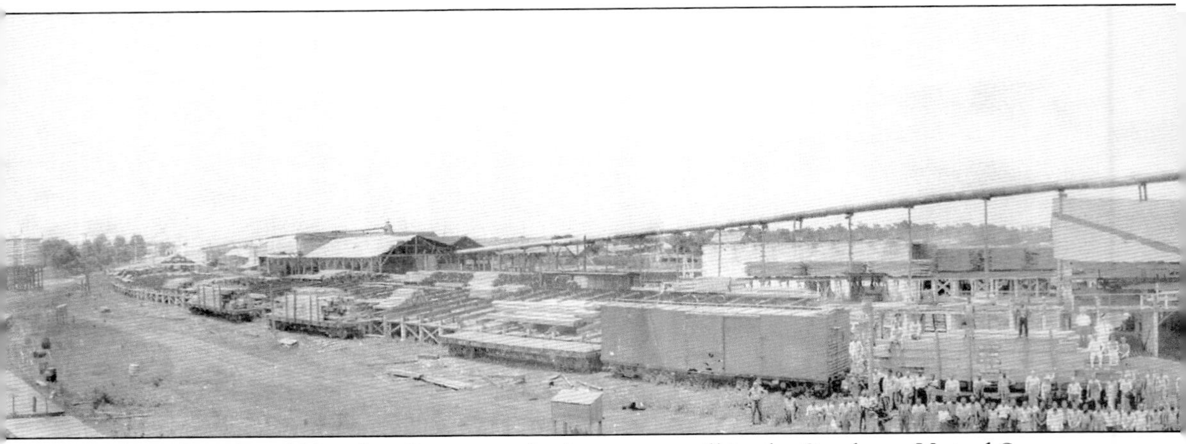

The J. Ray Arnold Lumber Company, the largest sawmill in the Southeast United States, gave Taylorville an international presence. The lumber mill originally was started by Elliott "E. E." Edge, who formed a partnership in 1908 with Robert Dowling from Live Oak, Florida. Arnold, a sawmill machinery salesman, married Dowling's daughter, Eva Lee Dowling. He bought out Edge's interest and renamed the mill in 1920. Arnold, along with his brothers Luther and Baker,

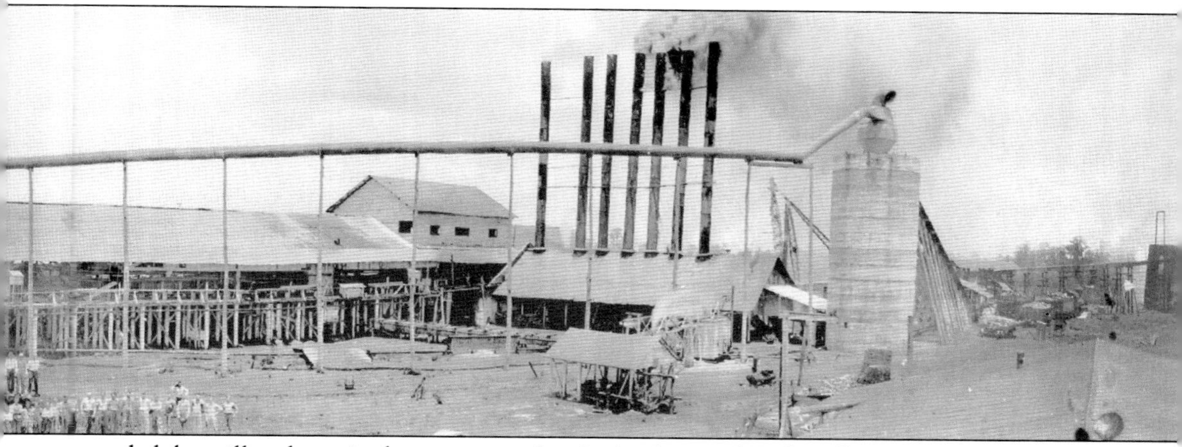

expanded the mill and acquired many acres of timberland around Taylorville and throughout the state. At its peak, the mill was the largest employer in the county, with more than 500 workers and a monthly payroll of $70,000. It ran two 10-hour shifts daily, producing 300,000 feet of highly sought after heart pine lumber that was shipped to 48 nations. (Courtesy of the Marion Baysinger Memorial Library.)

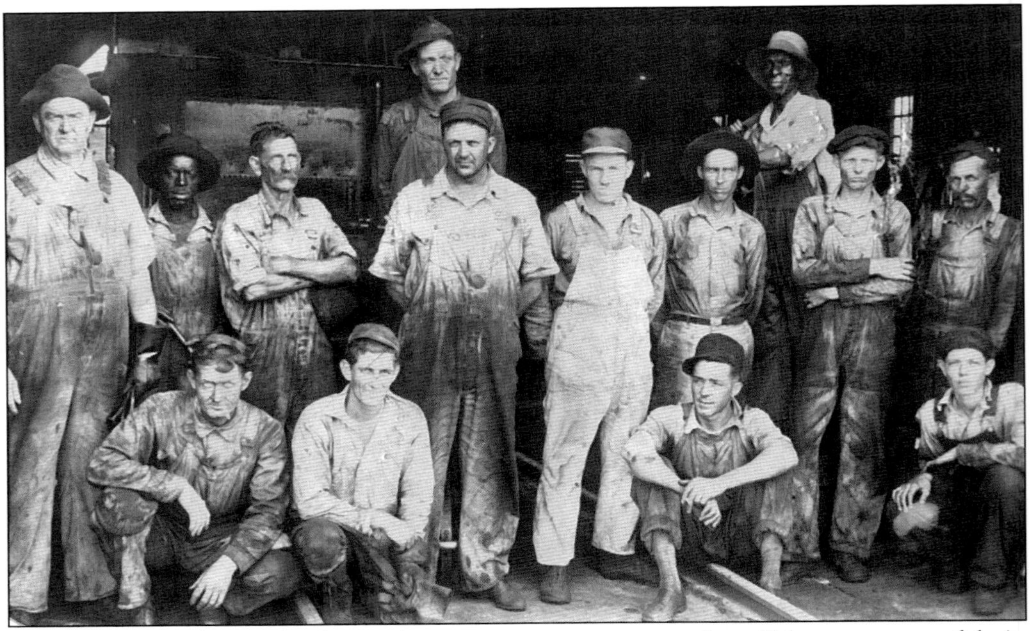

Taylorville started as a whistle-stop but grew in importance as the mill became successful. At the roadhouse, from left to right, are (first row) Bryant Tomlinson, Harley Rice, Ed Conley, and Claude Varn; (second row) O. H. Ingils, Harmon Johns, Ithiel Weir, Frank Williams, Clayton Weir, Louis Tomlinson, Wesley Rugerherford, and Spurgeon McDuffie; (third row) B. J. Williams and Sam Williams. (Courtesy of Imogene Weir Tallant.)

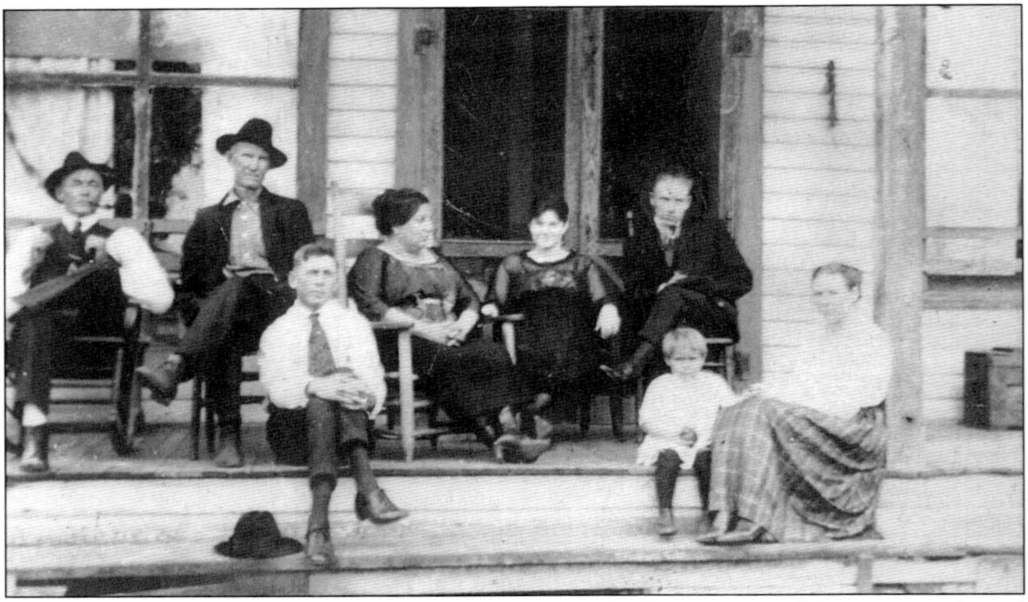

The Arnold brothers, who ran the sawmill, built this boardinghouse on Broad Street so members of their extended family and business visitors would have a place to stay. The boardinghouse, Arnold homes, and the mill were all within a block of each other. From left to right are unidentified, A. W. Cashwell, Atticus Carter, Quinnie Pate, Eva Mae Pate Weir, Clayton Weir, and two unidentified. (Courtesy of Imogene Weir Tallant.)

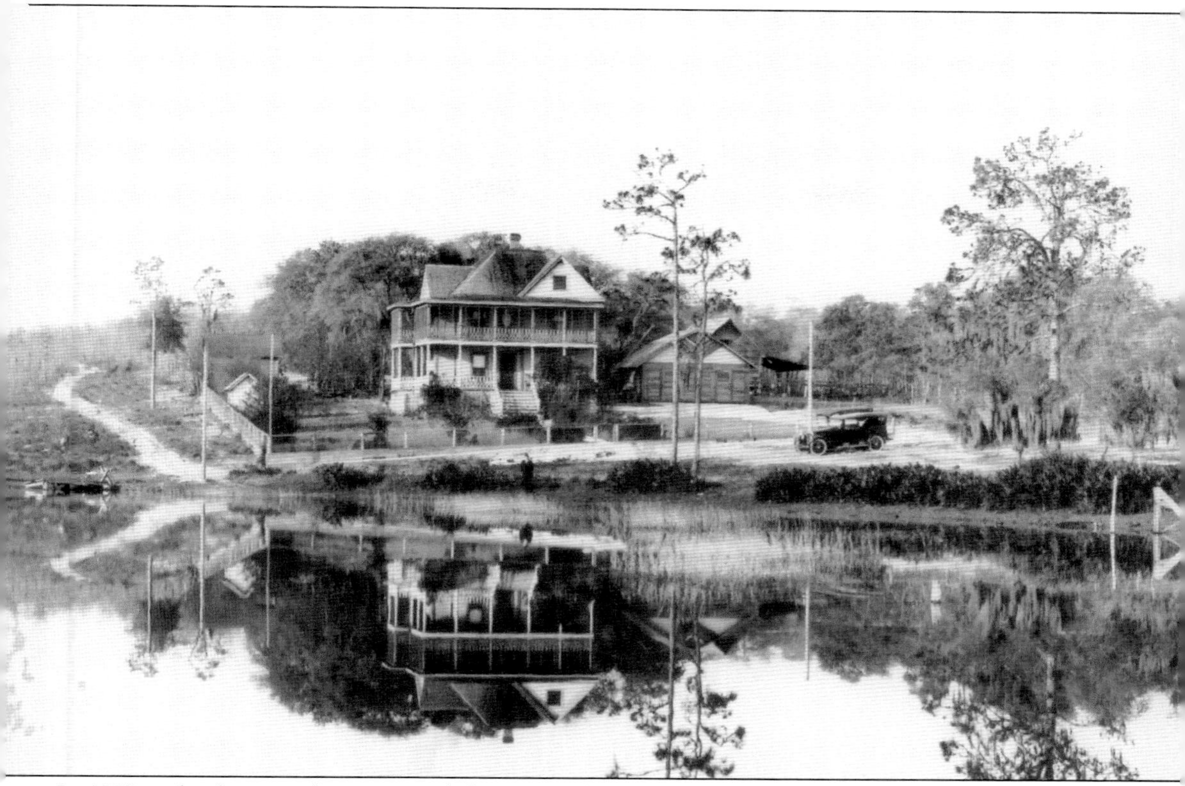

In 1910, a third major player entered the scene when John Washington Beach, from Rockford, Illinois, visited Taylorville and was impressed with the town's potential. He settled his family—wife Hattie, son Hubert, and daughters Audrey and Camille—in Tampa, while building this home that overlooks a lake he named after daughter Audrey. He bought 30,000 acres and had it platted. He enthusiastically promoted his "Groveland Farms" with glitzy brochures that touted an enviable lifestyle and money-making opportunities in Taylorville, population 500. He promised to pay the train fare of anyone who purchased land. Around 1912, the town became known as Groveland, although it would be 10 more years before it would be officially incorporated. Beach generously donated land to Groveland High School, the Edge Memorial United Methodist Church, and Lake David Park. The refurbished Beach home remains as a reminder of the city's boom era and Beach's vision. (Courtesy of the State Archives of Florida.)

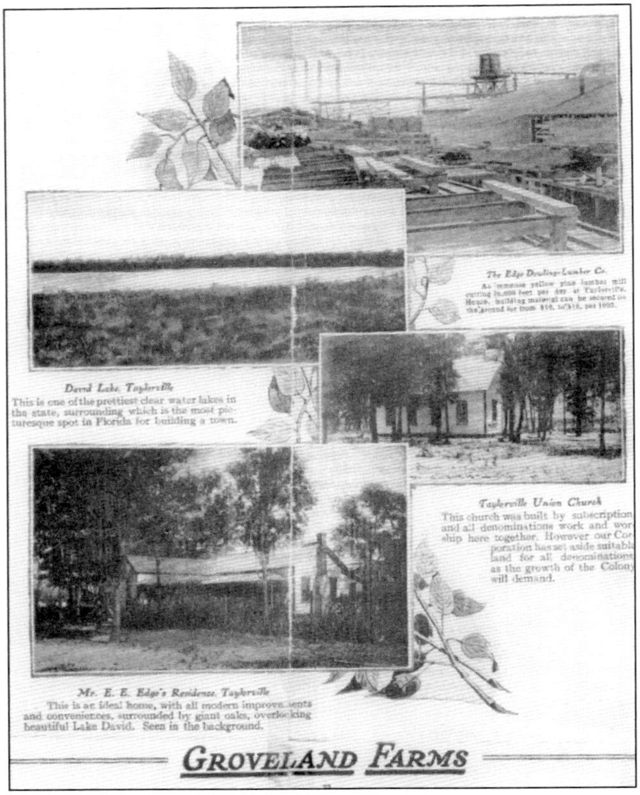

J. W. Beach's glowing picture of life in Taylorville lured many families to the town. He called his tracts of land Groveland Farms. The brochures painted an idyllic lifestyle, from "lakes teeming with fish" to crops that were "great profit producers." The brochures even noted Florida "has a lower death rate than any other state." (Courtesy of the Lake County Historical Society.)

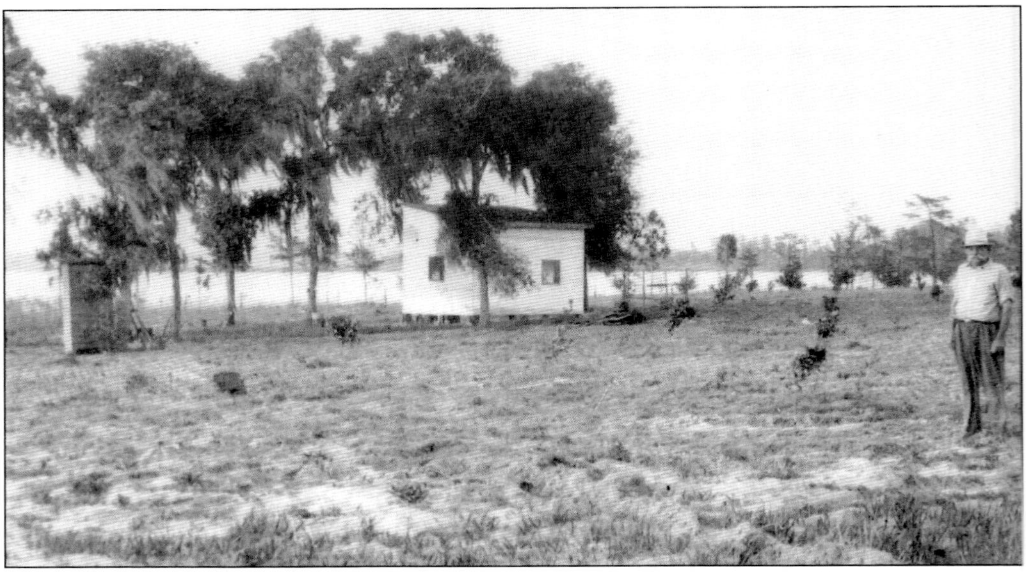

John Langenbach was one of the Northern settlers attracted to Taylorville. He arrived in 1911 from Terre Haute, Indiana, and started clearing land by hand. By 1916, when this photograph was taken, he had planted a small grove and built a shelter and outhouse. The property was on the corner of present-day Highway 33 and Boys Ranch Road on Pine Island Lake. (Courtesy of Ellen Langenbach Thompson.)

While Taylorville grew, so did surrounding pockets of smaller settlements. James Lee (left) and his wife, Lavina, pictured here in 1878, came from Berrien County, Georgia, three years earlier and homesteaded 160 acres in the Monte Vista Road area east of Taylorville. Their granddaughter is Cyleta Lee Austin, Groveland's historian emeritus. (Courtesy of Cyleta Lee Austin.)

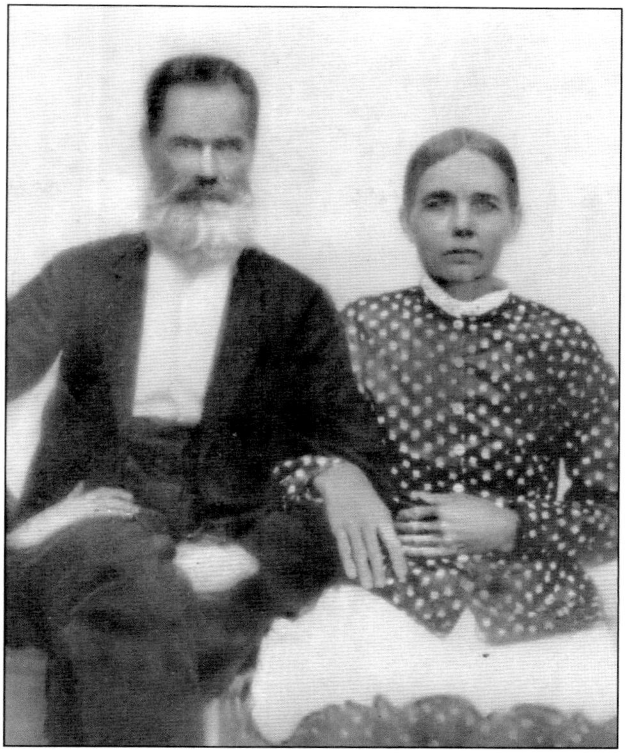

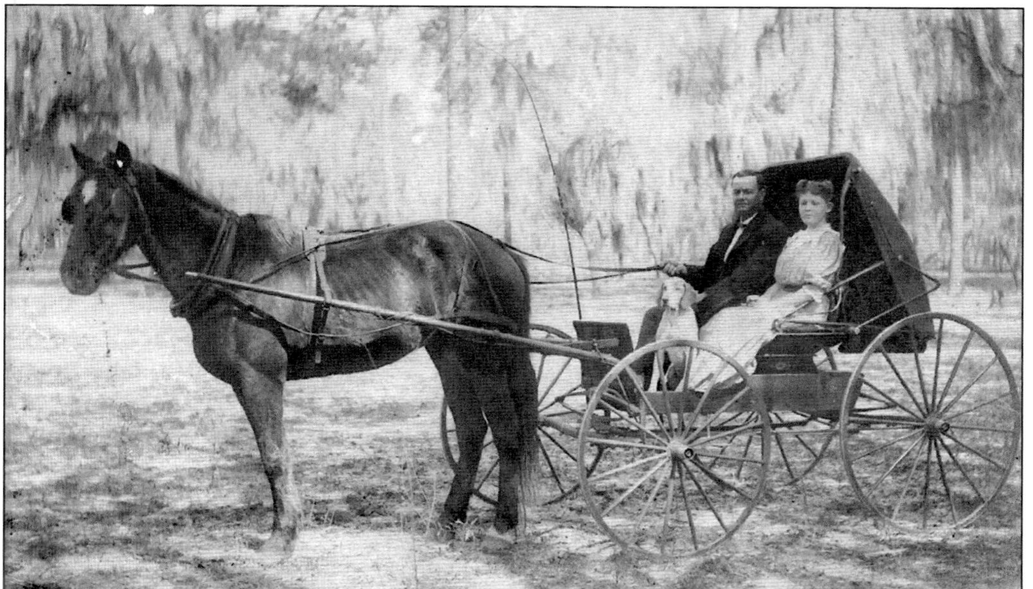

Joseph Lee (left) and his future wife, Bessie, are shown enjoying a buggy ride with his dog, Jack, in the early 1900s. After marrying in 1908, the couple lived in the Monte Vista area of east Taylorville. Once a month, Lee traveled to Leesburg to trade deer hides and sugarcane syrup for ammunition, coffee, flour, and salt. (Courtesy of Cyleta Lee Austin.)

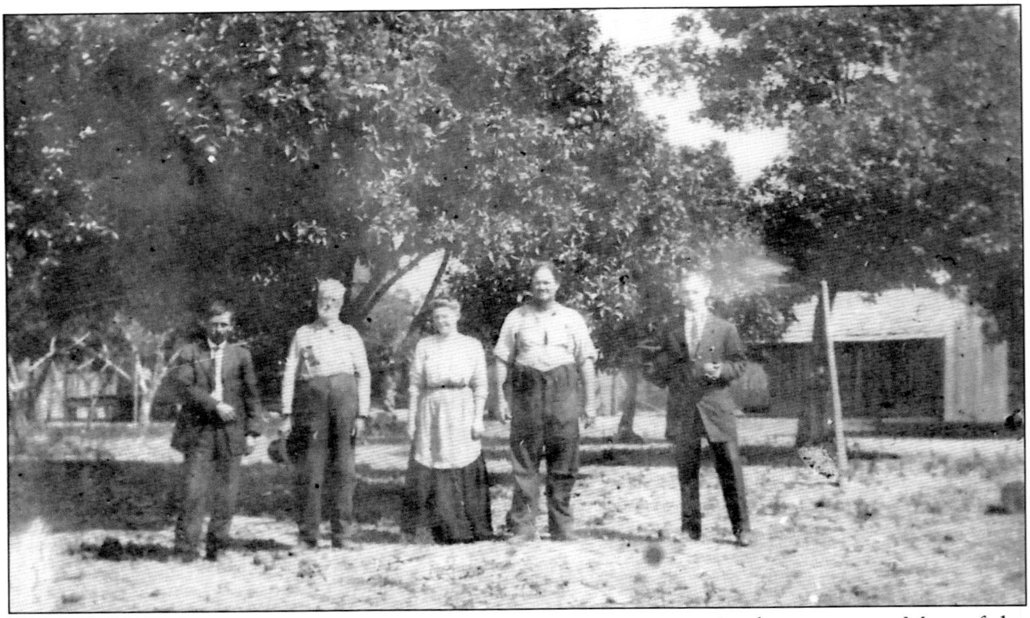

The Lee family is showing off their Monte Vista orange grove to Northern visitors. Most of the land in South Lake was once covered by longleaf or yellow pines. But after the trees were harvested for turpentine and lumber, farmers turned to citrus. From left to right are unidentified, James Lee, Bessie Lee, Joseph Lee, and unidentified. (Courtesy of Cyleta Lee Austin.)

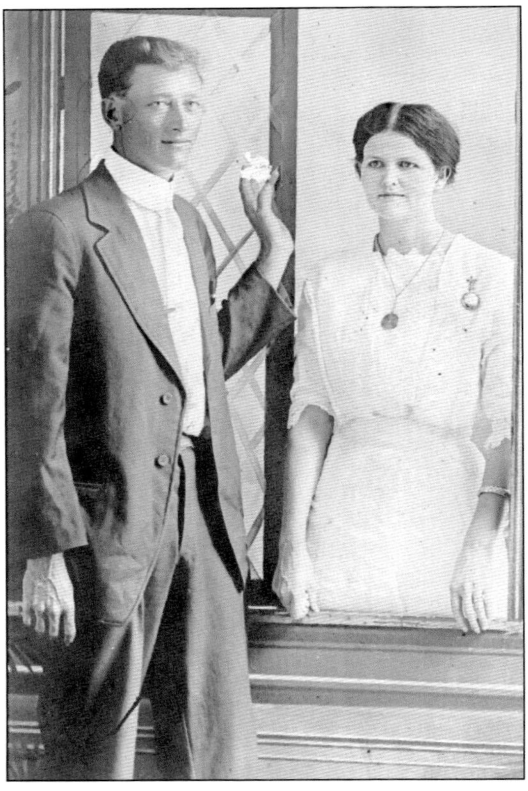

Dave Sloan, the grandson of Daniel Sloan, was born in 1892. He and Cornelia "Nelia" Bridges Sloan are pictured on their wedding day, August 20, 1919. The couple lived in Taylorville before moving to Slones Ridge, named after Confederate veteran William Slone. (Courtesy of Peggy Parrish Sloan.)

Dave Sloan (left) is pictured in his World War I uniform alongside an army buddy. After the war, he became a successful cattle rancher. He and his wife, Nelia, raised five children. He was the son of Gibson P. Sloan. (Courtesy of Peggy Parrish Sloan.)

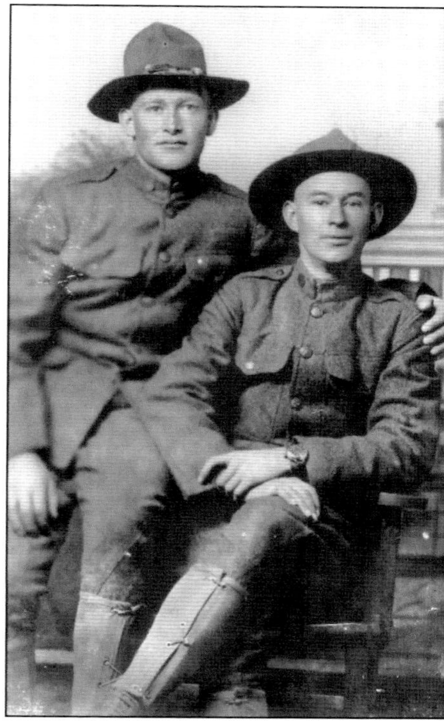

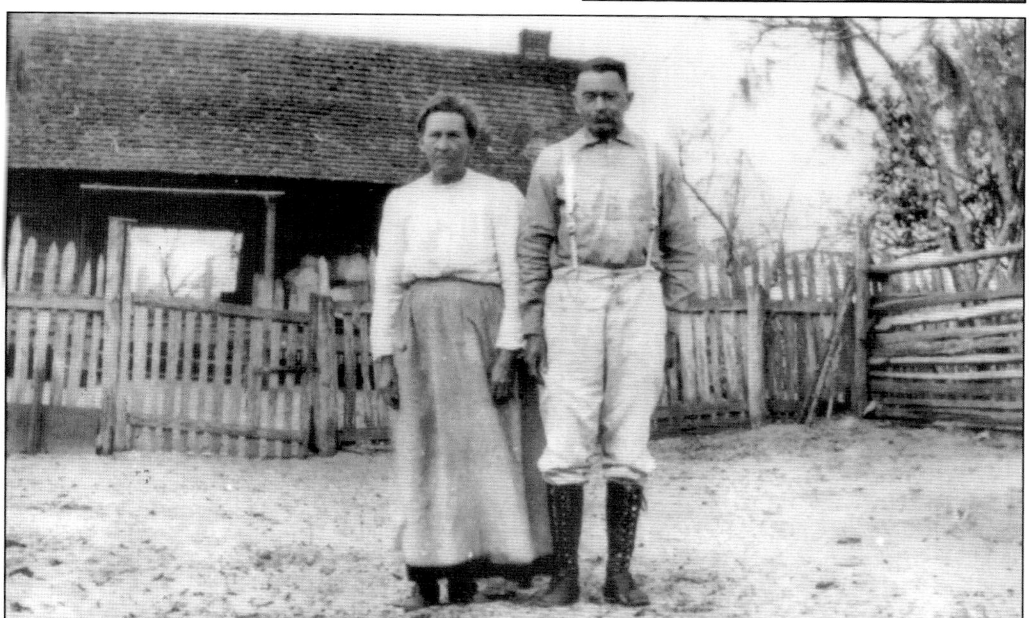

Serena Carlton Sloan (left) and her husband, Gibson P. Sloan, born in 1857, are shown at the Bay Root Richloam Management Reserve in front of their home. The couple had 10 children: Doshia, Phoebe, Mary Jane, Marion, Dave, Manuel, Elizabeth, Sarah, Aaron, and Perry. His father, Daniel Sloan, an early settler and Baptist minister, married the couple. (Courtesy of Carol Murray Tomlinson.)

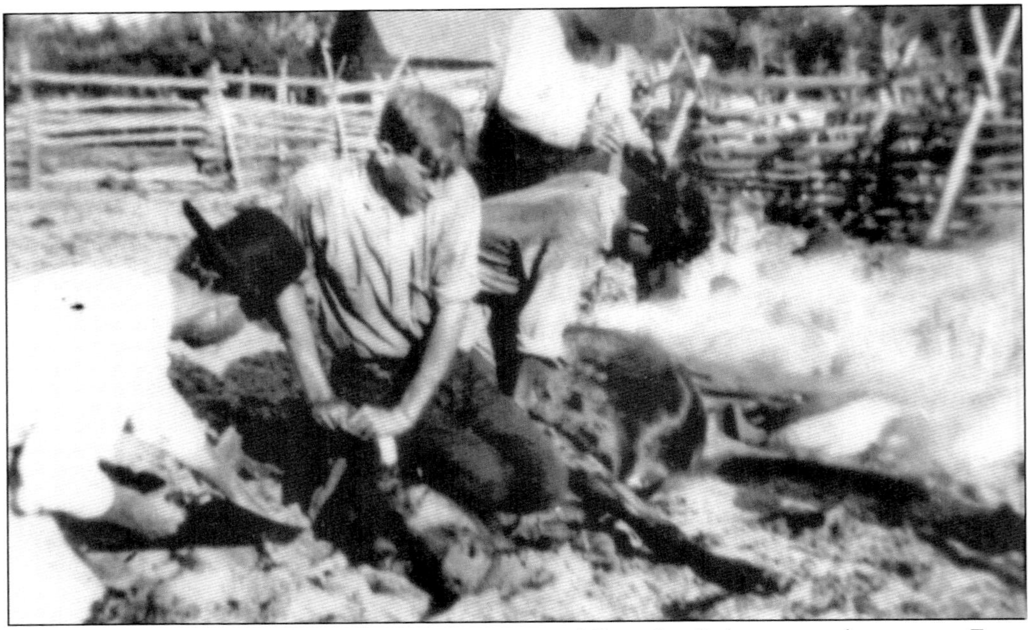

Cattle-ranching has long been an important part of Groveland's history and economy. From left to right are John Brady, overseer for the Bay Root turpentine distillery; Dave Sloan; Manuel Sloan; and Gibson Sloan (standing). The photograph, taken during the early 1900s, shows the men branding cattle and sawing off the animals' horns. John Brady is the man for whom Brady Trail is named. (Courtesy of Carol Murray Tomlinson.)

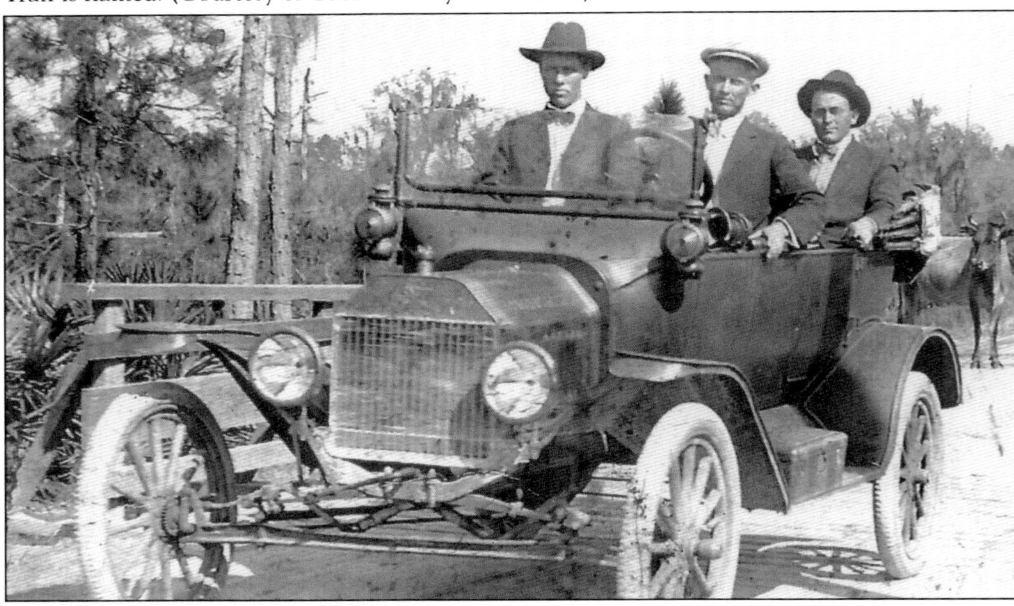

From left to right are front seat passenger Lucius Tomlinson, driver Virgil Tomlinson, and backseat passenger Marion Sloan taking a joyride in a Model T Ford as a cow in the road watches the Bay Lake men in this 1917 photograph. The roads were mostly sand or dirt covered with pine needles until county commissioners spent $500,000 to build clay roads around the area. (Courtesy of Cyleta Lee Austin.)

Wade Stewart (left), born in 1890, and his wife, Bertha Smoak Stewart, born in 1896, are pictured in front of an orange grove. The couple was married in 1914. Wade was the son Jasper "Jack" Franklin Stewart, born in 1871, of one of the first settlers in the Cherry Lake area north of Taylorville. (Courtesy of Cookie Stewart Beard.)

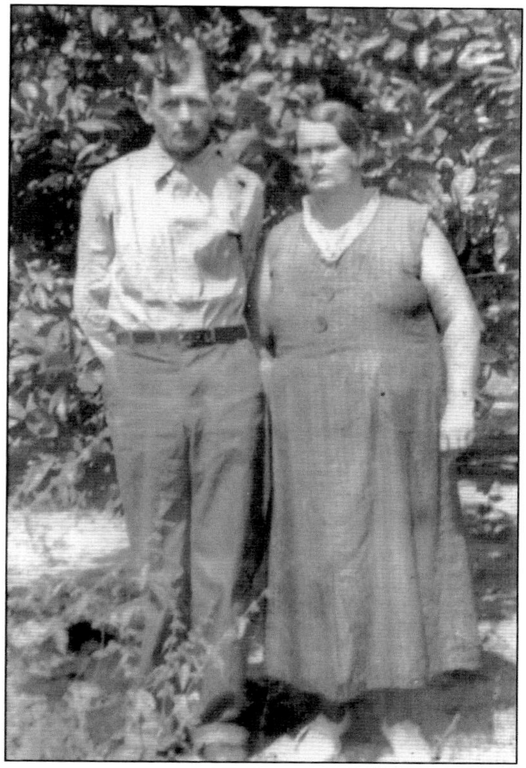

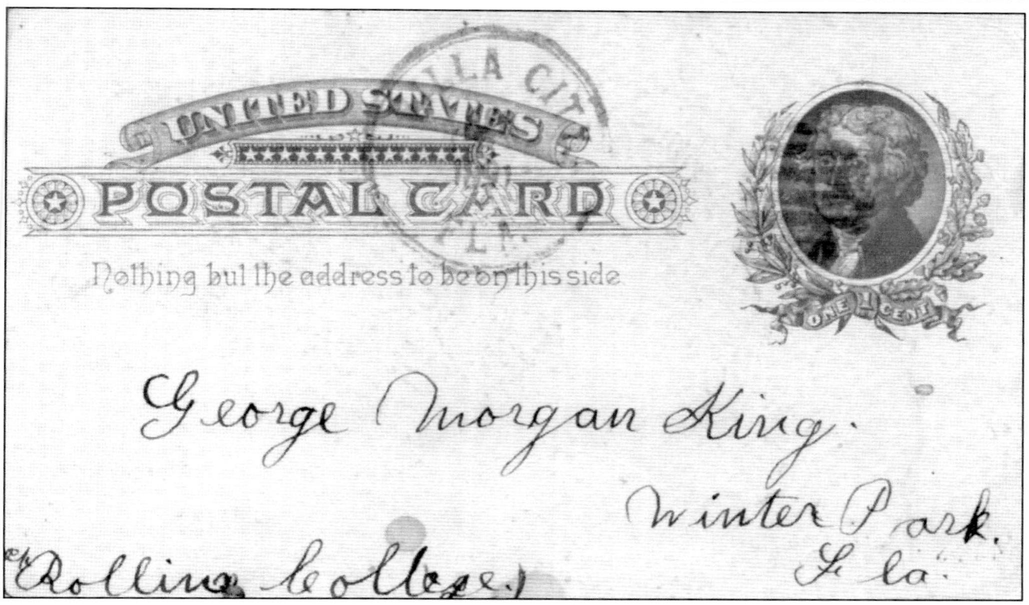

While Taylorville thrived, an almost magical community a few miles north, named Villa City, blossomed and then disappeared after a devastating freeze in February 1895, still referred to as the Great Freeze of 1894–1895. The city was founded by George T. King, a wealthy Baltimore salesman. Villa City once had its own post office, as evidenced by the postmark on this 1891 postcard. (Courtesy of Howard King.)

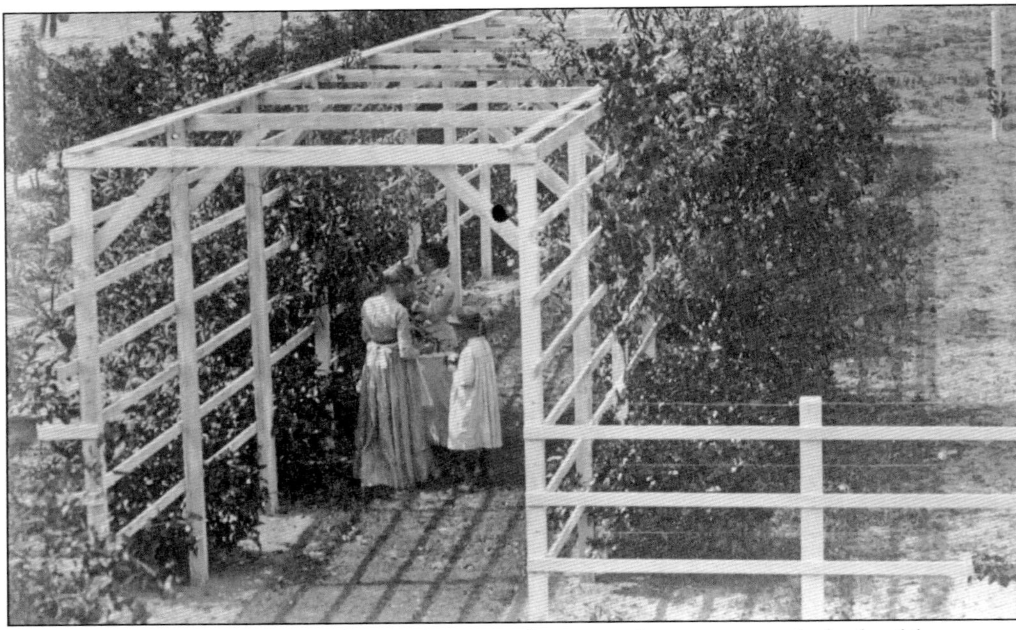

George T. King, a wealthy Colgate salesman who wanted to move south for health reasons, dreamed of a city of European-style villas, which gave the town its name. In November 1884, the King family left Baltimore for their grand home built on the shore of Lake Emma, named after his wife, Emma (center), seen in the 1886 photograph above with their daughter, Desire, and an unidentified woman. King was joined by relatives and other wealthy Northerners who built estates with pineapple-lined walkways and lavish gardens with oranges, strawberries, exotic flowers, and fountains. The city eventually included a hotel, church, store, photography studio, post office, and dozens of homes, such as Dr. John Hood's (below). A sudden, deep freeze in February 1895 wiped out the gardens and citrus. The families moved back north, leaving behind a ghost town. (Both courtesy of Howard King.)

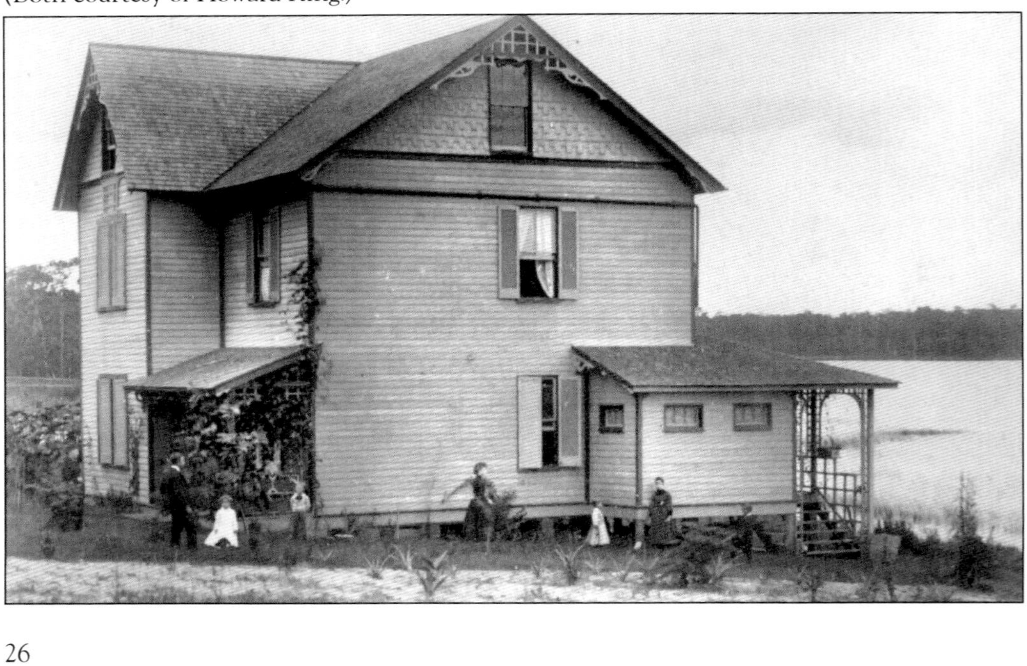

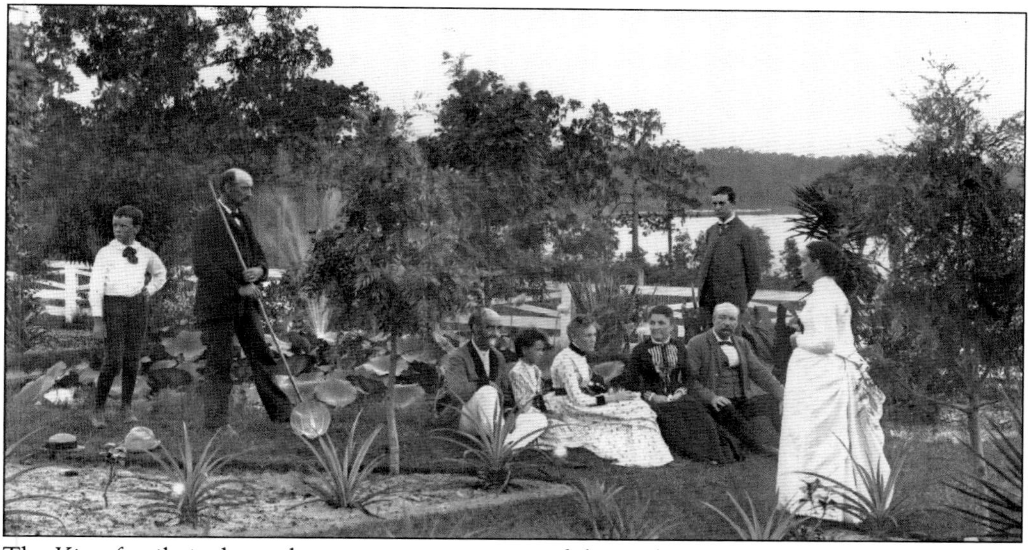

The King family is shown here entertaining some of their relatives and friends. The Villa City lifestyle was captured by photographer George Parlow, a famous Civil War photographer from Massachusetts and the brother-in-law of founder George King. From left to right are Morgan King, George King, Frank Parlow, Desire King, Ella Graham, Jennie King, William King, Arthur King (standing), and Emma King. (Courtesy of Howard King.)

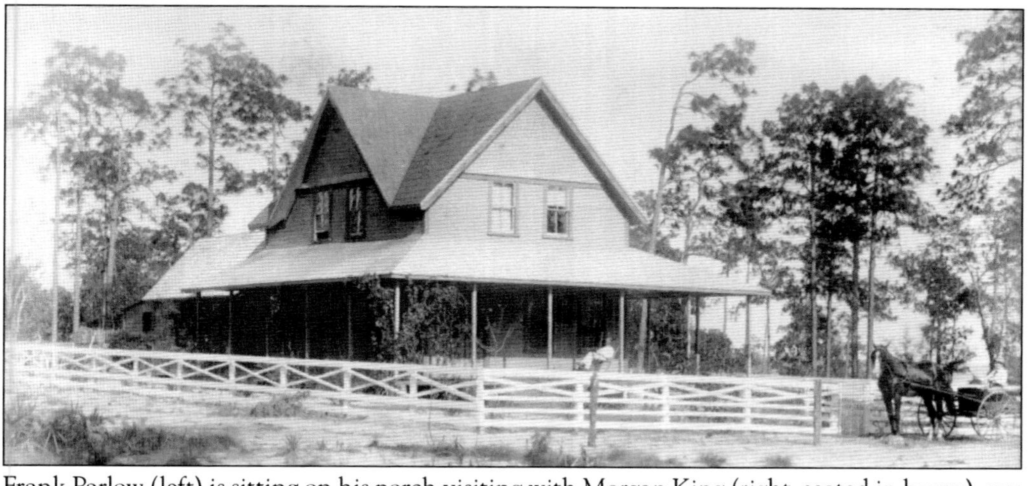

Frank Parlow (left) is sitting on his porch visiting with Morgan King (right, seated in buggy), son of Villa City founder George King, in this 1886 photograph. Parlow was the brother of George's wife, Emma, and renowned photographer George Parlow. Frank Parlow served as the town's postmaster. The post office was on the front porch. Lake Lucy was named after Frank Parlow's first wife, who died from illness. (Courtesy of Howard King.)

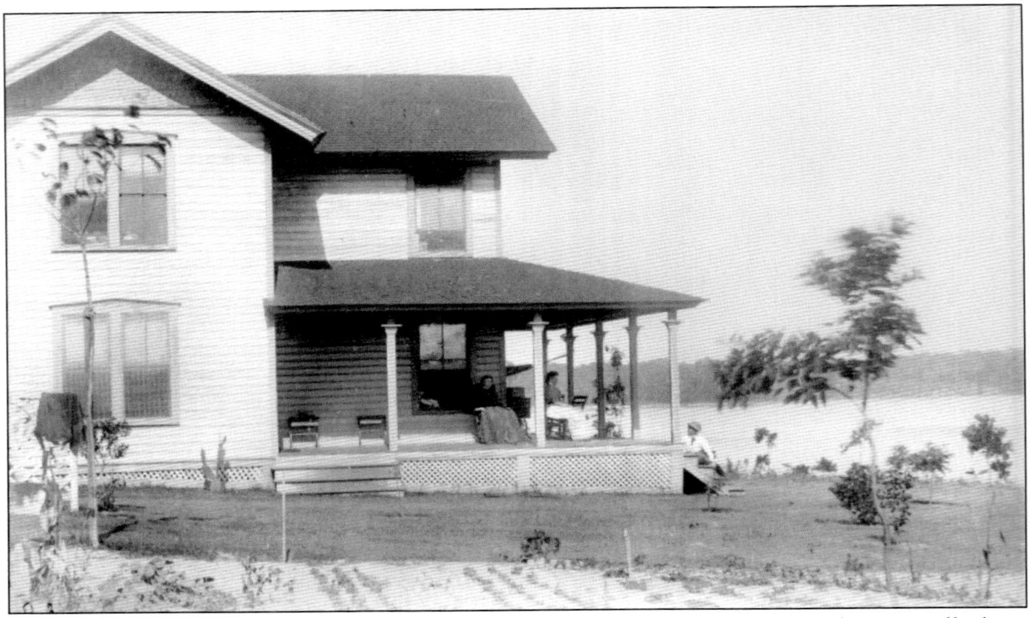

The Villa City lakeside home of Archibald Gano, owner of a sawmill and a popular gristmill where people ground corn, remained standing until about 1968. Gano came from New Jersey around 1878. He and his wife, Sallie, had 10 sons. Gano moved to Clermont after some angry neighbors reportedly blew up the dam that provided power to his mill. (Courtesy of Howard King.)

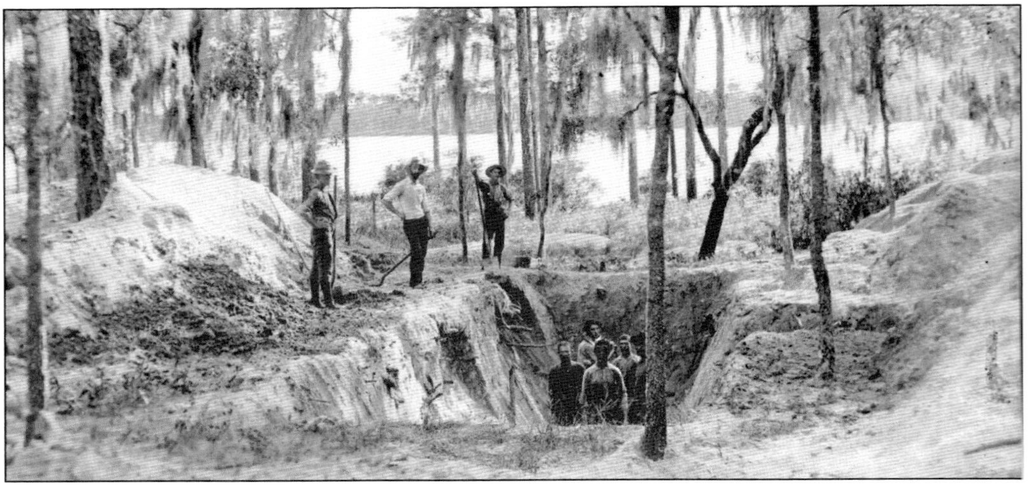

The spring-fed lakes, bountiful fish and game, and ideal climate attracted the Timacua Indians long before any white settlers arrived in south Lake County. Pictured here, William Hardy Boyd (third from left) and other unidentified early settlers dug up a mound to unearth artifacts that included fish bones, arrowheads, and pottery shards. Some tomahawks were made from Arkansas blackstone, suggesting the tribe traded with others. (Courtesy of Howard King.)

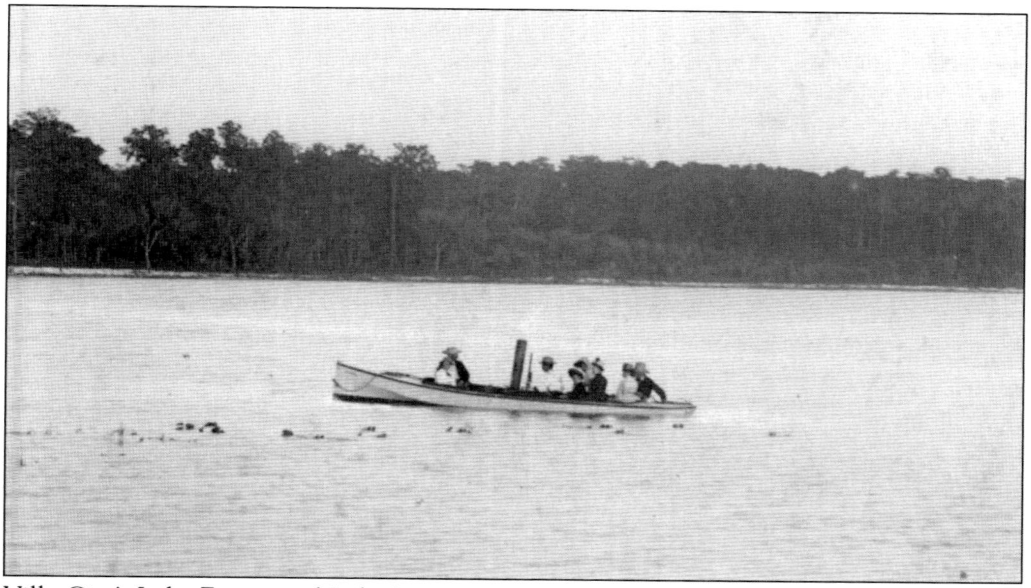

Villa City's Lake Emma and Lake Lucy connected to the Clermont chain of lakes via the Palatlakaha River. Steamboats connected the two settlements as residents traded goods. George King's sons, Arthur and Morgan, were in charge of maintaining the family's steamboat, pictured here with unidentified passengers. (Courtesy of Howard King.)

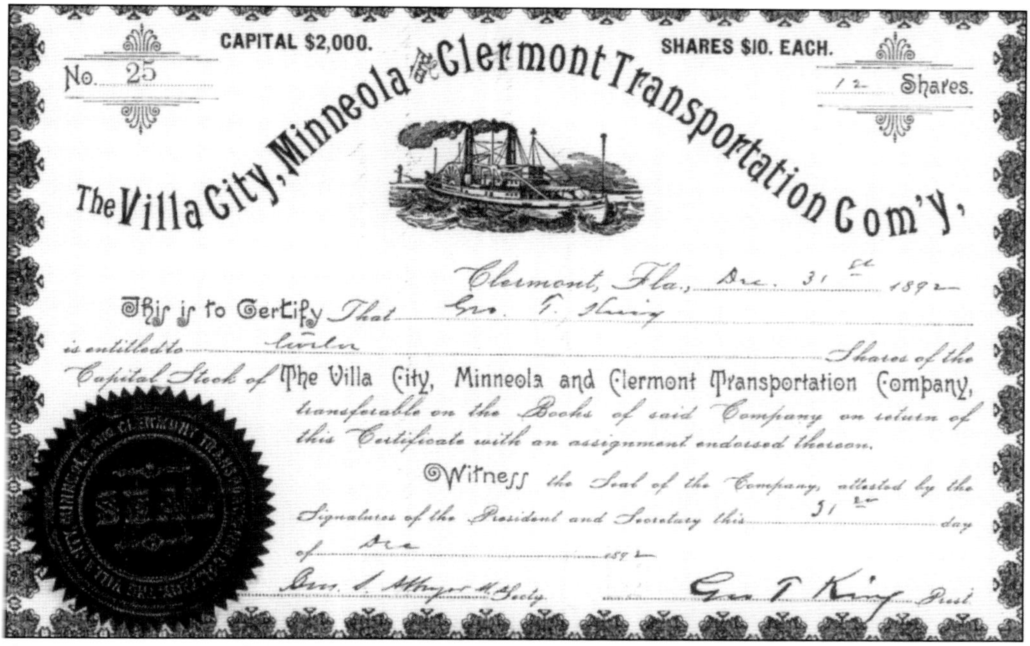

CAPITAL $2,000. SHARES $10. EACH.

No. 25 12 Shares.

The Villa City, Minneola and Clermont Transportation Com'y.

Clermont, Fla., Dec. 31st 1892

This is to Certify That Geo. T. King is entitled to twelve Shares of the Capital Stock of The Villa City, Minneola and Clermont Transportation Company, transferable on the Books of said Company on return of this Certificate with an assignment endorsed thereon.

Witness the Seal of the Company, attested by the Signatures of the President and Secretary this 31st day of Dec 1892

Secty Geo T King Prest

George King was one of the shareholders of the Villa City, Minneola, and Clermont Transportation Company. His 1892 stock certificate for 12 shares was worth $10 a share. Boaters once could travel from Villa City to the Atlantic Ocean through a chain of waterways that included Silver Springs and the St. Johns River. But a series of dams and locks now prevents such travel. (Courtesy of Howard King.)

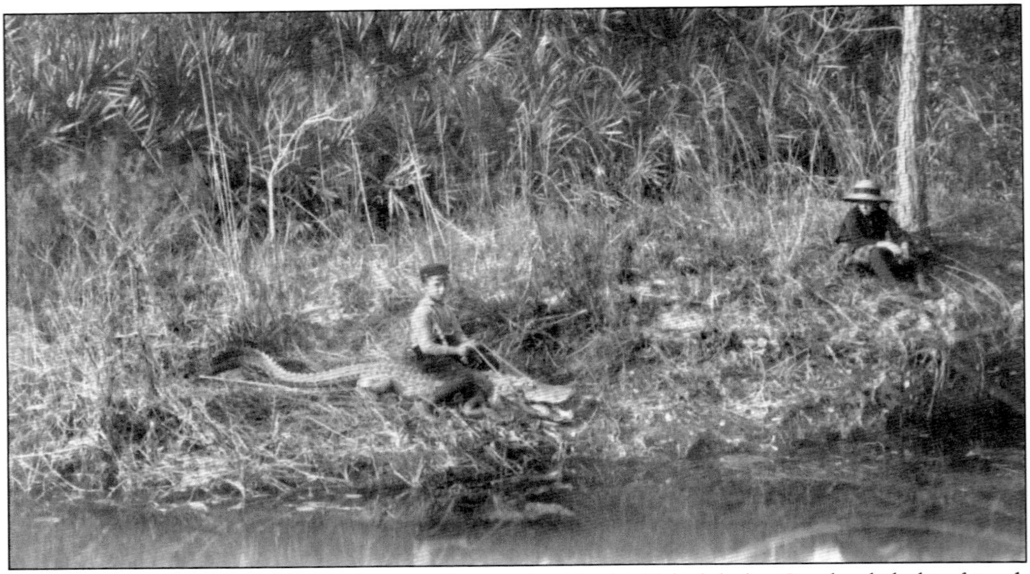

Harry Wilson (left) straddles a 10-foot alligator beside the Palatlakaha Creek while his friend, Desire King, watches in this 1888 photograph. A stick props open the mouth of the alligator that was killed earlier by adults. Visitors of the King family took an alligator with them on a trip home to Baltimore. (Courtesy of Howard King.)

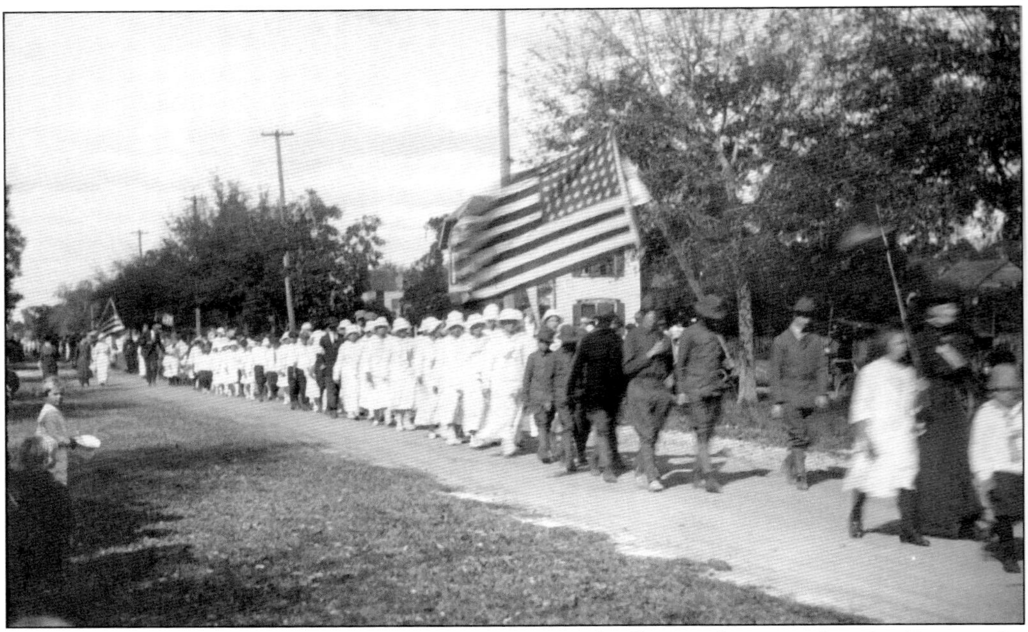

The Great Freeze of 1895 may have ended the dreams of Villa City for many decades. But nearby Taylorville was booming. In 1922, the town incorporated and officially changed its name to Groveland. Community pride was high, as shown in this early-20th-century photograph, when the city won first place in Tavares's George Washington Day Parade. (Courtesy of the Lake County Historical Society.)

Two

GROVELAND
BOOM ERA AND THE GREAT DEPRESSION 1912–1940

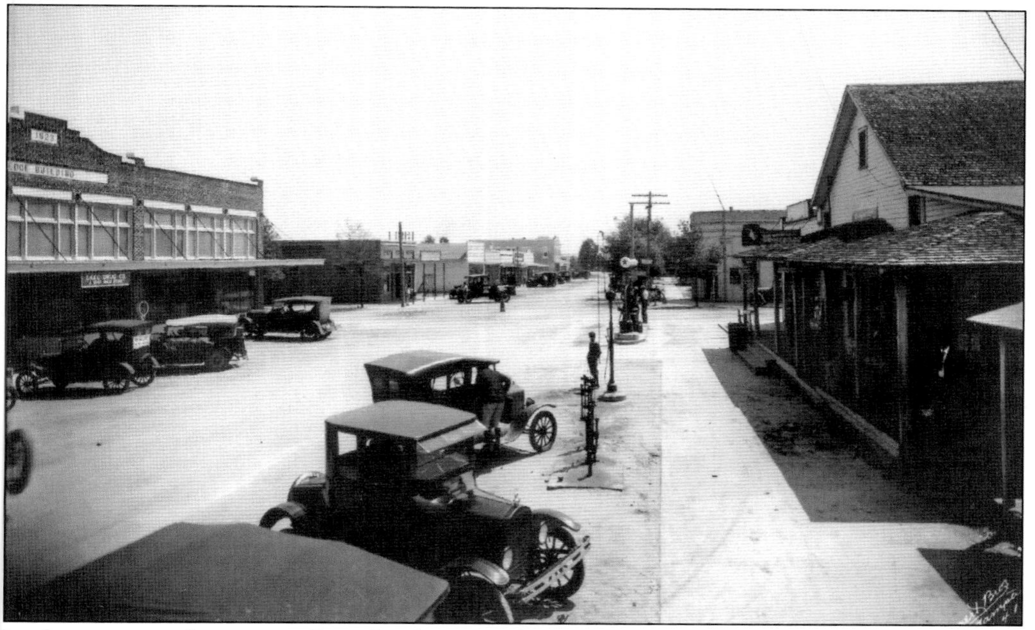

Looking east at downtown Groveland in March 1924, a photographer caught the town at its boom-era peak. The new Edge Mercantile store and Lake Drug Company (left) had opened the previous year; and in the background, the Arnold sawmill smokestacks reflect a company running around the clock producing record revenues. Taylorville was becoming a memory. Groveland was making a name for itself as the home of the largest sawmill in the Southeast and home to the youngest Florida Speaker of the House. There was a new school and gymnasium on Cherry Street. These were heady days, and it was all recorded in the town's newspaper, the *Groveland Graphic*, published at its new press pictured on the left side of the street in the center of this photograph, between the two largest businesses in town. (Courtesy of the Tampa-Hillsborough County Public Library System.)

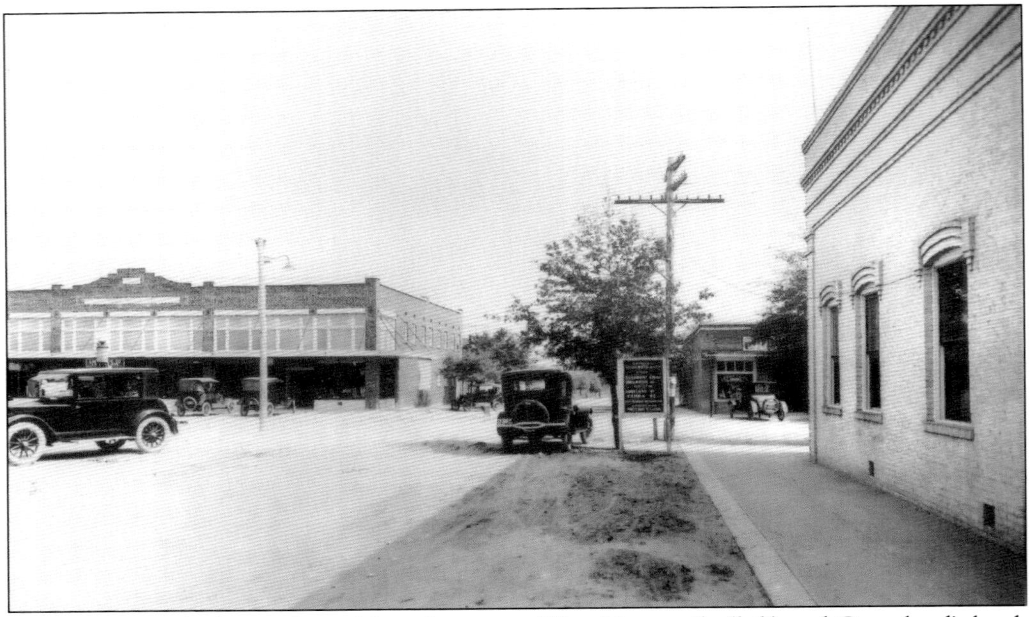

This 1924 view looks north on Main Avenue at Edge Mercantile (left) and Groveland's bank (right), along the heart of Groveland's business district. The photograph was taken by Burgert Brothers, renowned commercial photographers from Tampa who chronicled Florida living from 1899 to 1963. Their photographs appeared in *Life* and *National Geographic* magazines. (Courtesy of the Tampa-Hillsborough County Public Library System.)

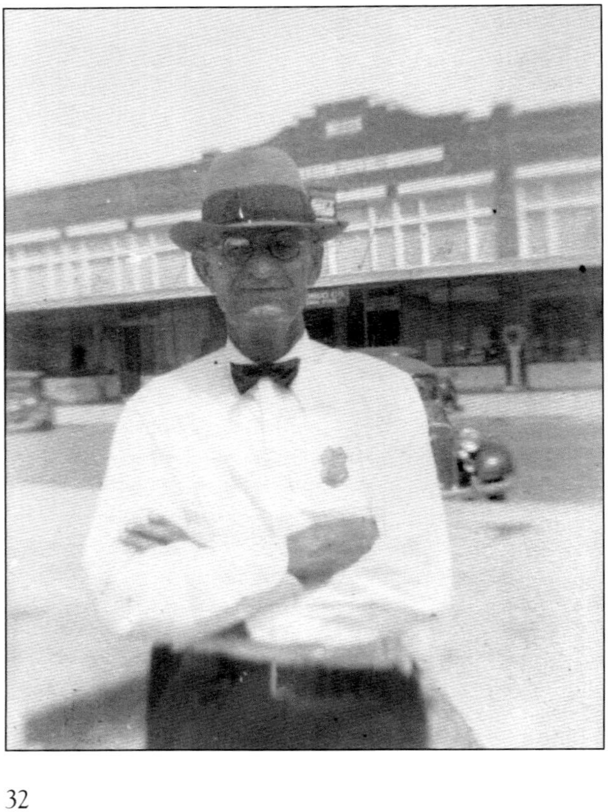

One of Groveland's first law officers was town marshal George Myers, pictured here in front of Edge Mercantile around 1928. Myers once served as a federal marshal in the Wild West, where he won a horsehair bridle from legendary Apache warrior Geronimo in a horse race. Myers did not carry a gun while on duty as town marshal, preferring a club instead. He and his wife, Susan Myers, ran the Groveland Hotel. (Courtesy of Dolores Gano Walker.)

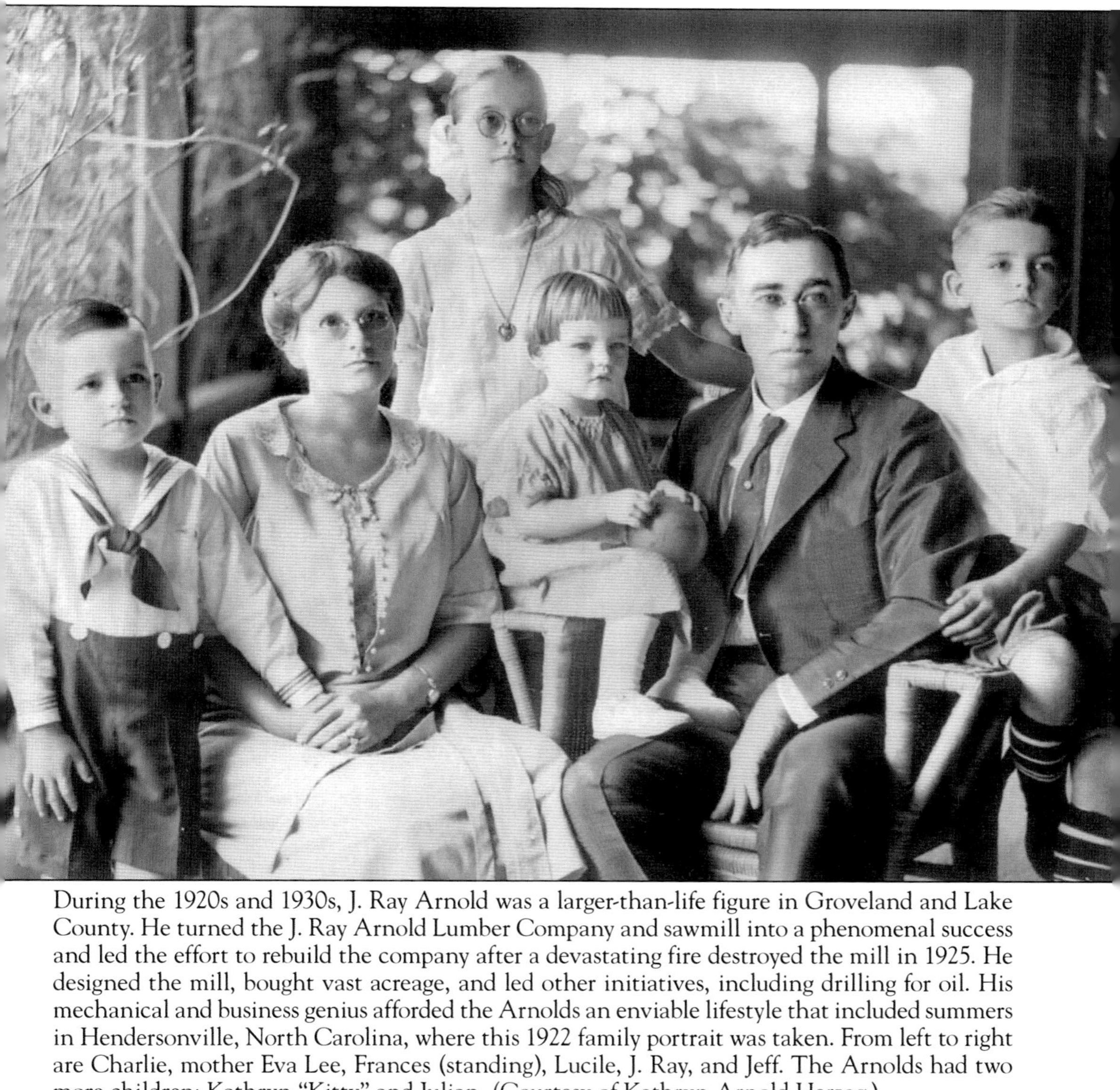

During the 1920s and 1930s, J. Ray Arnold was a larger-than-life figure in Groveland and Lake County. He turned the J. Ray Arnold Lumber Company and sawmill into a phenomenal success and led the effort to rebuild the company after a devastating fire destroyed the mill in 1925. He designed the mill, bought vast acreage, and led other initiatives, including drilling for oil. His mechanical and business genius afforded the Arnolds an enviable lifestyle that included summers in Hendersonville, North Carolina, where this 1922 family portrait was taken. From left to right are Charlie, mother Eva Lee, Frances (standing), Lucile, J. Ray, and Jeff. The Arnolds had two more children: Kathryn "Kitty" and Julian. (Courtesy of Kathryn Arnold Herzog.)

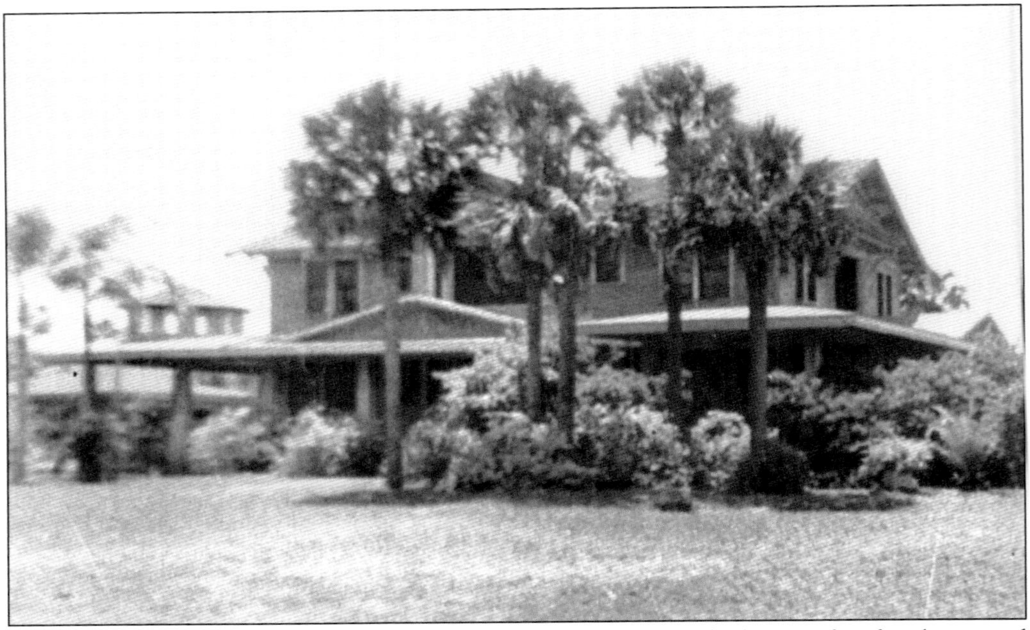

The J. Ray Arnold home, designed for cross-ventilation, had five bedrooms, five fireplaces, and a commercial-size refrigerator. Azaleas were brought from out of state. He built an elaborate gym (left rear) for his extended family's recreation. The gym included a swimming pool, two bowling alleys, pool tables, and rifle range. The home was at the corner of present-day Indiana Avenue and eastbound Highway 50. (Courtesy of Kathryn Arnold Herzog.)

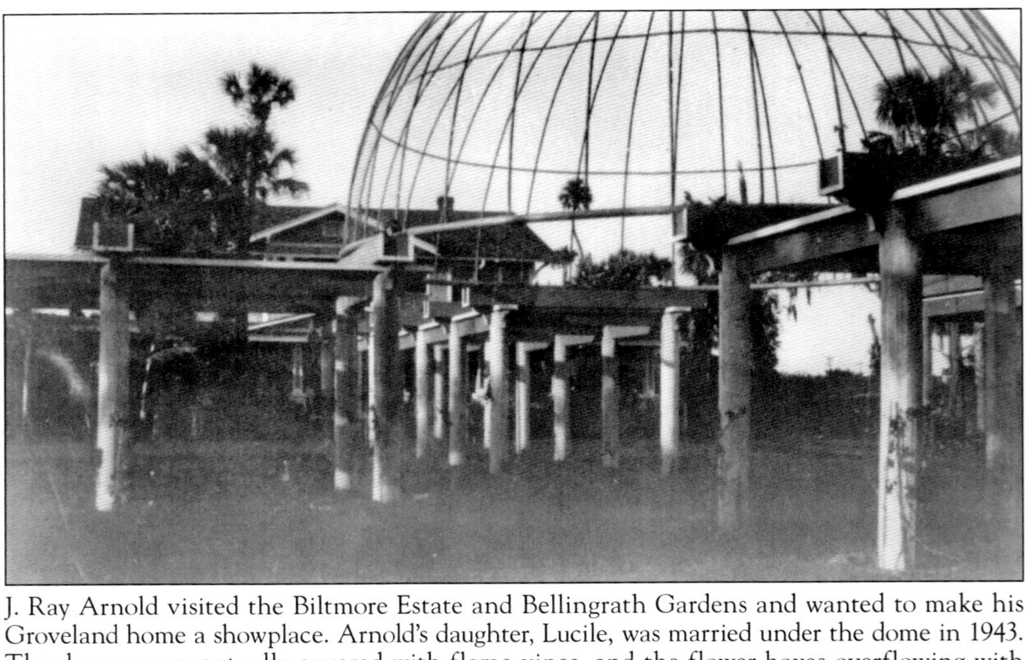

J. Ray Arnold visited the Biltmore Estate and Bellingrath Gardens and wanted to make his Groveland home a showplace. Arnold's daughter, Lucile, was married under the dome in 1943. The dome was eventually covered with flame vines, and the flower boxes overflowing with confederate jasmine. (Courtesy of Kathryn Arnold Herzog.)

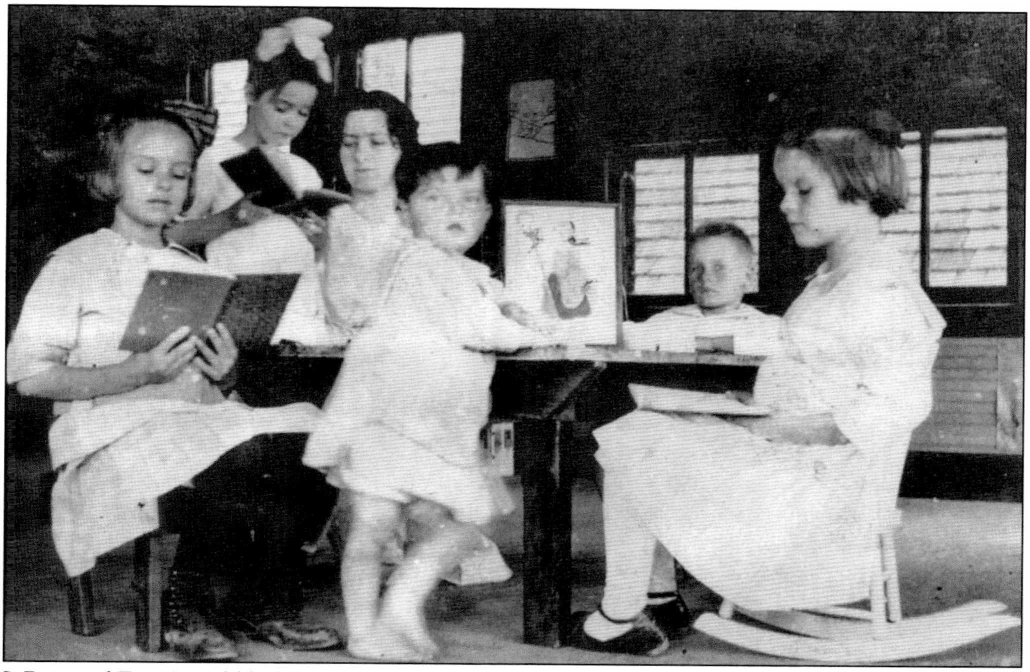

J. Ray and Eva Arnold believed strongly in the importance of education. They brought teachers to their home for academics and music lessons. Then they focused their resources on improving schools in Groveland and at neighboring Montverde Academy. Every night, the parents would read by the upstairs fireplace while the children sat around a large conference table doing their homework. (Courtesy of Kathryn Arnold Herzog.)

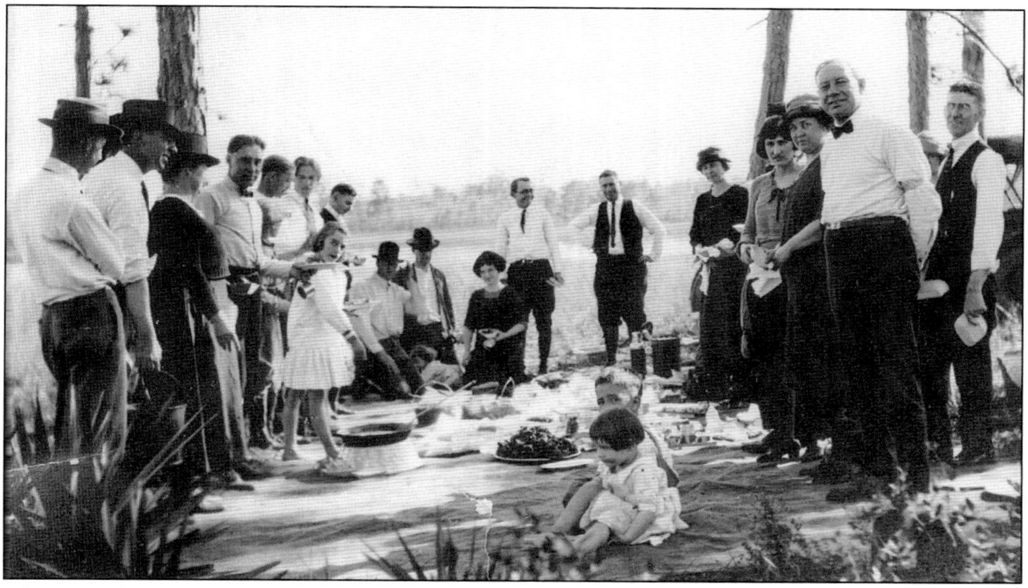

The extended family of brothers J. Ray Arnold, Luther Arnold, and Baker Arnold enjoyed picnics. This early-1920s picnic followed a day of hunting. The Reverend Walter Meade, pictured right in a bow tie, was pastor of the First Baptist Church of Groveland, which the Arnolds helped establish. (Courtesy of Kathryn Arnold Herzog.)

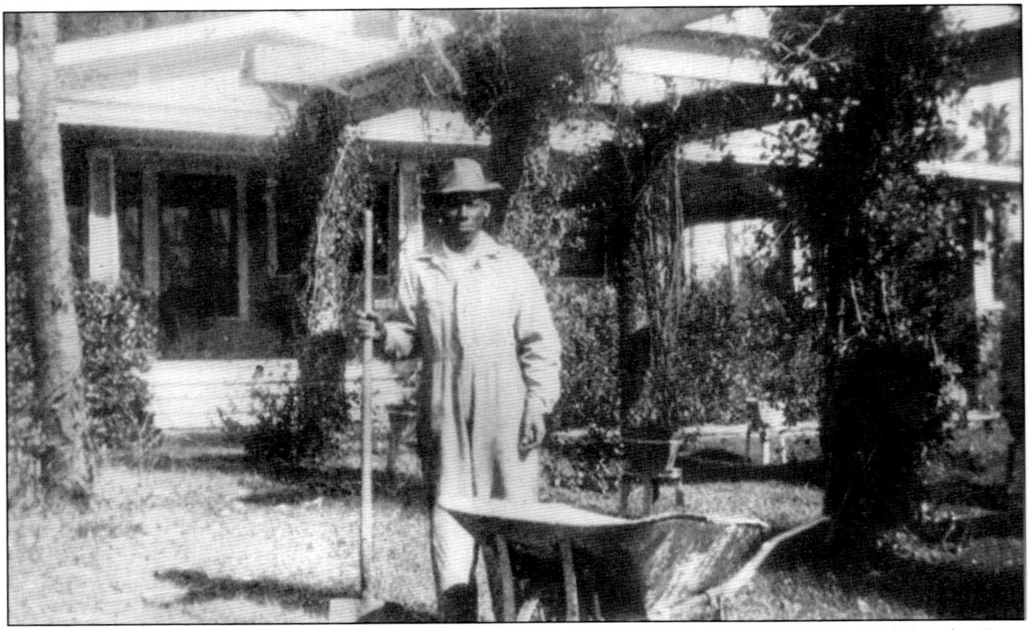

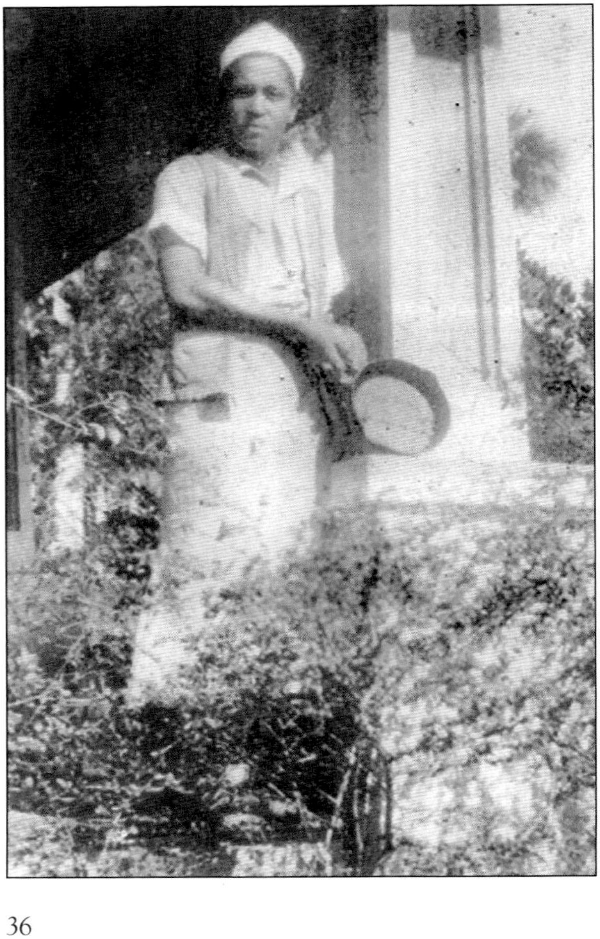

Arthur Robinson worked for the J. Ray Arnold family for many years. Before Arnold and Eva Lee Dowling were married, he had worked for the Dowling family in Live Oak, Florida. Robinson occasionally gardened and was a butler and chauffeur. Cat (left) was a highly skilled cook. The Arnold family had formal dinner every day. Arnold had a foot pedal under the dining room table that could summon Robinson, who wore a starched white coat when he served the family's dinner. Desserts were served daily, often with heavy cream that came from the fresh milk brought twice a day to the household. (Both courtesy of Kathryn Arnold Herzog.)

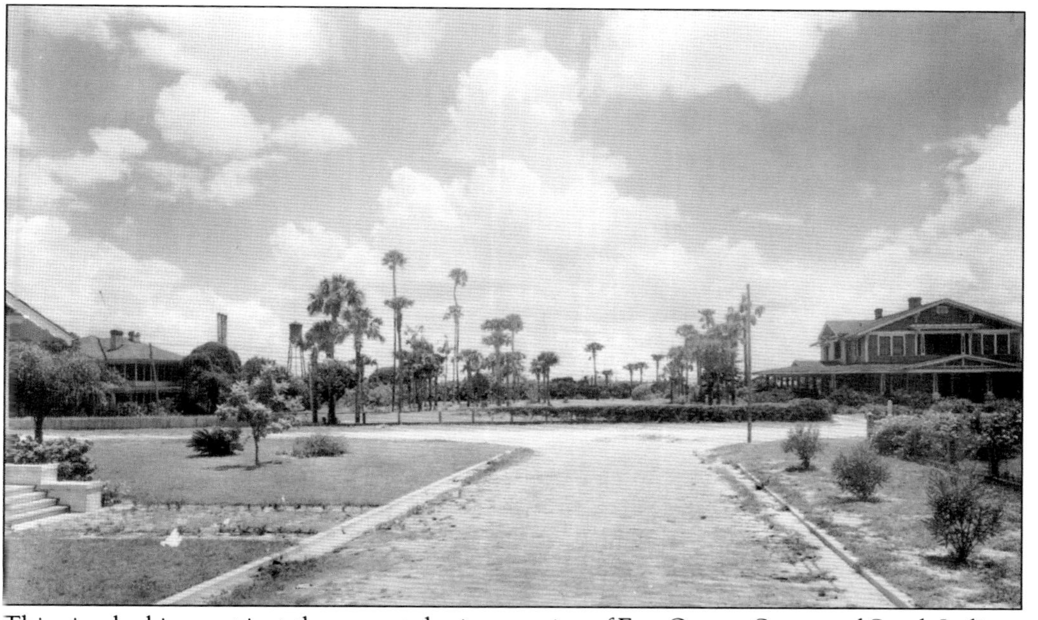

This view looking east is at the present-day intersection of East Orange Street and South Indiana Avenue. To the right is the J. Ray Arnold family home. At the far left is the Luther Arnold home. Barely visible are the sawmill's smokestacks. Although this road dead-ended into J. Ray Arnold's front yard, it was later extended to become eastbound Highway 50. The palm trees were brought by train. (Courtesy of Kathryn Arnold Herzog.)

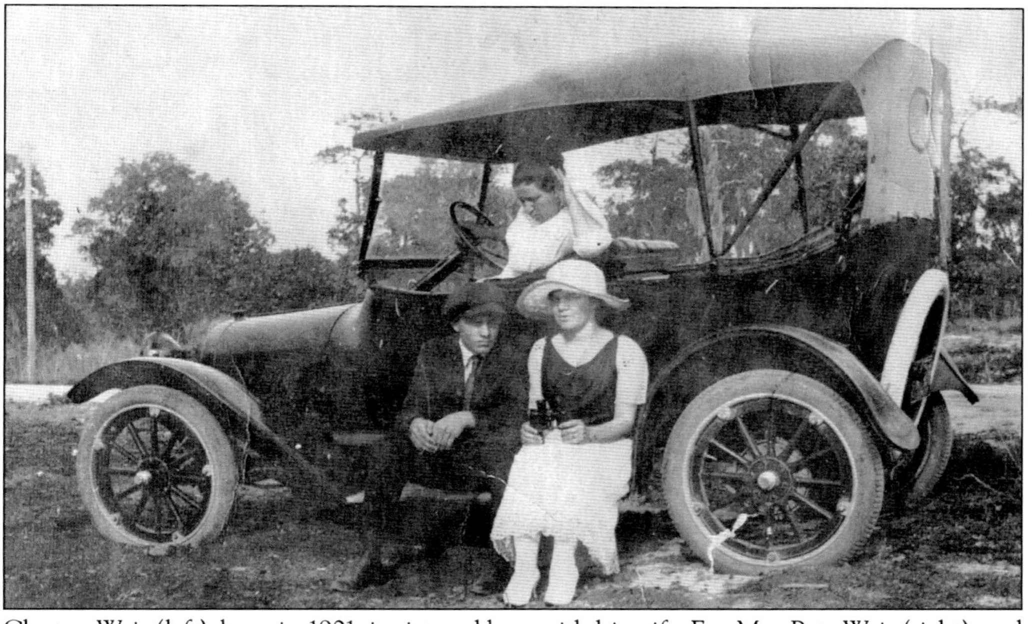

Clayton Weir (left), born in 1901, is pictured here with his wife, Eva Mae Pate Weir (right), and her mother, Quinnie Watson Pate (rear). Clayton Weir worked as a machinist at the Arnold sawmill before he became a well-known Groveland attorney. In the 1940s, he was elected mayor. He and Eva Mae married in 1923 and had a daughter, Imogene, and son, James. (Courtesy of Imogene Weir Tallant.)

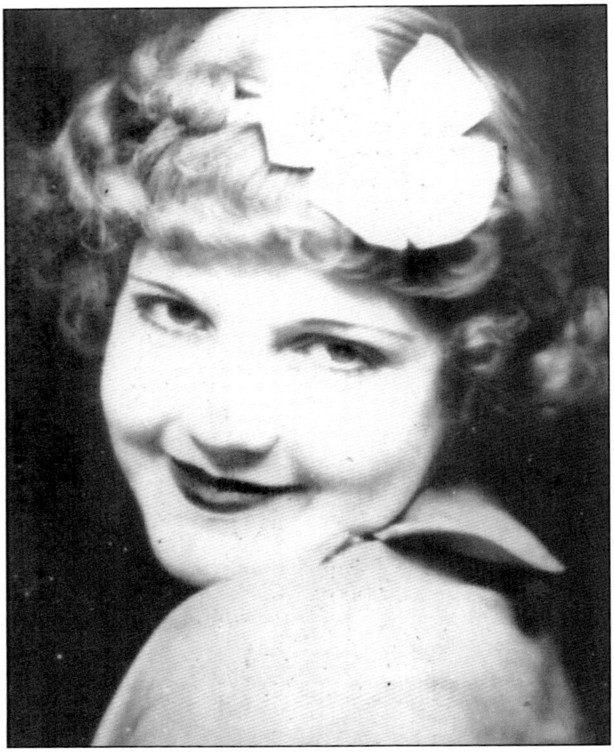

Cyleta Lee Austin, shown in this 1935 photograph, is recognized as Groveland's historian emeritus. Her long ties to Groveland go back to 1869, when her grandparents Allen and Matilda Carter settled Carter's Island, several miles southwest of Groveland. Her interest in history began as a child when she enjoyed looking through her grandmother Matilda Carter's photographs. (Courtesy of Cyleta Lee Austin.)

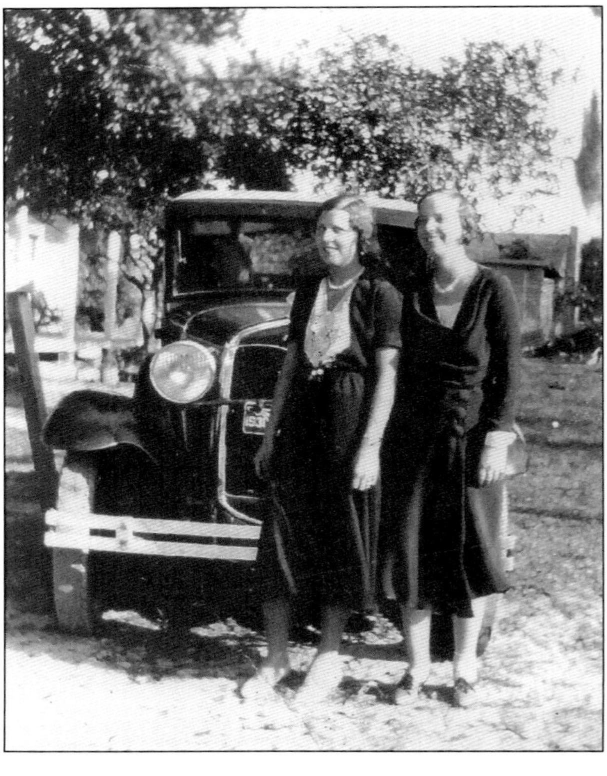

Lois Merritt (left) and Jessie Mae Rice Barmore, shown in this 1931 photograph, were teenagers during Groveland's 1920s boom era. Barmore, a lifelong resident, became an elementary teacher and was well known as the pianist and organist at Edge Memorial United Methodist Church. She was born in 1913 and died in 2000. Her children, Charles, Marvin, and Betty Barmore, also attended Groveland High School. (Courtesy of Cyleta Lee Austin.)

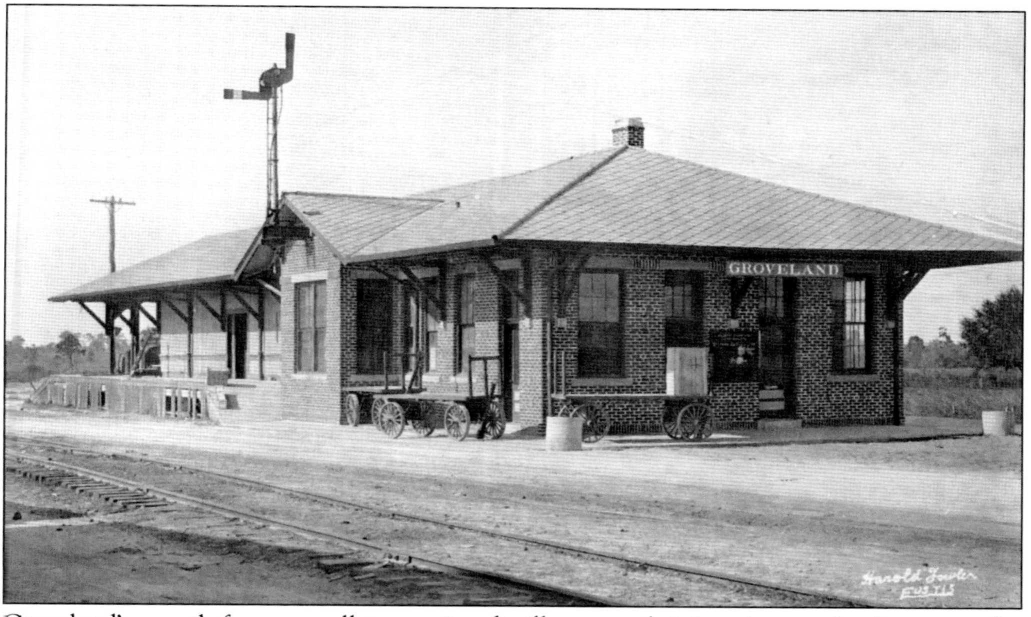

Groveland's growth from a small turpentine distillery to a thriving city was due in part to the Orange Belt Railway that ran from Sanford to St. Petersburg. This brick station was built in 1925 near the peak of Florida's rail system. The train track that once ran parallel to Highway 50 was pulled out by 1984. The station was used by the citrus processing plant next door. (Courtesy of State Archives of Florida.)

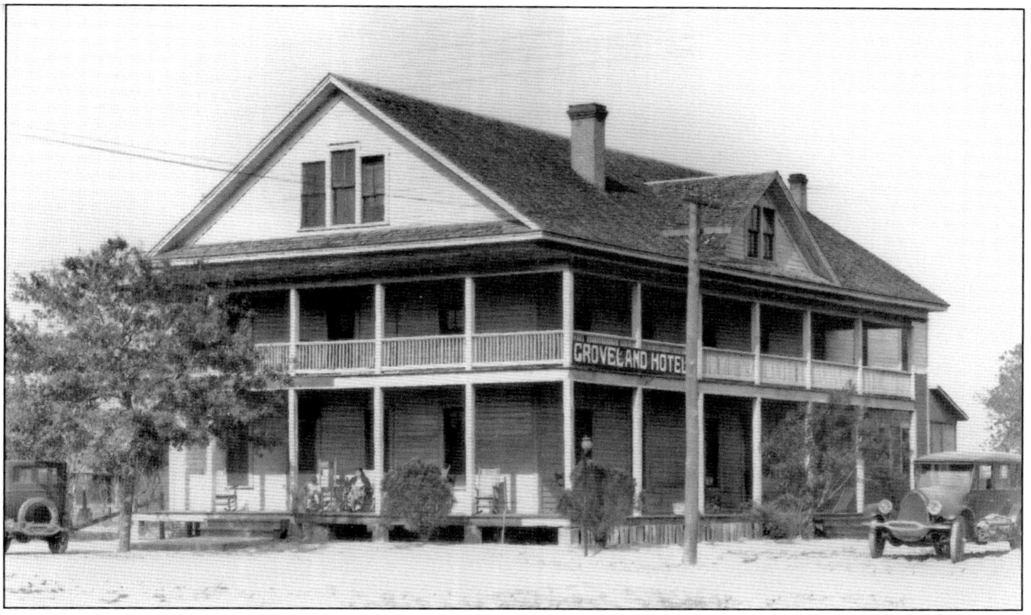

The Groveland Hotel was built around 1911 by developer J. W. Beach to house prospective land buyers visiting from the North, where he advertised extensively. While the hotel was being constructed, Beach housed tourists in Pullman cars along sidetracks. The Lake David Hotel, as it is currently known, still stands at the corner of Cherry Street and Main Avenue. (Courtesy of the Tampa-Hillsborough County Public Library System.)

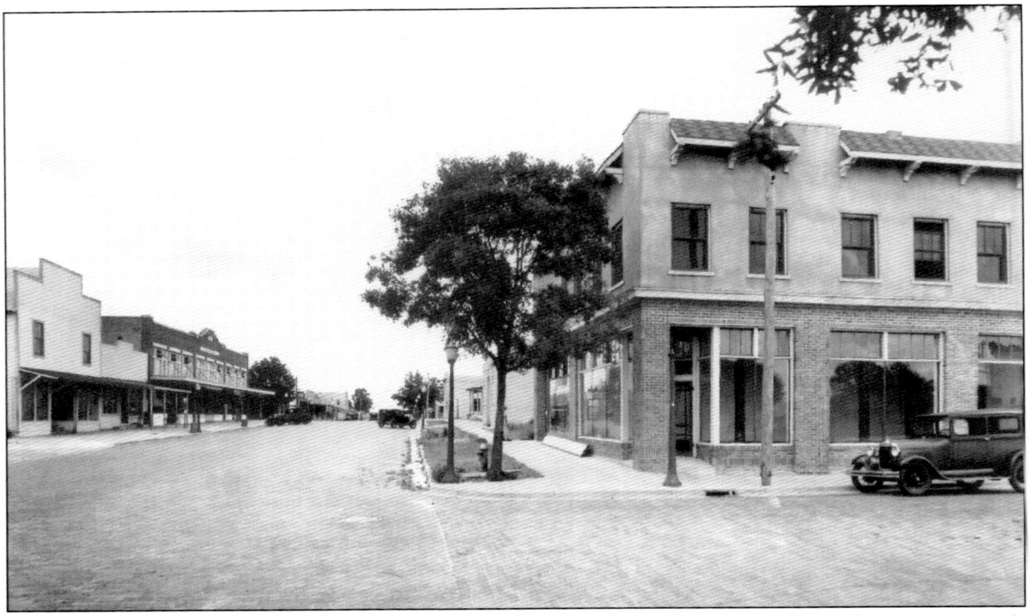

By the late 1920s, Groveland boasted brick-lined streets, street lamps, and new businesses, such as the two-story Charles Anderson real estate office shown on the right. Anderson, a journalist and real estate agent who became mayor, arrived in 1918. Groveland had such a large Swedish population that he started two Swedish newspapers: the *Florida Posten* and *Svenska Journalener*. (Courtesy of the Tampa-Hillsborough County Public Library System.)

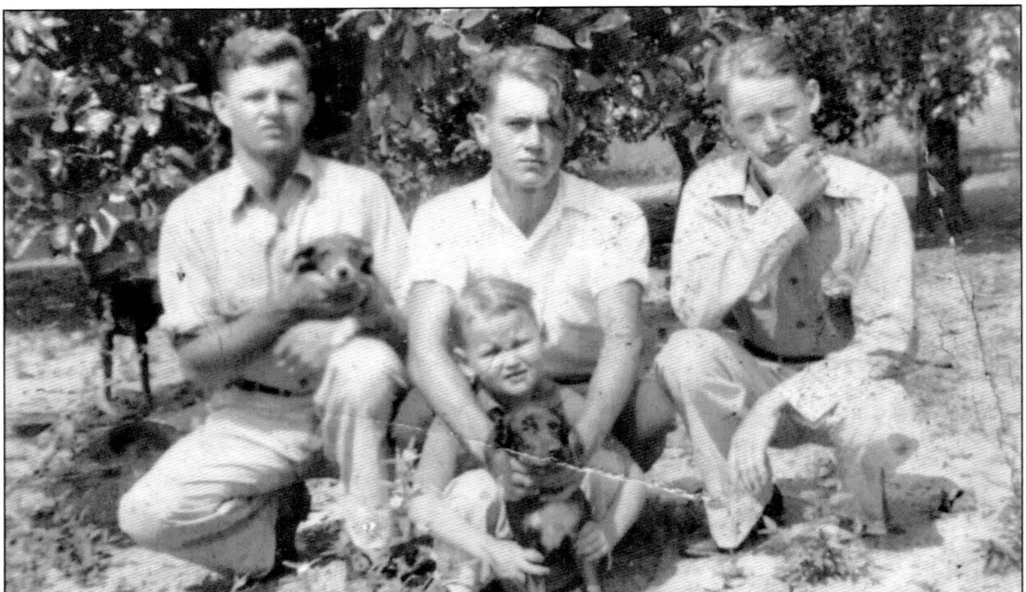

The Stewart brothers, pictured here in front of the family's grove during the 1930s, were the grandchildren of original settlers near Cherry Lake. Alvin Stewart (first row) was born in 1933. From left to right are Franklin Stewart, born in 1922, Galey Stewart, born in 1919, and James Stewart, born in 1921. (Courtesy of Cookie Stewart Beard.)

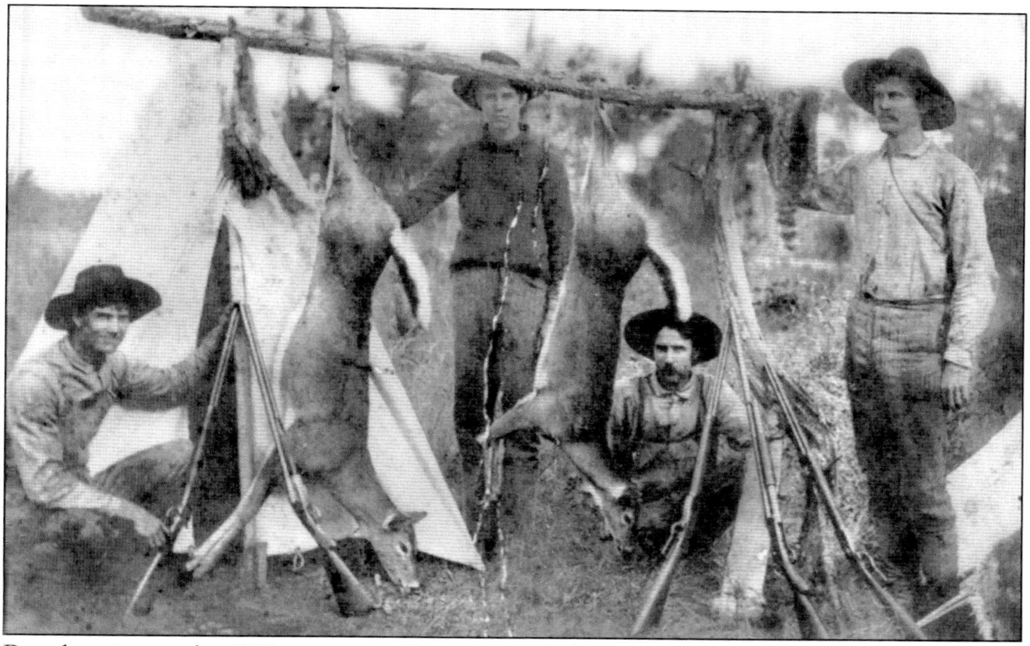

Deer hunting in the 1920s was a popular activity and source of food. Pictured here from left to right are brothers Lorem Brown, Bud Brown, William Jesse Brown, and John Brown, all sons of pioneer Simon Brown. Because of the bountiful wild game, it was common to hear people say, "There's no reason to go hungry in Groveland." (Courtesy of Peggy Parrish Sloan.)

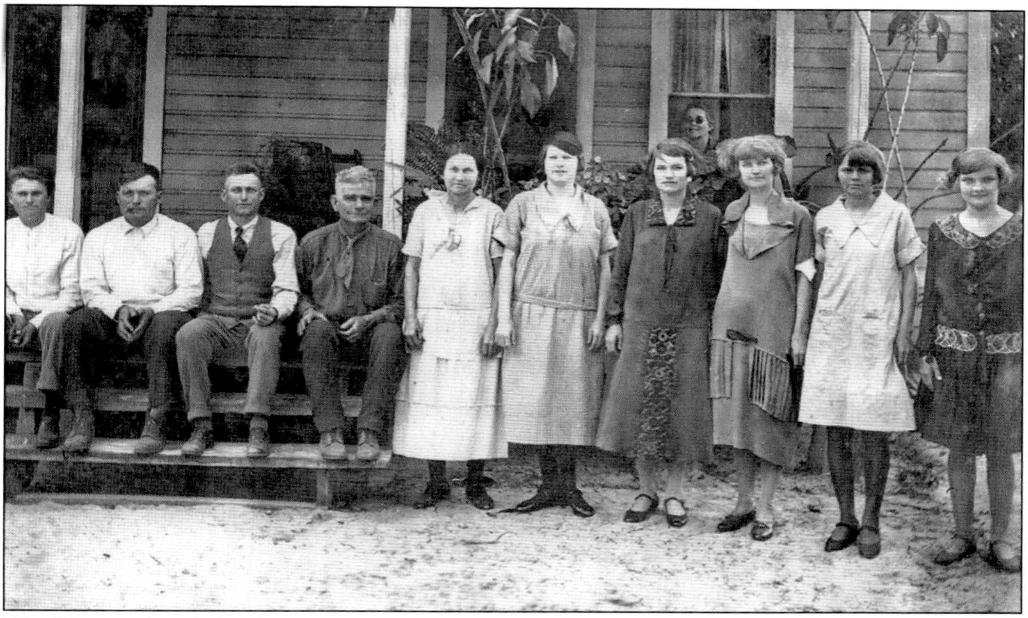

The Watson family has long roots to the Groveland and Tuscanooga area. Pictured in this 1925 family reunion photograph, from left to right, are Rovin Watson, Thomas Watson, William Watson, Hiram Joseph Watson, Mahetibel Sloan Watson, Nancy Watson Hunt, Bertha Watson Jenkins, Hattie Watson Hortsan, Claudia Watson Calvechio, and Teril Rose Watson. (Courtesy of Peggy Parrish Sloan.)

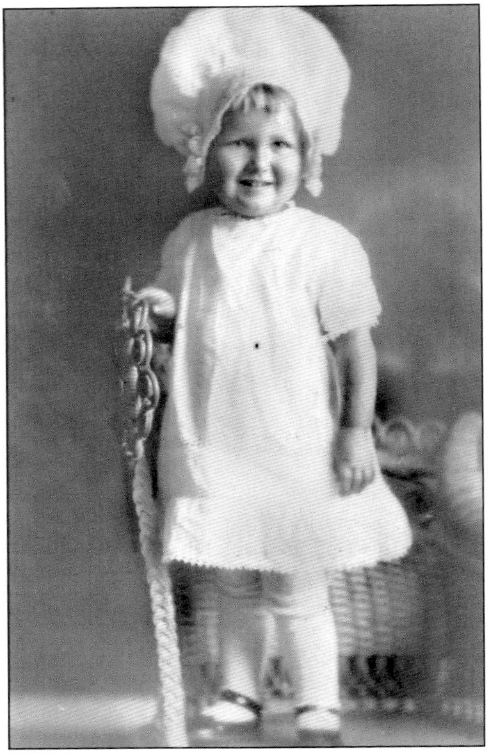

Thelma Sloan Knight, a lifelong Bay Lake resident, is pictured dressed up for her one-year-old birthday photograph in 1921. She is the daughter of Dave and Nelia Bridges Sloan and the great-granddaughter of early settler Daniel Sloan, who developed a special breed of corn. Her children, also lifelong residents, are Carolyn Knight, David Knight, and Theresa Knight. (Courtesy of Carol Murray Tomlinson.)

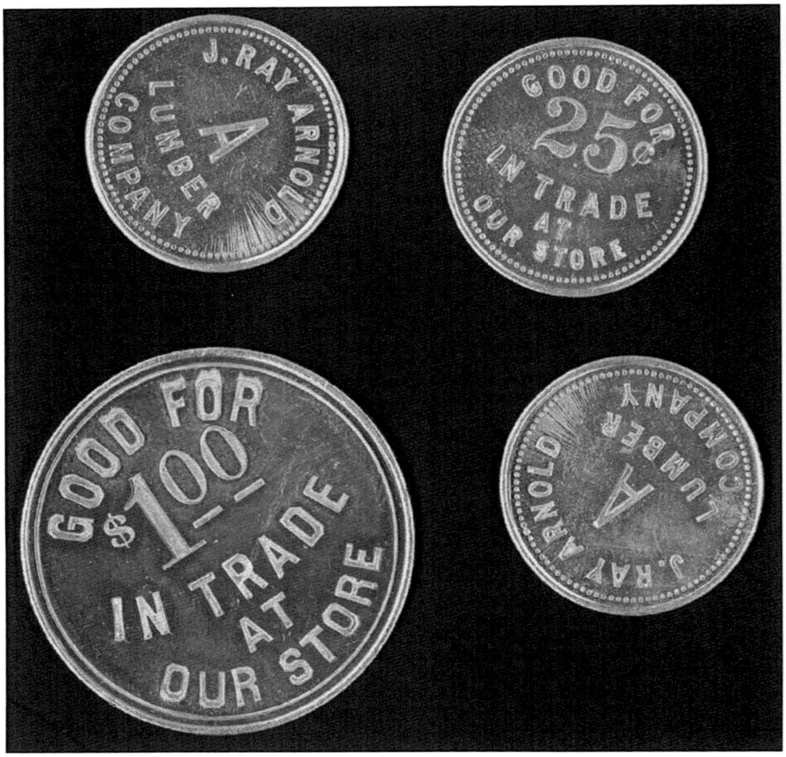

In the 1920s and 1930s, sawmill owner J. Ray Arnold and business baron E. E. Edge issued their own currency. The coins, which townspeople called "lumies" because they were made from aluminum, were good at the local stores. The company-store currency provided stability after back-to-back banks failed. Eventually, the companies were ordered to stop, and U.S. currency was used once again. (Courtesy of Kathryn Arnold Herzog.)

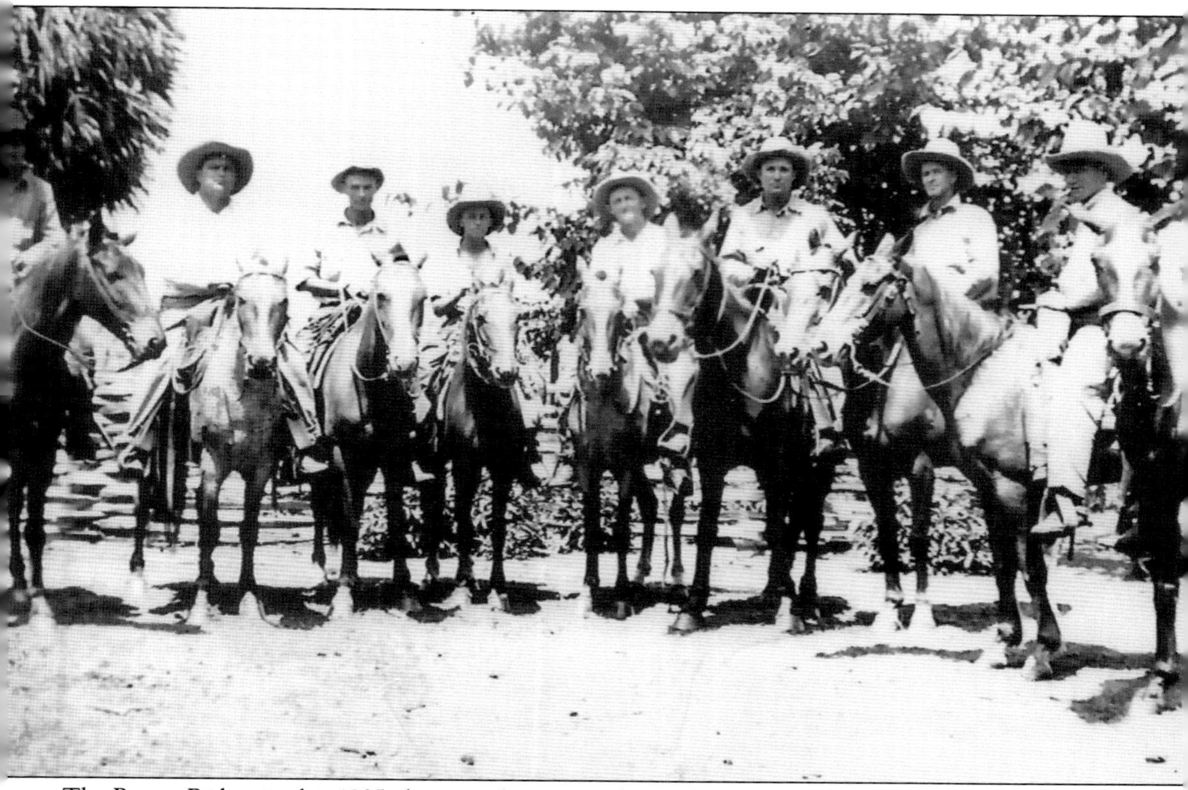

The Range Riders in this 1935 photograph were cowboys who helped with the cattle on ranches throughout South Lake, including the Bronson family's 30,000-acre ranch. From left to right are Allison Story, Alfred Story, Buster Story, Walter Bridges, Oliver Knowles, Lewis ?, Charles Knowles, unidentified, and Jim Tomlinson. The Bronson name is one of the most famous in Florida. Irlo Bronson is the namesake of the highway leading to Walt Disney World. He served in the Florida House and Senate. Since 2001, Charles Bronson has been the Florida Commissioner of Agriculture. The Bronson family has been in agriculture continuously since 1635. (Courtesy of Dennis Bronson.)

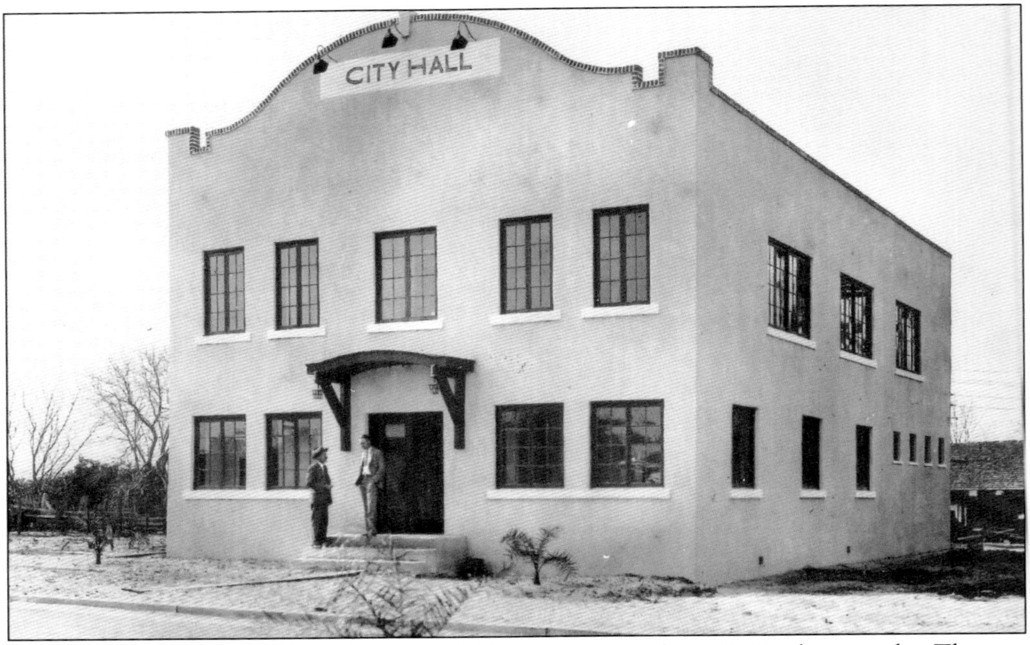

Groveland's city hall is shown from two different views in these 1930s photographs. The city headquarters, then as now, is on Lake Avenue one block south of Broad Street (Highway 50). During the Depression-era 1930s, the once bustling city was hard hit. The Arnold sawmill failed to recover, business titan E. E. Edge died suddenly in 1934, and two banks failed, taking with them many people's life savings. Unemployment was high, and people moved away in droves. One reporter wrote, "It should have become a ghost town. But there was a deep and vital root system beneath Groveland. There's a stubbornness in Groveland citizens that wouldn't let conditions prove fatal." (Above courtesy of Cyleta Lee Austin; below courtesy Tampa-Hillsborough Public Library System.)

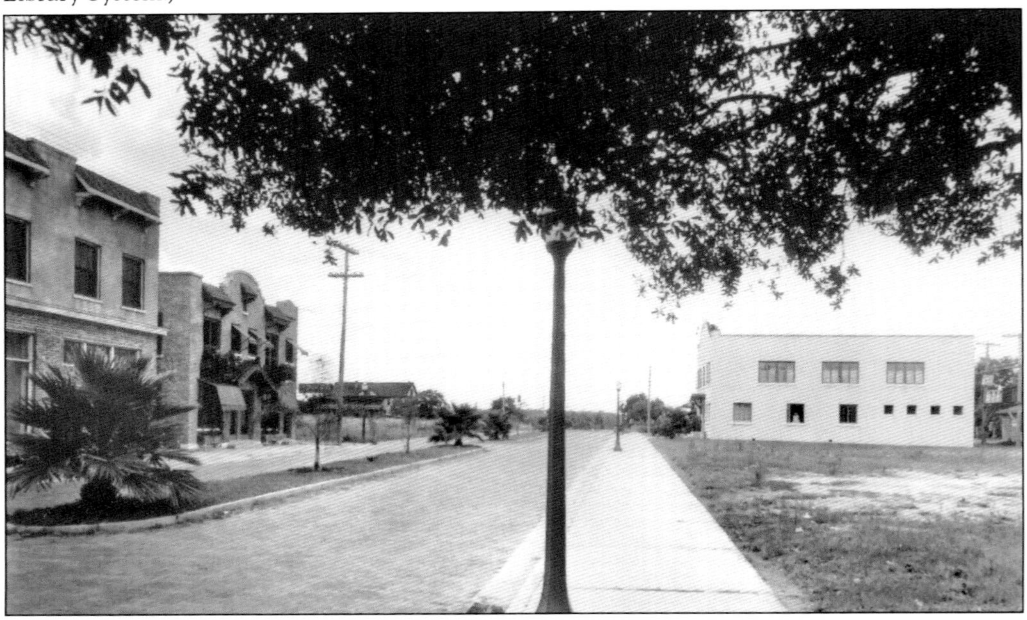

Three

Next Generations
War Years and the Space Race 1941–1969

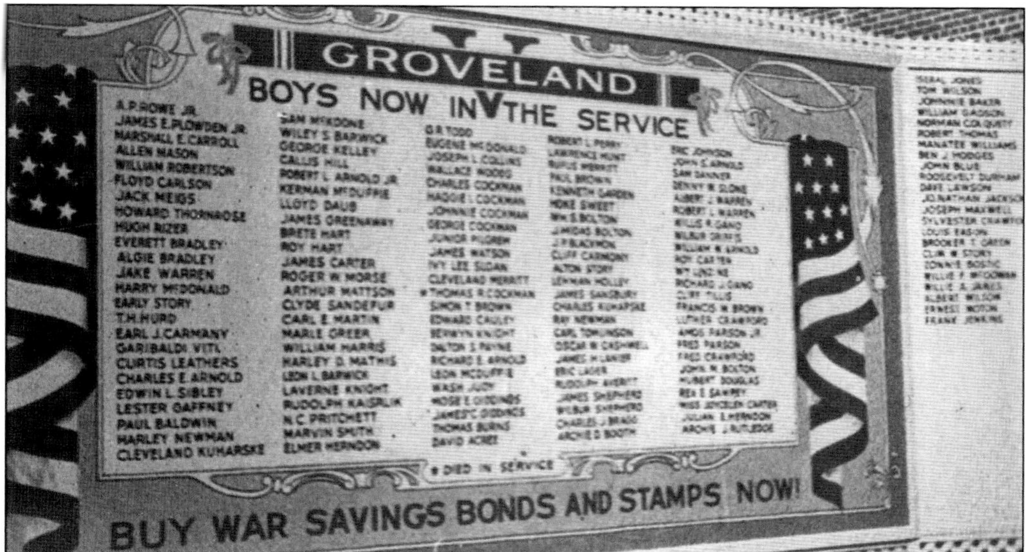

After the Great Depression, Groveland's next generations were sandwiched by World War II and the space race. The community erected this sign west of town in a show of patriotism during the war. The Cochman family sent eight sons into the armed forces, more than any other Florida family. Joycelen Carter became one of the first Florida women to serve in the U.S. Navy. At home, people prayed, endured rations, and bought war bonds. In the years that followed, Groveland steadily gained its economic legs back. Thanks to the WPA (Works Progress Administration), major improvements added to the quality of life. The 1950s saw a baby boom with new families moving into Groveland, filling classrooms and church pews. The downtown business district hummed, while cattle ranching and the citrus industry grew. The 1960s were a mixed blessing, with concerns over the cold war tensions balanced by the unlimited possibilities of the space race. (Courtesy of Vernell Lee.)

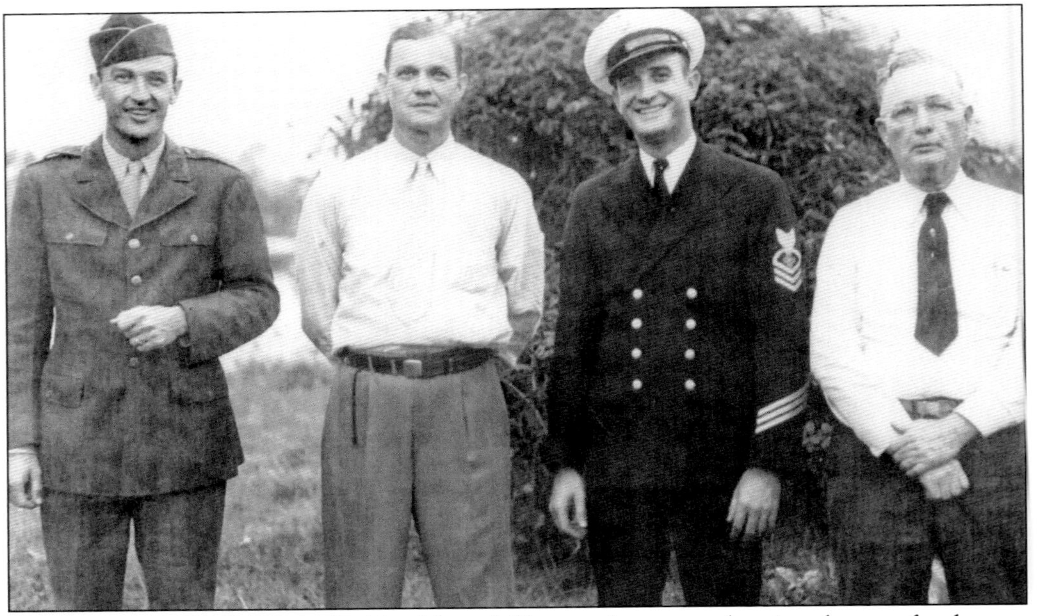

Comdr. Abner "Butch" Rowe Jr. (third from left) came home to a hero's welcome after he was released from a Japanese prisoner-of-war camp following four years of captivity during World War II. Rowe's letters home during his prison years were printed on the front page of the *Groveland Graphic* newspaper. From left to right are Rowe's brother, Julian Rowe, who also served; M. L. Roberts; Butch Rowe; and L. Day Edge. (Courtesy of Julian Rowe.)

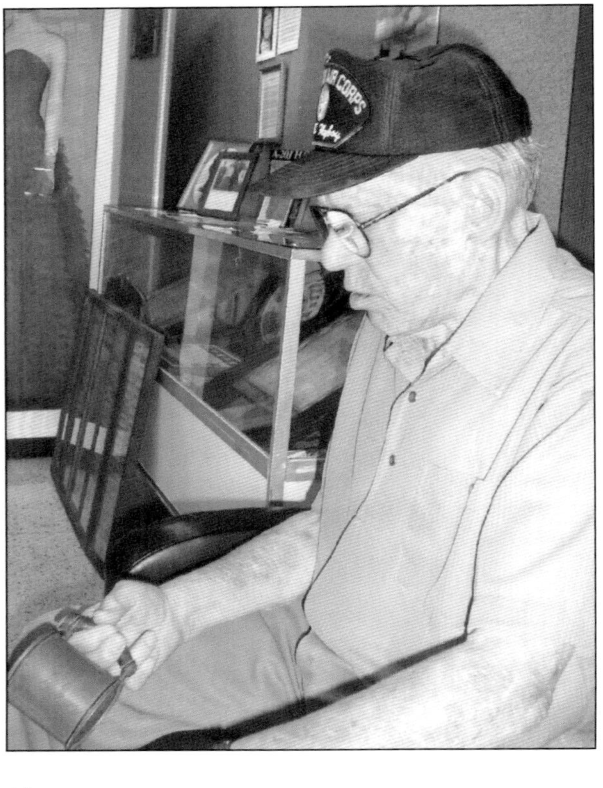

Rex Winn, a pilot with the U.S. Army Air Corps during World War II, looks at a tin cup, twig, and wire he fashioned into a cup while being held in a German prisoner of war camp. One of Winn's fellow prisoners had the cup engraved with the date they were rescued. (Courtesy of the Groveland Historical Museum.)

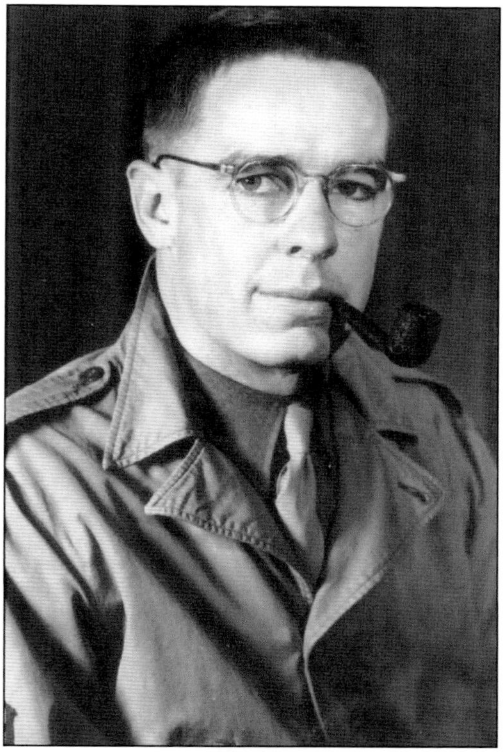

Several Arnold family members served during World War II, including Richard Arnold (right) who fought in the Battle of the Bulge. Below, from left to right, are Charles Arnold, who was a bombardier instructor, and Julian Arnold, who flew a B-29 Super Fortress for 25 missions over Japan and was awarded two Distinguished Flying Crosses. John Arnold (not pictured) was awarded the Navy Cross for his heroic acts. After his tanker was torpedoed, he ran through flames to reach the forward gun mount. He returned to Groveland and served as city clerk for many years. (Above and below left courtesy of Kathryn Arnold Herzog; below right courtesy Lindsay Keegan.)

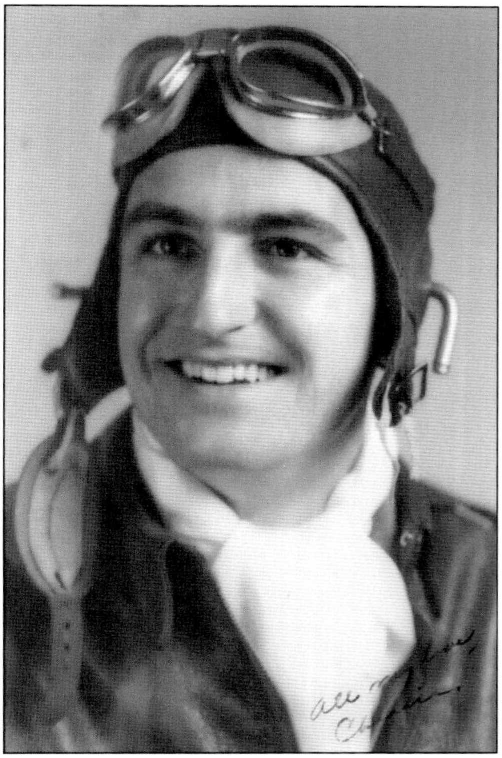

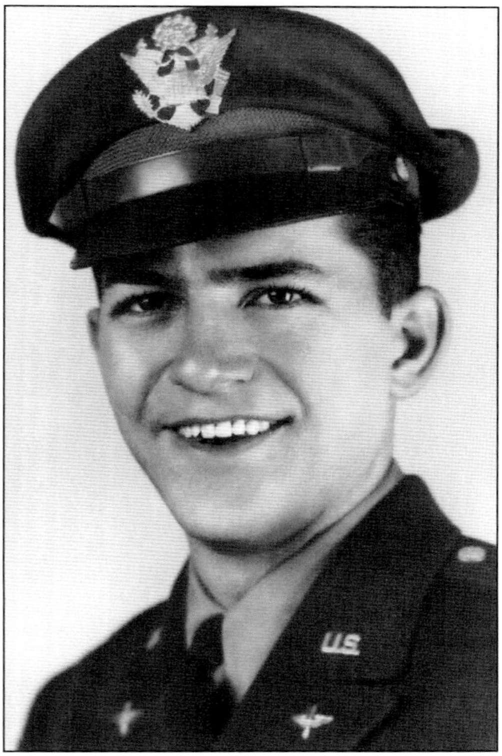

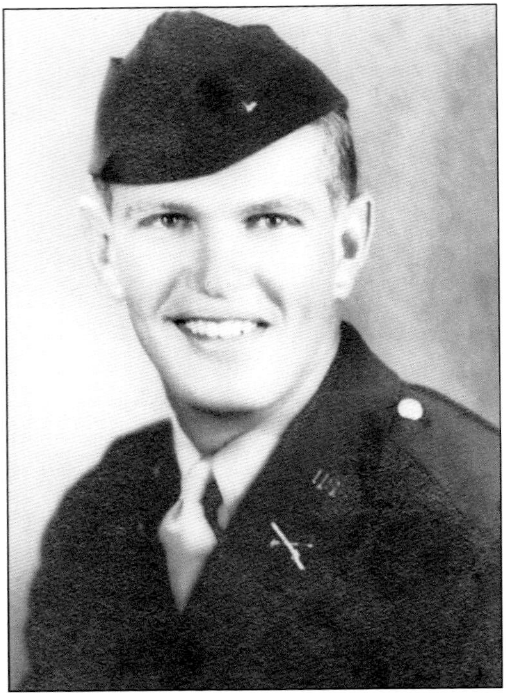

Lt. Forrest Earl Myers, son of George and Susan Myers, received the Silver Star for heroism while serving with the army's 86th Infantry Division against Germany. When his company commander was captured, Myers led his unit nearly 29 miles facing heavy enemy fire. He destroyed or captured many enemy troops along the way. (Courtesy of Dolores Gano Walker.)

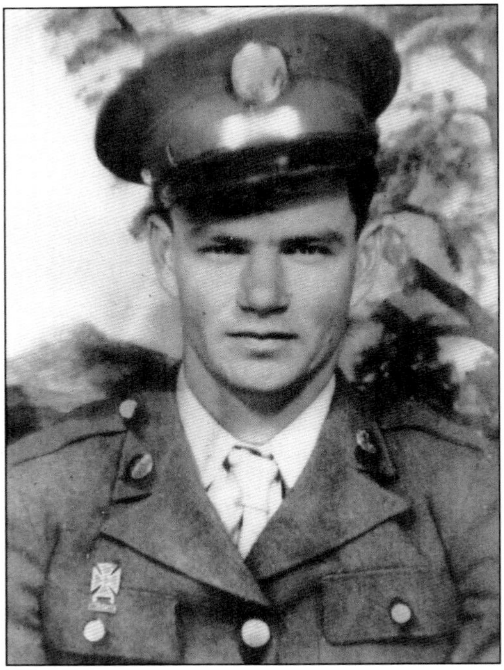

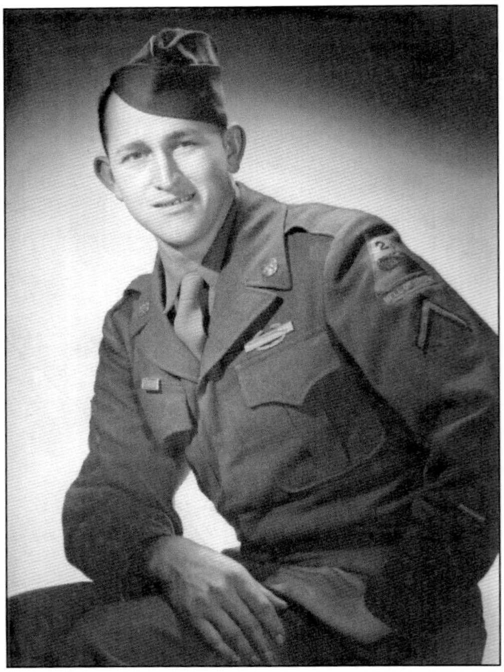

Groveland's rural settlements sent their sons to serve during World War II. From left to right are PFC Charles Franklin Stewart, who served in the 25th Infantry Division of the U.S. Army and was a descendant of Cherry Lake settlers; and Pvt. J. B. Sloan, the great-grandson of early Groveland settler Daniel Sloan. J. B. Sloan was 19, serving in Berlin when this photograph was taken. (Left courtesy of Cookie Stewart Beard; right courtesy Donald Richard Sloan.)

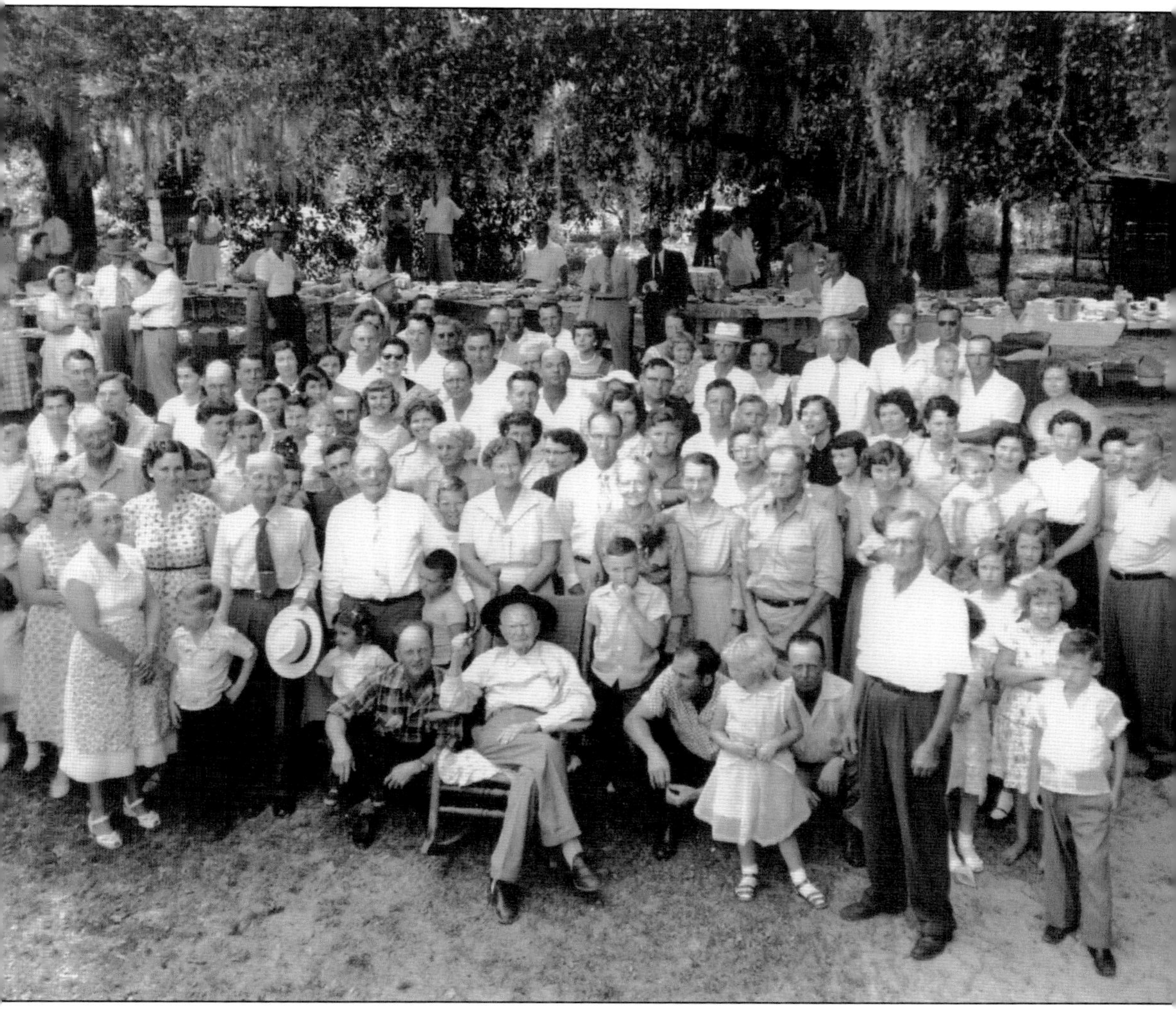

Walter Bridges is seen in this 1954 photograph celebrating his 100th birthday with family and friends. Bridges was born May 1, 1854. He married Mary Ann Brooks in January 1878. The couple had nine children: Pearson, Sally, Carrie, Nathan, Charles, Wallace, Mitchell, David, and Cornelia "Nelia." Bridges lived to be 101 before dying in July 1955. (Courtesy of Carol Murray Tomlinson.)

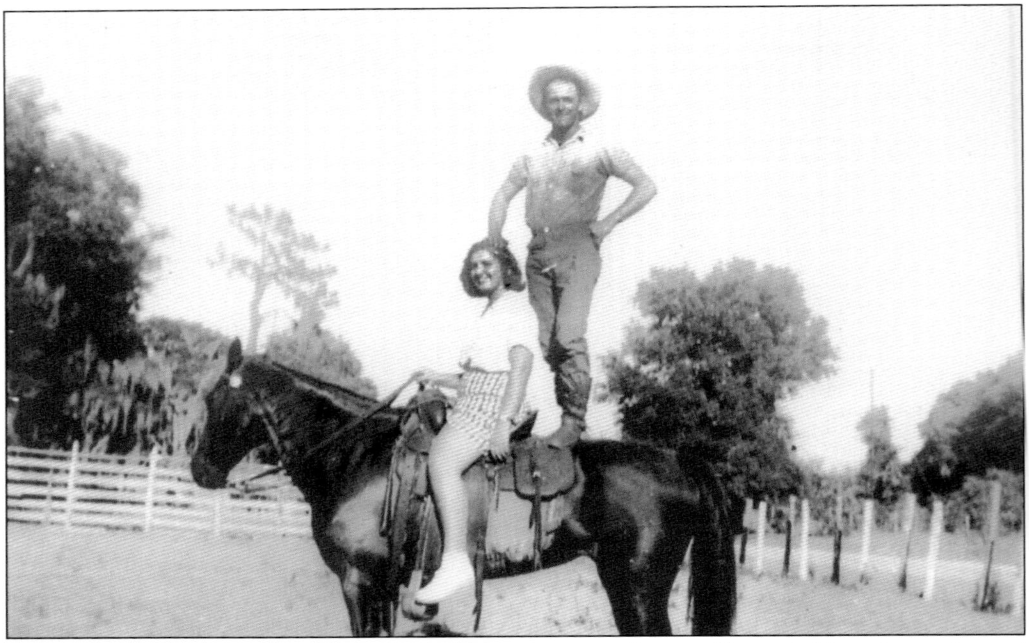

Even during the war years, life had its idyllic moments. Louise Sloan (left), a descendant of Groveland pioneer Daniel Sloan, is riding a horse named Billy in this 1941 photograph taken at Slones Ridge. Behind her stands Beryl Stokes, who worked for Allen's uncle, Dave Sloan. (Courtesy of Carol Murray Tomlinson.)

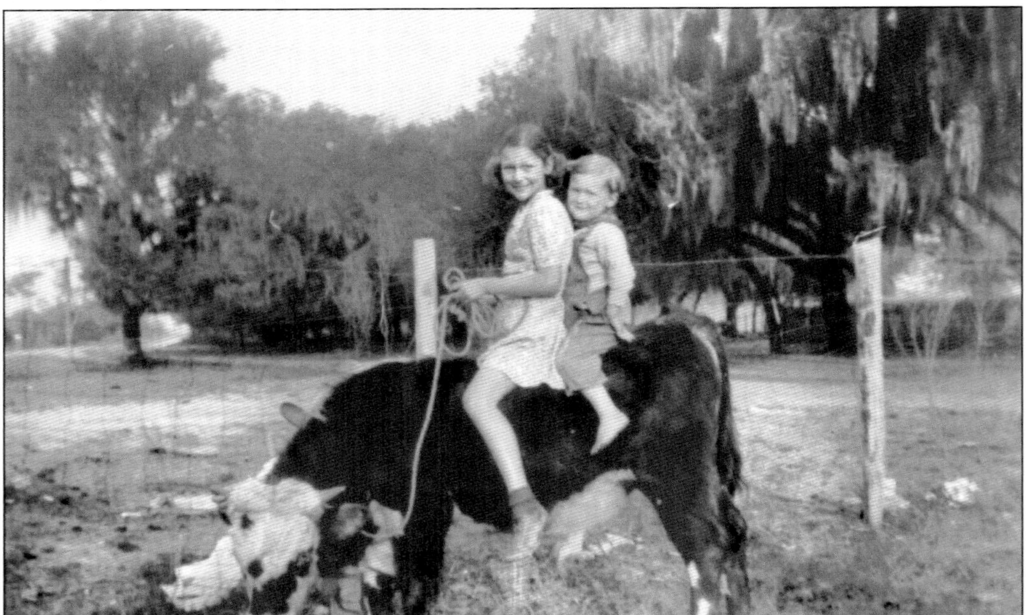

Jewell Sloan Stansell (left), 12, and Edward "Punk" Sloan, 4, are having fun pretending to ride one of her dad's prize cattle in this 1941 photograph taken at Dave and Nelia Sloan's farm on Slones Ridge. Although Dave Sloan raised cattle for show, many Bay Lake residents earned their living as cattle ranchers. (Courtesy of Carol Murray Tomlinson.)

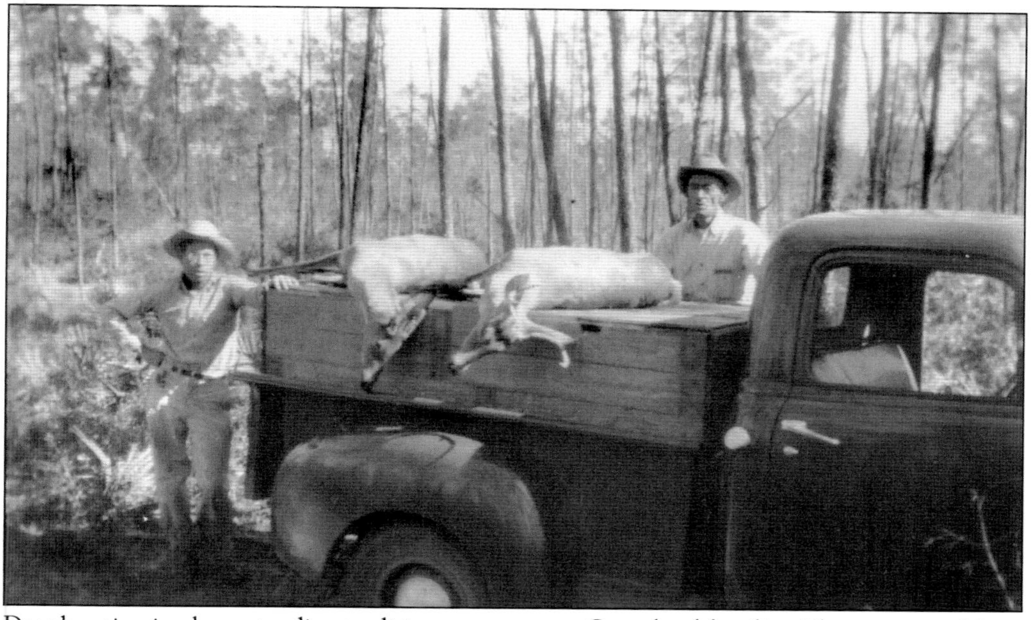

Deer hunting is a long-standing tradition among many Groveland families. The opening of deer-hunting season is looked forward to all year long. The deer provide venison for the family table. The most popular spot is the Ocala National Forrest, known as "the scrubs," where many hunters had permanent camps. Returning from a day's hunting are Lawton Joiner (left) and Perry Sloan. (Courtesy of Carol Murray Tomlinson.)

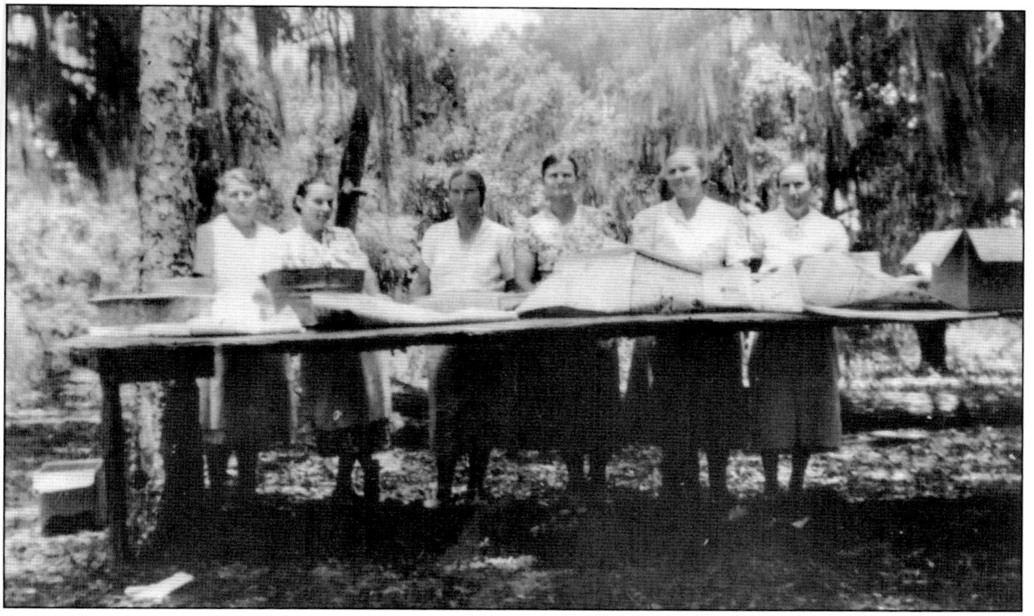

Women were part of cattle-ranching traditions as well. They usually prepared food and socialized while the men were out working the cattle. It is unclear what kind of food preparation was going on at the time this photograph was taken. From left to right are Molly Hunt Sloan, Anne Watson Sloan, Clara Tomlinson Carter, Cornelia Bridges Sloan, Sadie Sloan Merritt, and Lillie Tomlinson Sloan. (Courtesy of Carol Murray Tomlinson.)

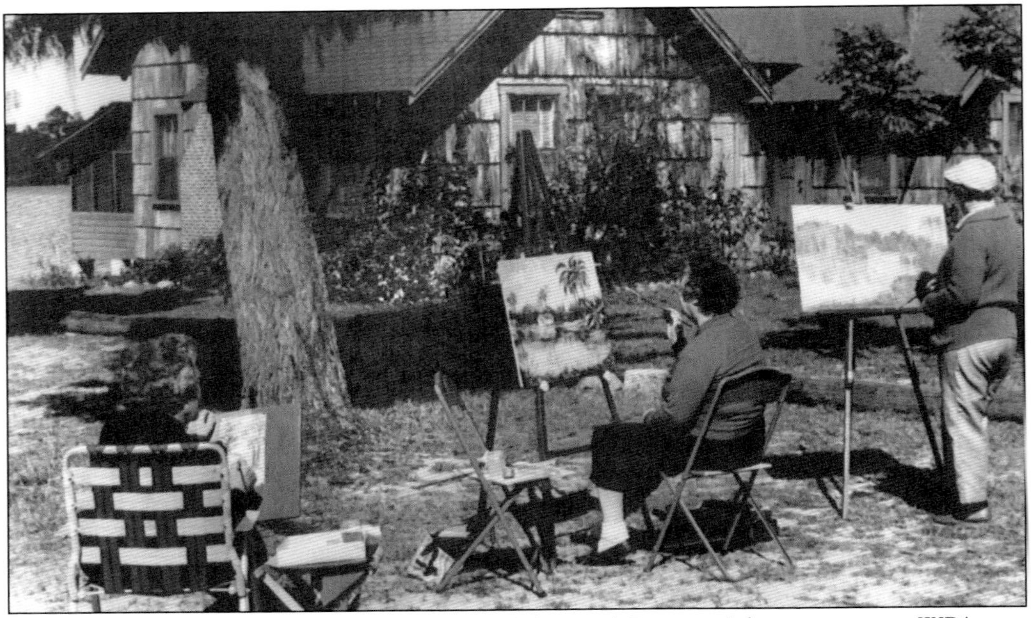

The Works Progress Administration, later called the Work Projects Administration or WPA, was a federally funded program that provided employment and major improvements to Groveland in the late 1930s. The WPA built the tennis courts and community center at Lake David, where these Groveland Women's Club members in the mid-1960s are enjoying oil painting. (Courtesy of the Marion Baysinger Memorial Library.)

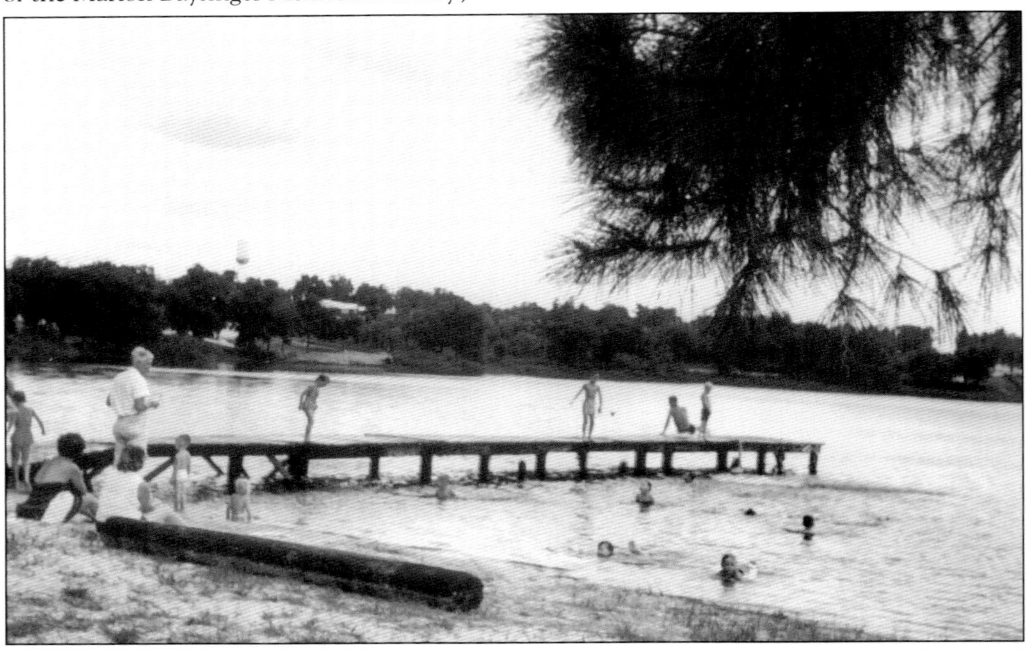

Lake David Park has always been the heart of the city's recreational life and where many Groveland children learn to swim. It is the site of the annual Fourth of July celebration and includes tennis courts built by the WPA. In more recent years, it has become a water-skiing haven, where several national ski-jumping records were set. (Courtesy of the Marion Baysinger Memorial Library.)

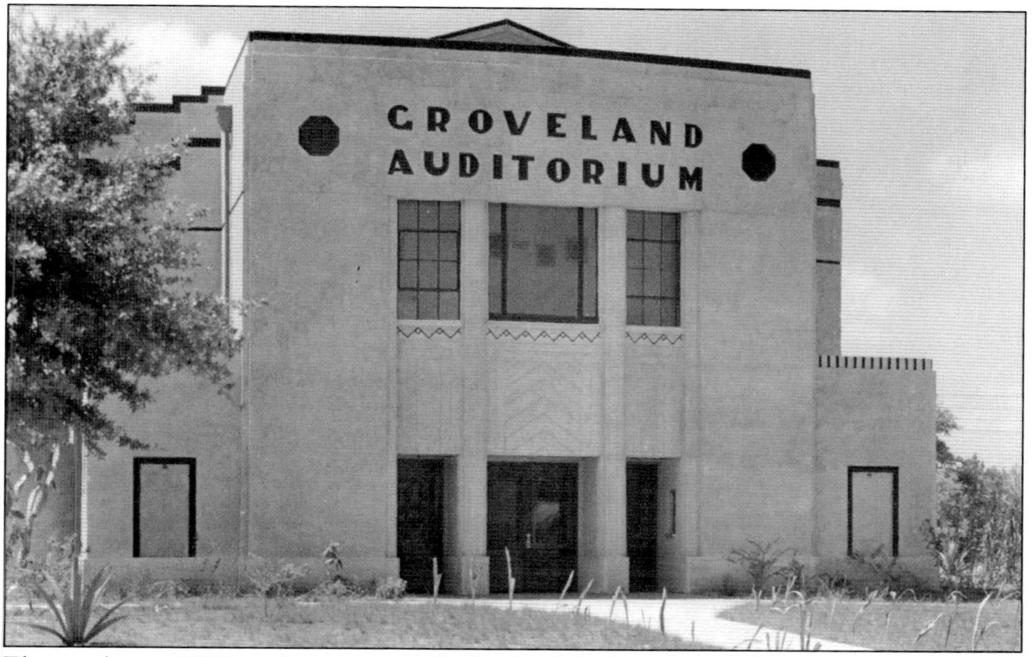

The two largest WPA projects were the high school, built in 1937 and currently home to Gray Middle School, and the Groveland Auditorium. As seen in these 1940s photographs, the auditorium had a front entrance for indoor programs (above) and a band shell in the rear used for outdoor concerts (below). The auditorium was located at present-day Lake Avenue and Orange Street where the Puryear Building and Veterans Park exist. In the 1950s and 1960s, the city leased the building to a private party to use as a movie theater. In the late 1960s, the building was torn down to make way for the Puryear Building and Veterans Park. Bystanders say the concrete walls were so thick that the first wrecking ball had no impact. (Both courtesy of the Marion Baysinger Memorial Library.)

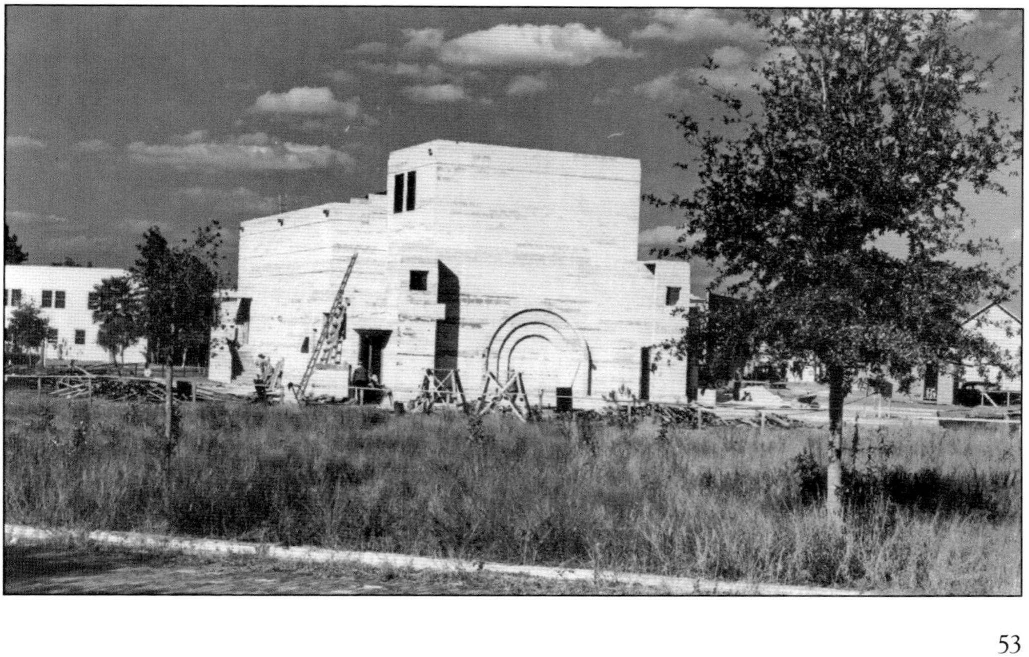

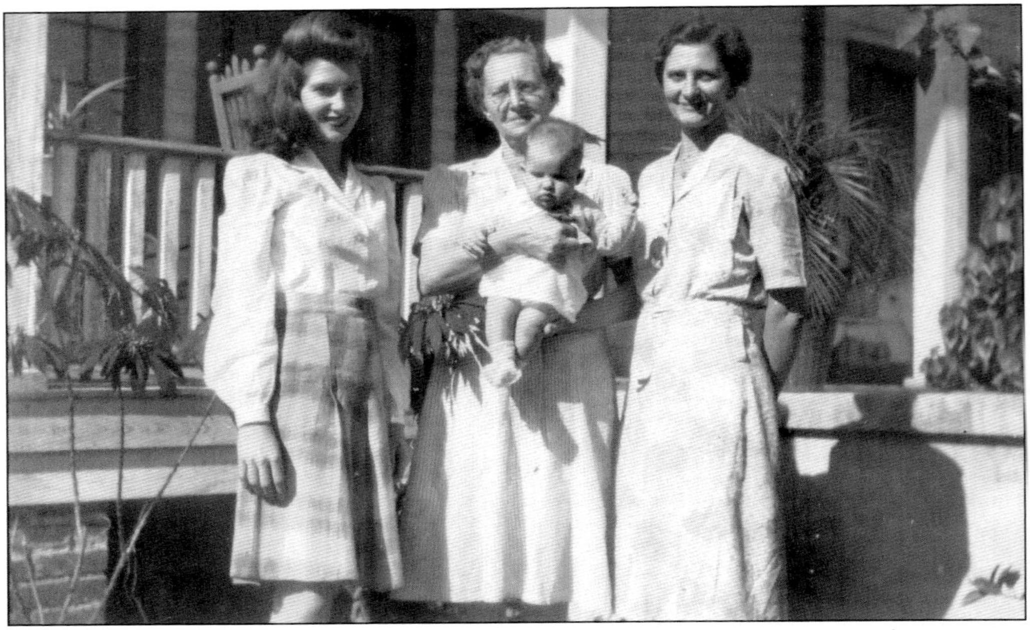

By the 1940s, Groveland was maturing into a well-established city in which several generations now lived. From left to right in this four-generation photograph taken in 1945 are Dolores Gano Walker; her maternal grandmother, Susan Williams Myers; Dolores Walker's mother, Opal Myers Gano; and Dolores's baby daughter, Sandra Eileen Walker. (Courtesy of Dolores Gano Walker.)

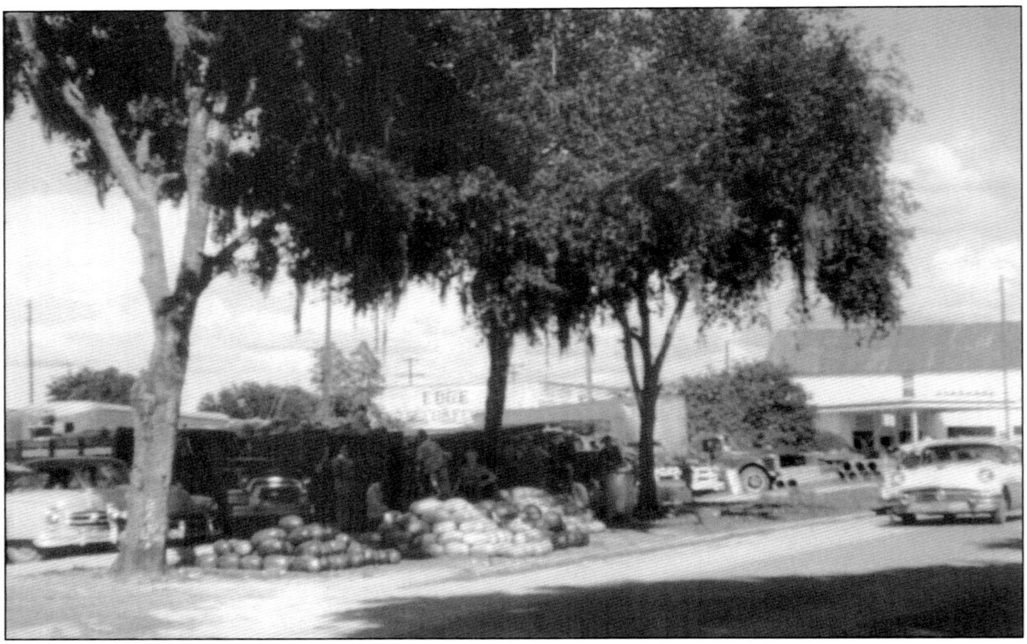

In the first half of the 20th century, Groveland was a prime watermelon producer. Local farmers would line up their watermelons along busy State Highway 50, as they did the day this photograph was taken in 1959, and sell to passing motorists. A few years earlier, more than 100 truckloads were sold in one day. More than 300 freight-car loads were sold in one year. (Courtesy of Ric Baysinger.)

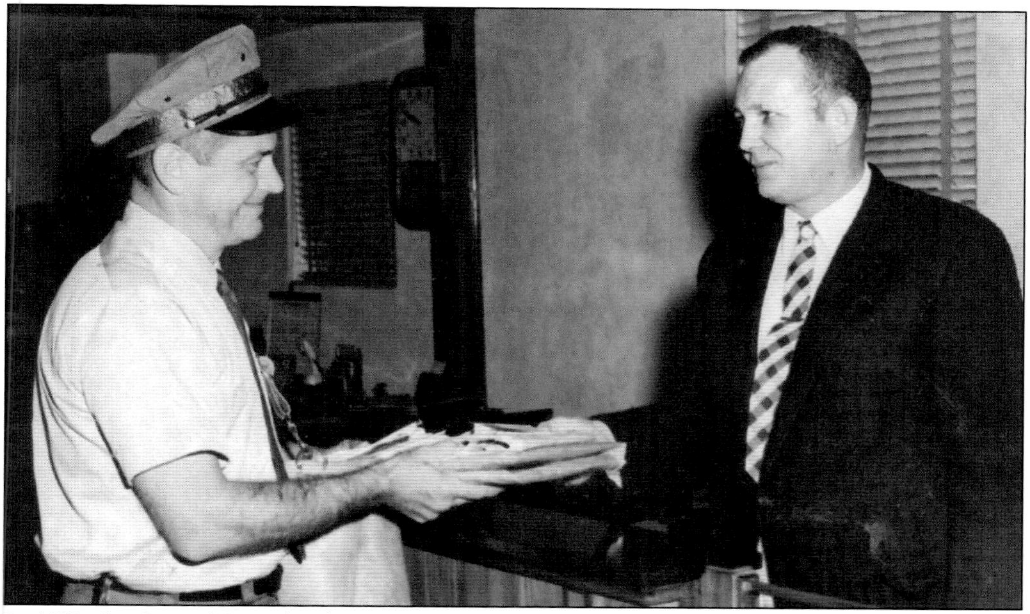

In 1959, the City of Groveland crossed another milestone when the Groveland Street Planning Committee made sure all streets were named, and eliminated any duplicate names, in preparation for house-to-house mail delivery. Pictured here on November 14, 1959, is Mayor Joe Fairchild (right), president of People's State Bank, accepting the town's first residential mail delivery from Stanley Koss. (Courtesy of June Fairchild.)

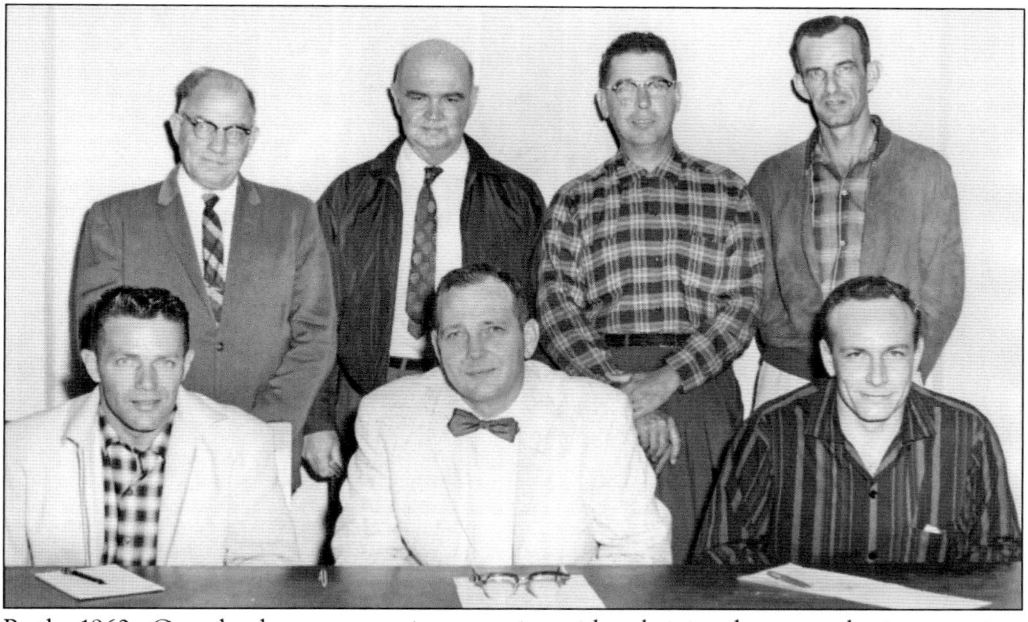

By the 1960s, Groveland was once again prospering with a thriving downtown business section. The newly elected city council, pictured here in January 1960, drew many of its members from the business sector. From left to right are (first row) Rex Winn, Mayor Joe Fairchild, and John Harb; (second row) Clayton Weir, Charles Ingalls, A. S. Davis Jr., and Joyce Gano. (Courtesy of the City of Groveland.)

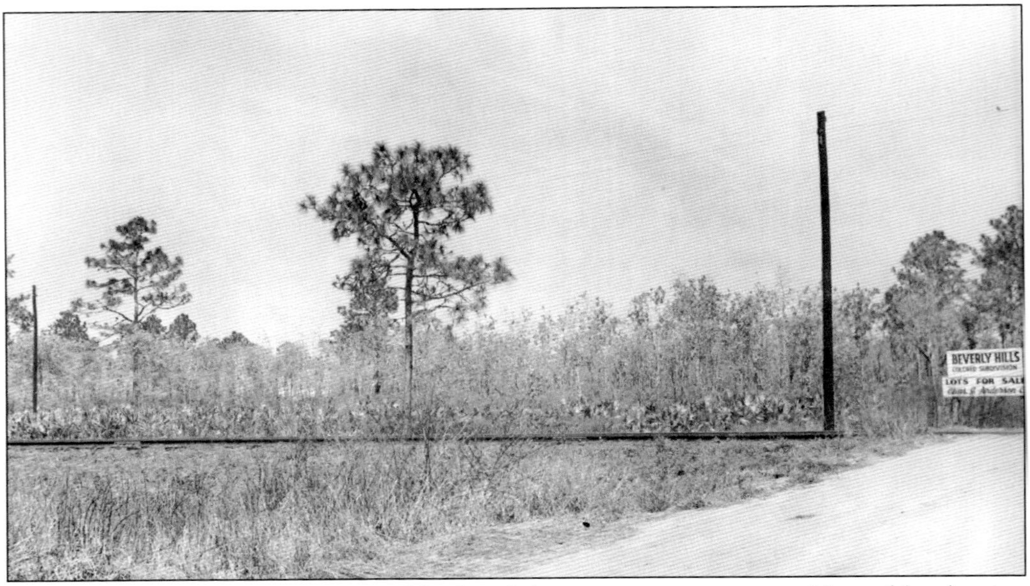

Groveland's African American neighborhoods began to grow, too, as evidenced by the sign advertising the Beverly Hills "colored subdivision" north of the train tracks in east Groveland. The real estate agent was Charles Anderson, who had been a driving force in attracting many Swedish Northerners to Groveland. (Courtesy of City of Groveland.)

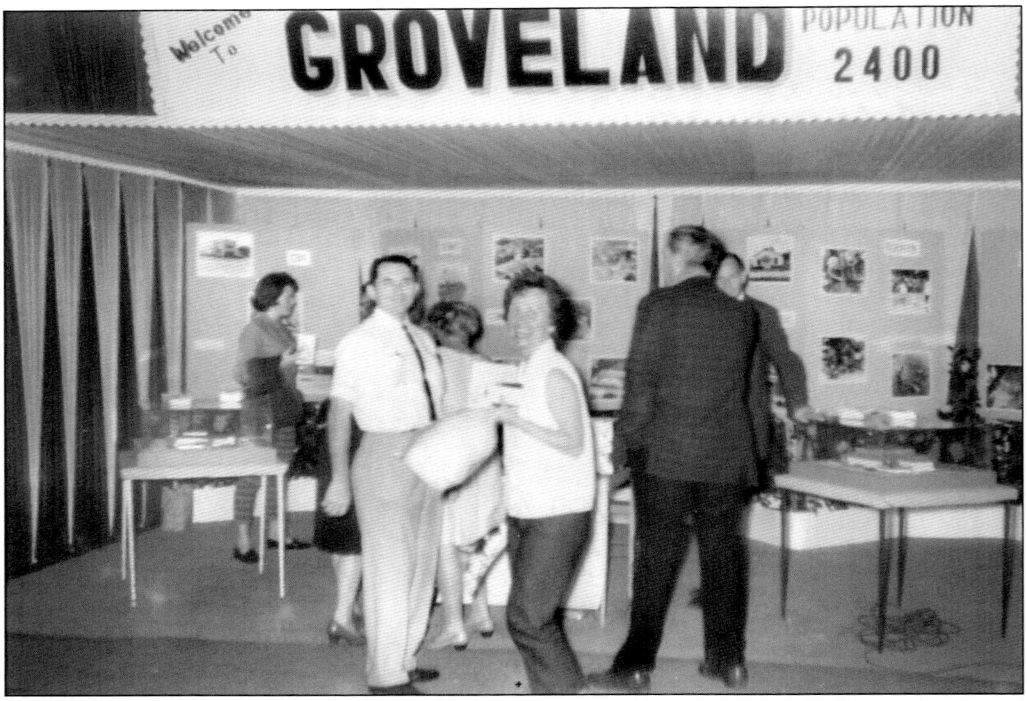

William "Brat" Brannon and his wife, Lou Brannon, visit the Groveland display at the annual Lake County Fair in March 1965. He was a former president of the Business Men's Luncheon Club. Brannon's grocery store was known for delivering groceries to a resident's doorstep. (Courtesy of Ric Baysinger.)

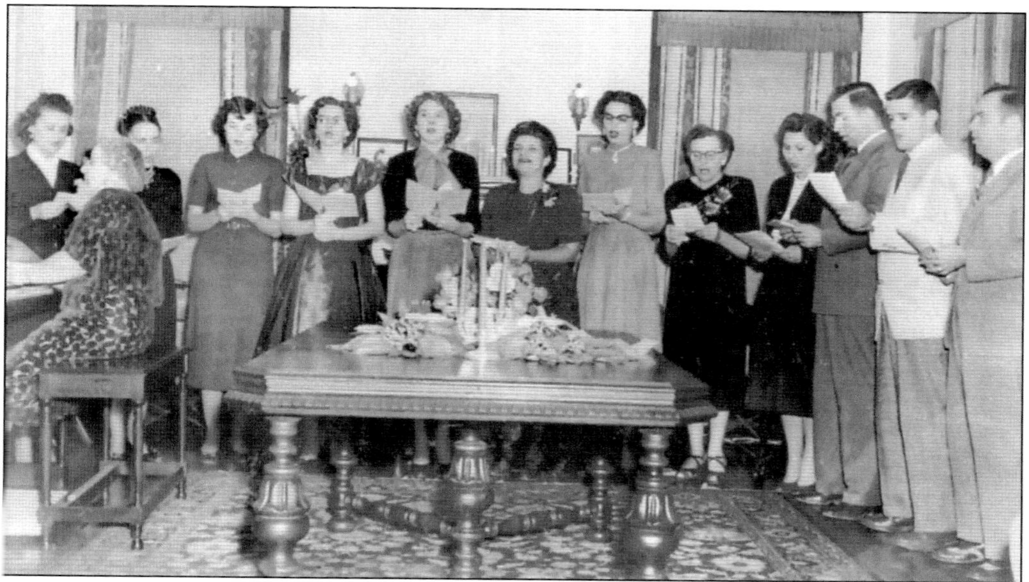

Alberta Simpson (left, at organ) was a popular music teacher who taught organ and piano lessons in Groveland during the 1950s. Singers surrounding Simpson are, from left to right, Doris Hogan, Frances Brice, Shirley Kinlaw, Marcia Hart, Elaine Williford, Eva Mae Pate Weir, Hazel Pennington, Nana Williford, two unidentified, Earl Kinlaw, and unidentified. (Courtesy of Imogene Weir Tallant.)

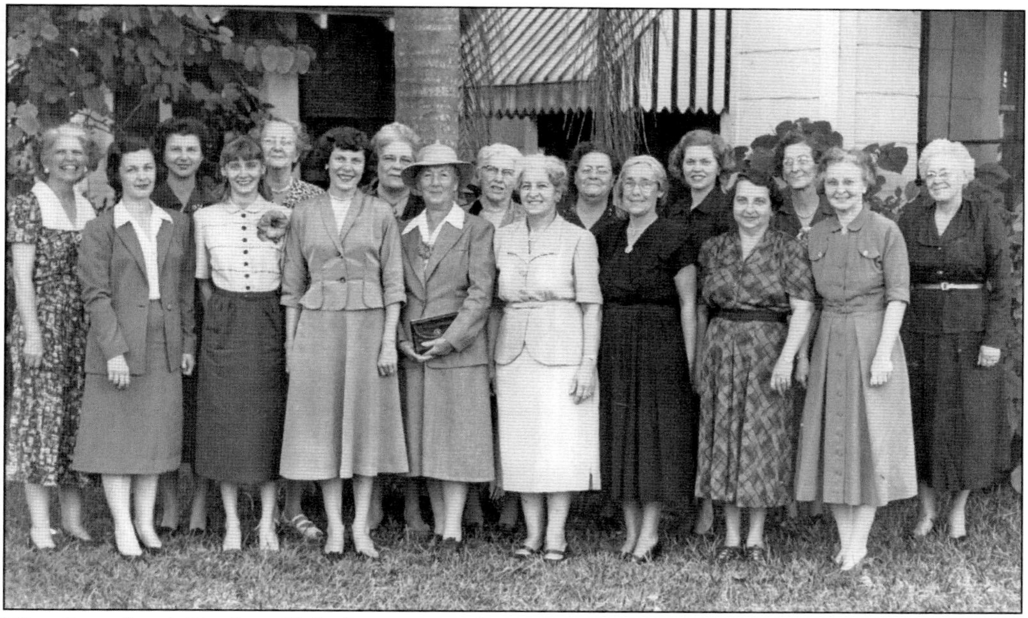

The Groveland Garden Club first met on January 21, 1953. In attendance at the Sheppard family's home on north Highway 19 from left to right are (first row) June Rowland, Joan Slade Rice, Lucile Arnold, ? Werner, Pearl Krahnke, Miriam Rice, Mildred Barnes, and unidentified; (second row) Miriam Thomas, June Fairchild, Susan Myers, Sophia Langenbach, Alice Jahries, unidentified, Esther Kurfiss, ? McDaniel, and Nellie Fletcher Smith. (Courtesy of the Groveland Historical Museum.)

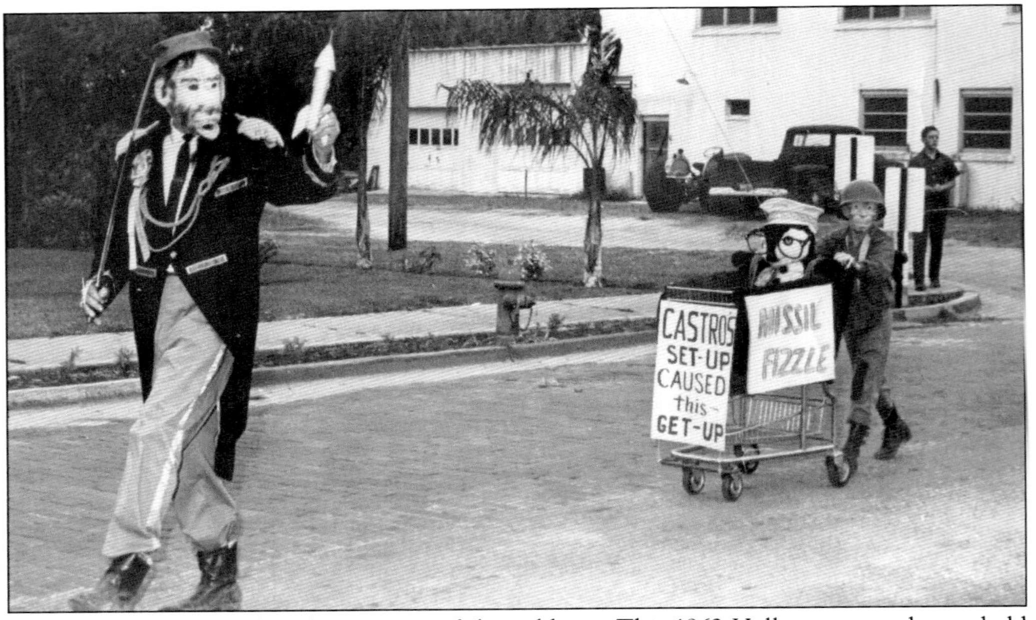

The 1960s also ushered in the tensions of the cold war. This 1962 Halloween parade was held only three days after the Cuban missile crisis ended. Principal Frank Farr (left) is leading the parade holding a missile in his hand. He is followed by Davis Elementary student Jeff Boswell, who pushed a cart with signs that read, "Castro's set-up caused this get-up" and "Missil Fizzle." (Courtesy of Jeff Boswell.)

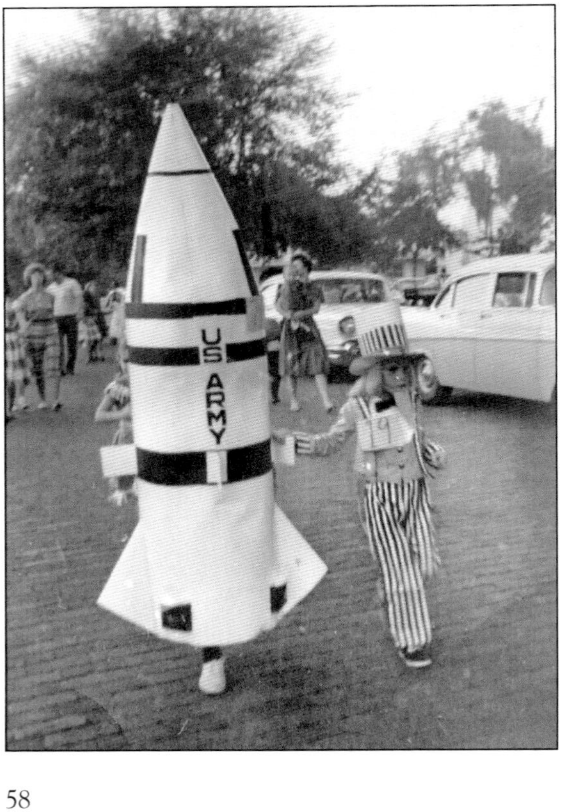

The same Halloween parade captured another sign of the times, the space race. Connie Woolum, whose father, Everett Woolum, worked at defense contractor Martin-Marietta, was dressed as a Pershing Bullpup missile. She was accompanied by her sister, Susan Woolum, who was dressed up as Uncle Sam. The costumes, made by the girls' mother, Doris Woolum, won first place. (Courtesy of Connie Woolum Fleetwood.)

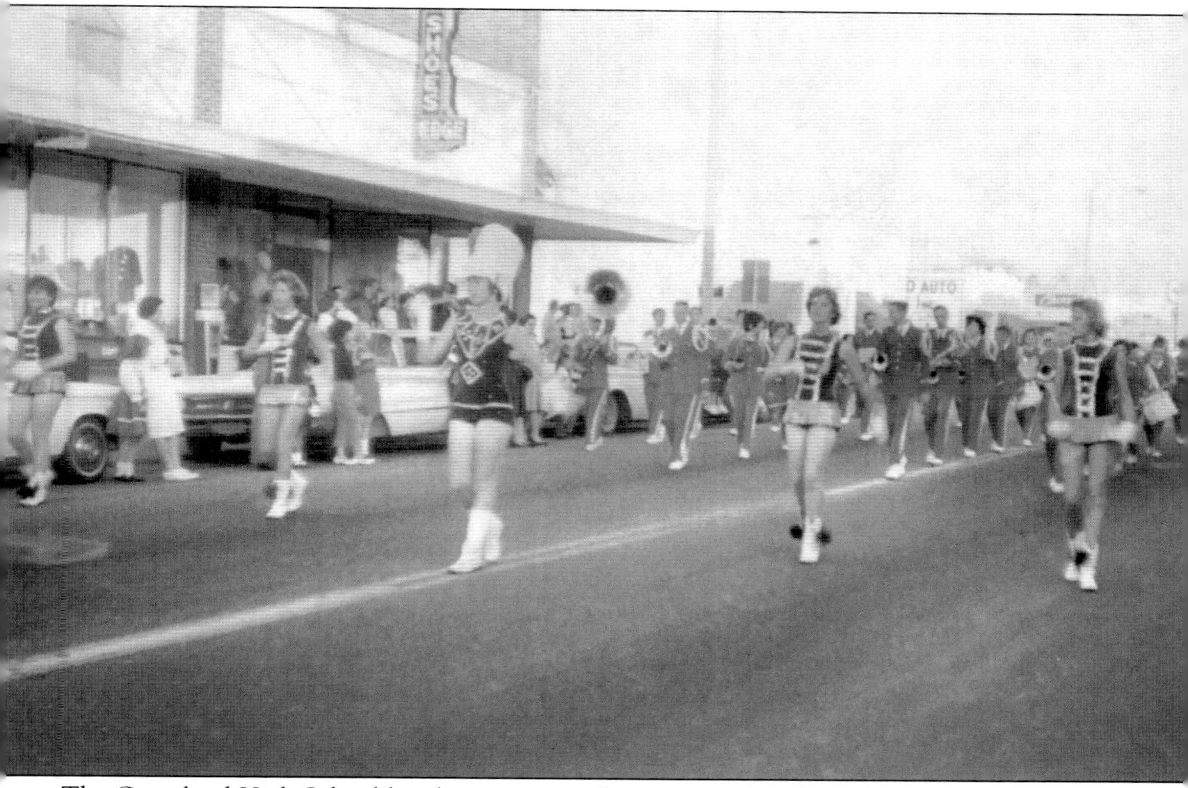

The Groveland High School band was a tremendous source of pride to the town and to the student body. This 1963 Halloween parade was led by head majorette Doris Mussato and her fellow twirlers, Ritchene Vowell, Susan Harb, Carol Speer, and Marla Schwan. The band, which for many years was led by band director Charles Caudill, often won rave ratings at high school band competitions. Some of its members started or played in some of the most popular garage bands of the day, such as the Nation Rocking Shadows, Ron and the Starfires, and the Originals. In this parade down Broad Street, the band marches past some of the city's most successful businesses: Edge's Mercantile Company, Standard Auto Parts, Cherry's Fashions, and the Palm Restaurant. (Courtesy of Ric Baysinger.)

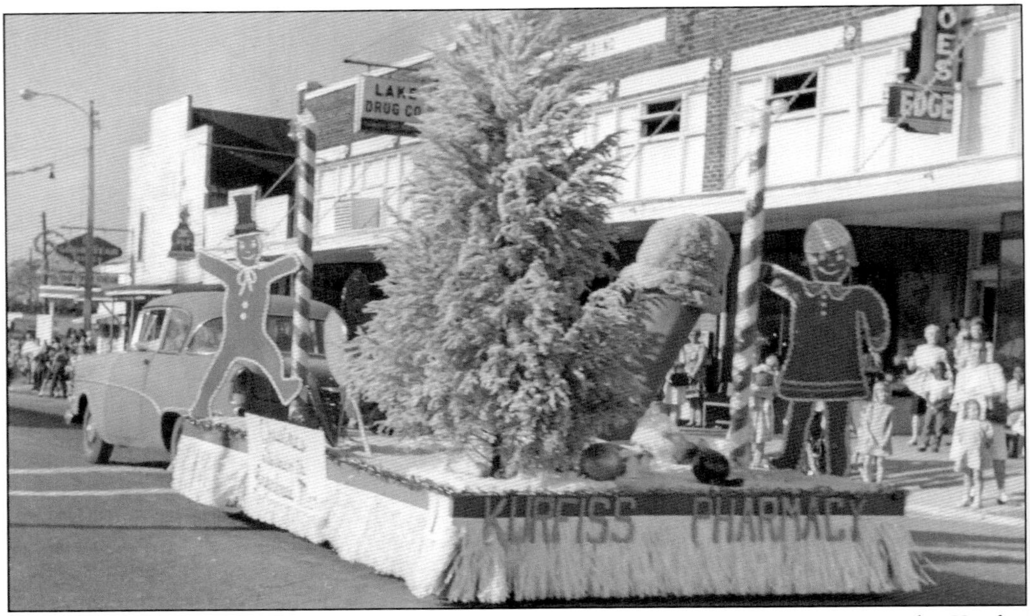

As this 1965 Christmas parade shows, Groveland could boast two pharmacies—the Kurfiss Pharmacy, which won first place among merchants' floats in this parade, and Lake Drug Company, which had been around since the 1920s. The sign for Lake Drug juts out from the Edge Building where the float is passing by. Kurfiss Pharmacy was run by Reggie Kurfiss, the son of Howard Kurfiss, the town's funeral director. (Courtesy of the Groveland Historical Museum.)

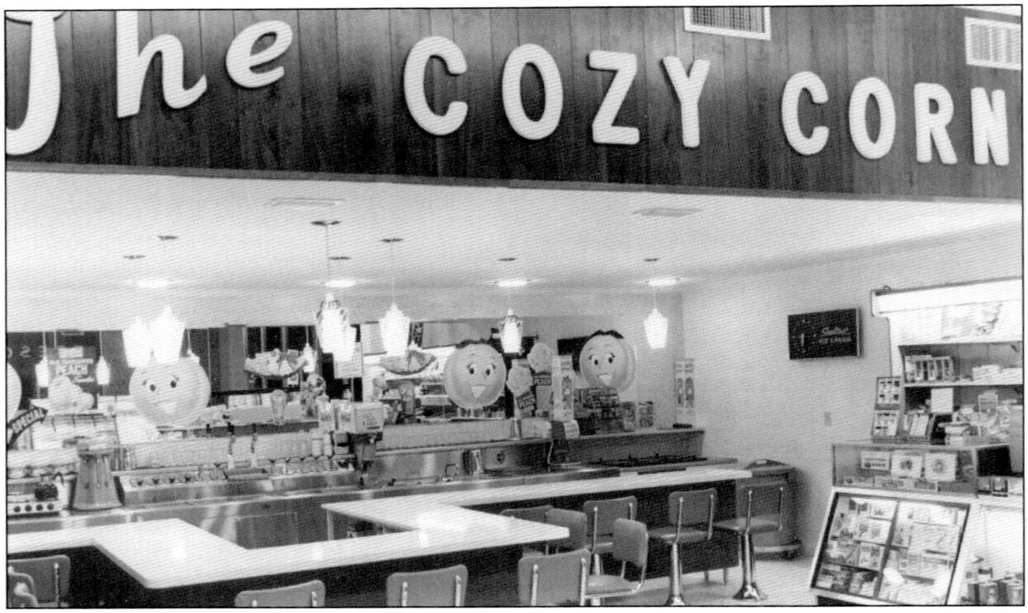

Kurfiss's shiny new pharmacy on Main Avenue included a soda fountain called the Cozy Corner. Since the 1920s, hanging out at rival Lake Drug Company's soda fountain after school had become a well-established tradition. Friends shared the news of the day over hot fudge sundaes, cherry Cokes, and suicides—a hometown specialty of crushed ice with a squirt of every flavoring. (Courtesy of the Groveland Historical Museum.)

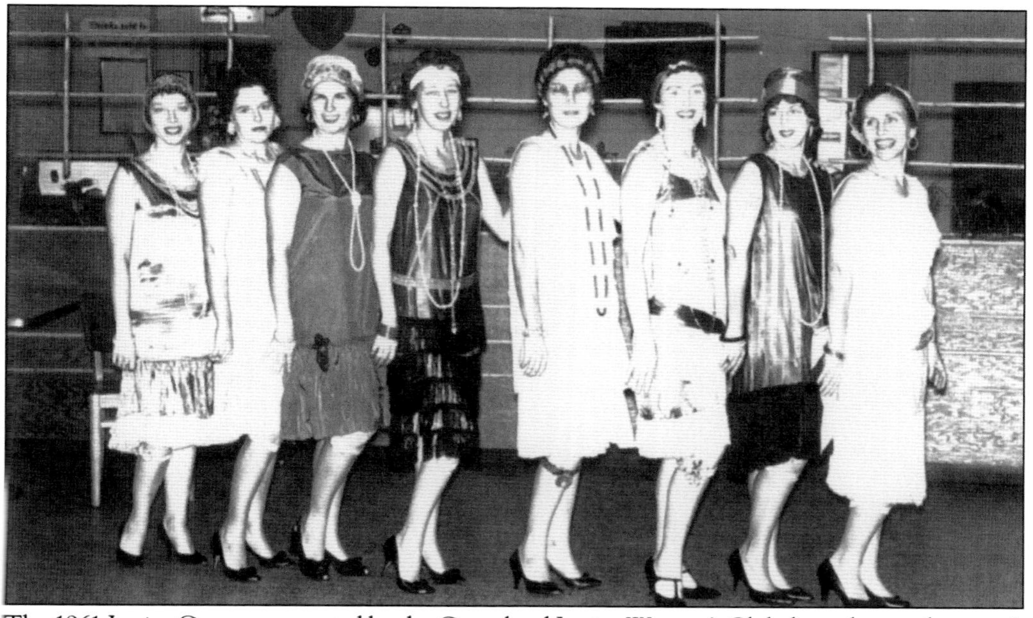

The 1961 Junior Capers, presented by the Groveland Junior Woman's Club, brought out the town's talented and whimsical side. Dressed in Roaring Twenties flapper dresses and performing "Five Foot Two, Eyes of Blue" from left to right, are Sally Caudill, Claudia Sharpe, Jo Ann Seaver, Dot Maguire, Margaret Galassi, Gladys Kuharske, Bea Harb, and Lou Brannon. The event was held at the Groveland High School auditorium. (Courtesy of the Groveland Historical Museum.)

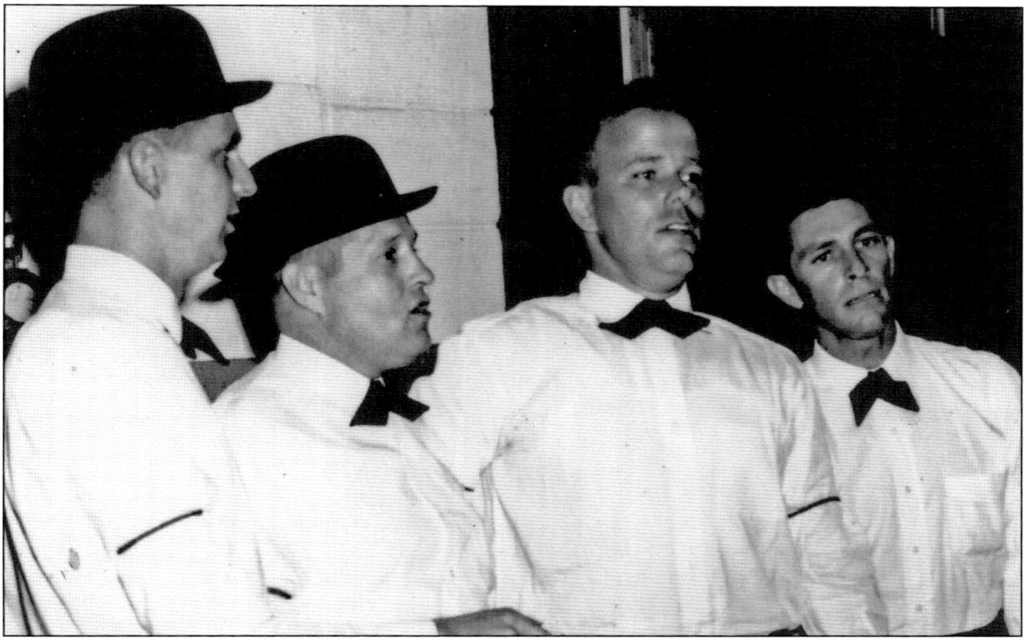

Also on the program at the 1961 Junior Capers was a barbershop quartet called the Four Pops. The four singers are, from left to right, Leonard Seaver, bass; Charles Caudill, baritone; Bill Conybear, lead; and Dick Willard, tenor. Bob Maguire was the master of ceremonies. E. W. "Scotty" McCalley directed the production. (Courtesy of Imogene Weir Tallant.)

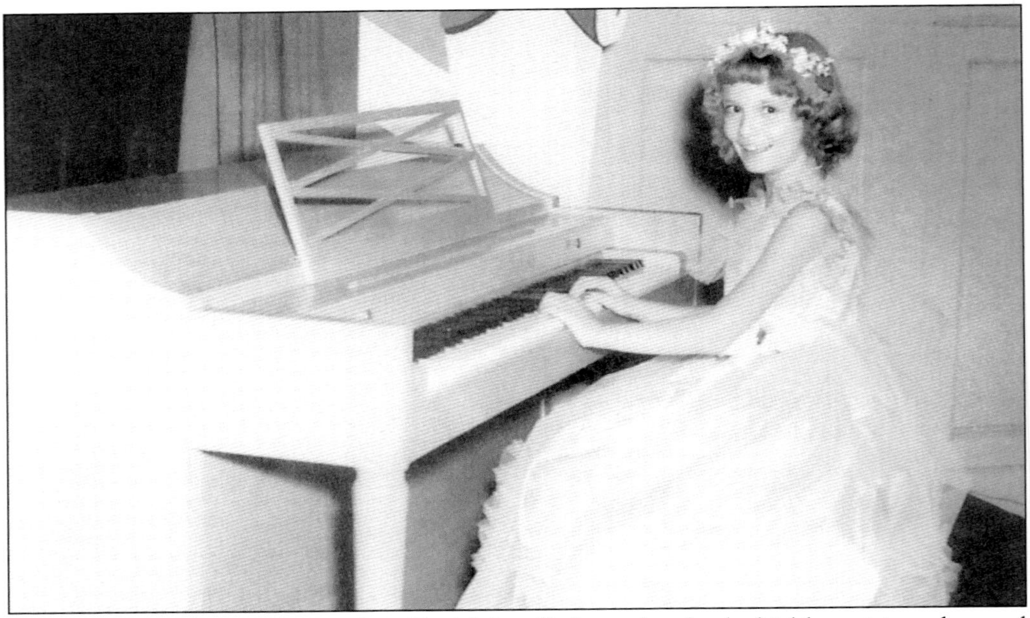

Students who took piano lessons from Beulah Ingalls dressed up for the highly anticipated annual recitals. Students walked to Ingalls's home studio once a week and practiced in between using the John W. Schaum lesson books. Pictured here in this late-1950s photograph is Hazel Langenbach, daughter of Fred and Lucy Langenbach and the great-granddaughter of one of the early Pine Island settlers. (Courtesy of Ellen Langenbach Thompson.)

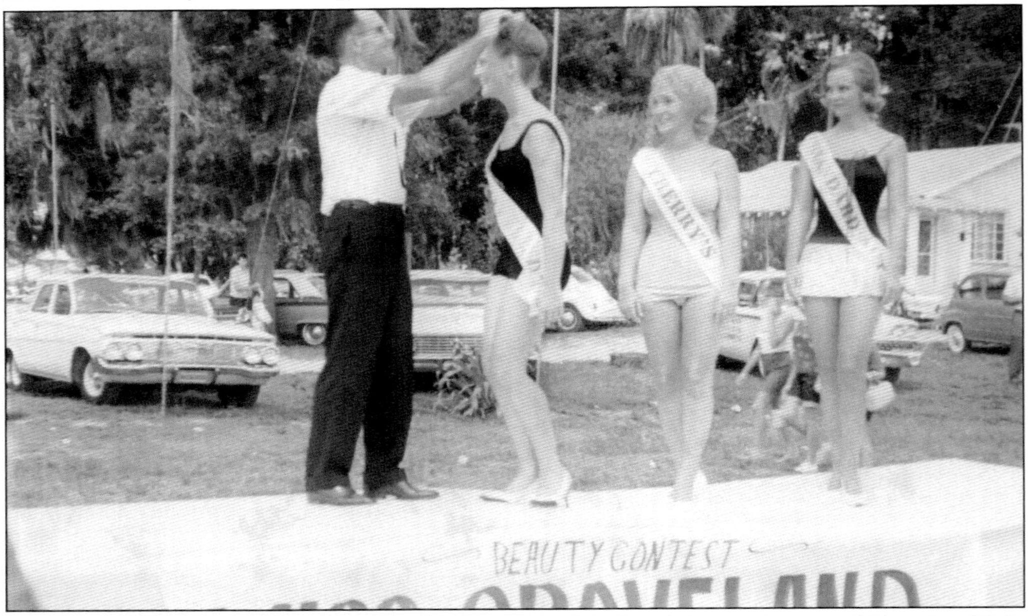

In 1965, the Miss Groveland Contest became a highlight of the city's annual Fourth of July celebration. Mayor Elma Puryear (left) is crowning the winner, Carol Speer, while runners-up Sandy Frontz (second from right) and Lauralee Payne (right) look on. The beauty contest crowned the city's beauties for decades to come. They met for a reunion on July 4, 2007, at the grand opening of the Groveland Historical Museum. (Courtesy of Ric Baysinger.)

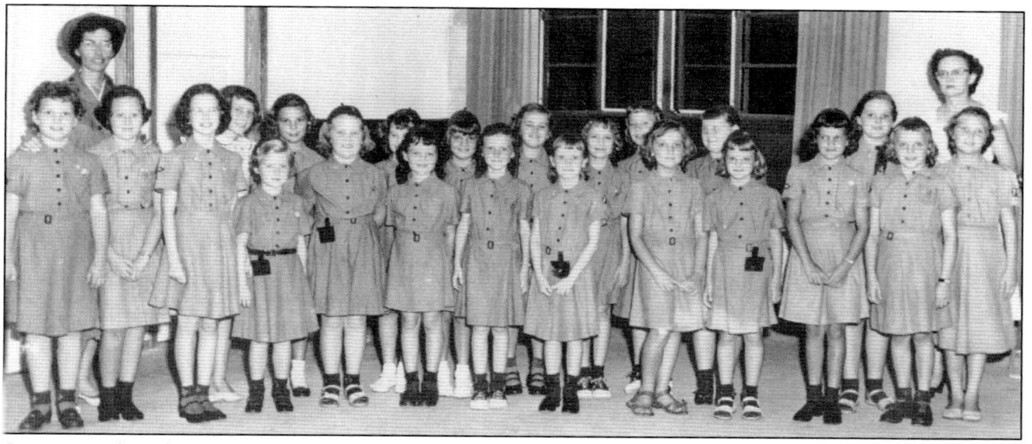

Scouting played a big role in the lives of many Groveland youth such as those in the 1958 Brownie troop above. From left to right are (first row) Carol Bradley, Doris Mussatto, Linda Schmidt, Linda Tillis, Nancy Kuharske, Gail Clay, Teresa Higdon, Charlene Bridges, Nora Lee Newman, Gloria Fairchild, Jeannie Gano, Cheryl Harb, and Peggy Evans; (second row) ? Glass (leader), Gayle Cowart, Jeannie Potter, Bunny Lord, Margaret Jost, Hazel Langenbach, Marla Schwan, Janice Smith, Clemie Fairchild, and Lucy Langenbach (co-leader). Scouting was an important part of the Baysinger family (below). The parents were den mother and assistant scoutmaster, and the sons became Eagle Scouts, the highest rank attainable in Boy Scouts. Attending the 1965 Eagle Scout ceremony at the Lake David Center below are, from left to right, Scoutmaster Paul Hoskinson, Ric Baysinger, Marion Baysinger, Jim Baysinger, and Bob Baysinger. (Above courtesy of Charlene Bridges Neel; below courtesy of Ric Baysinger.)

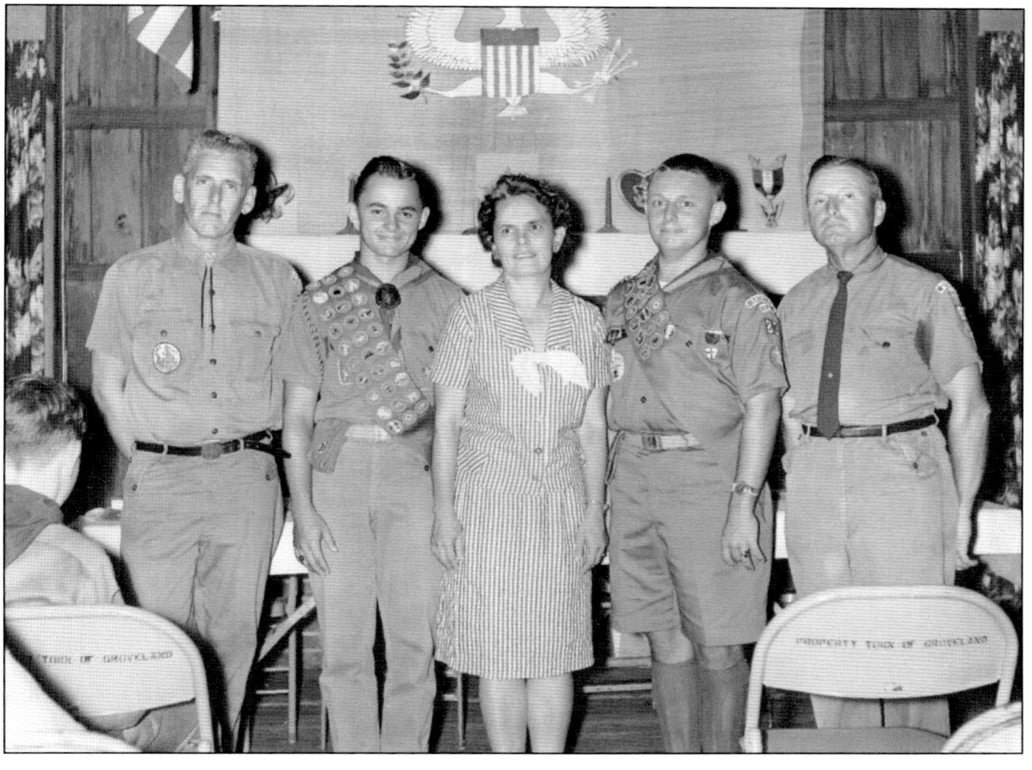

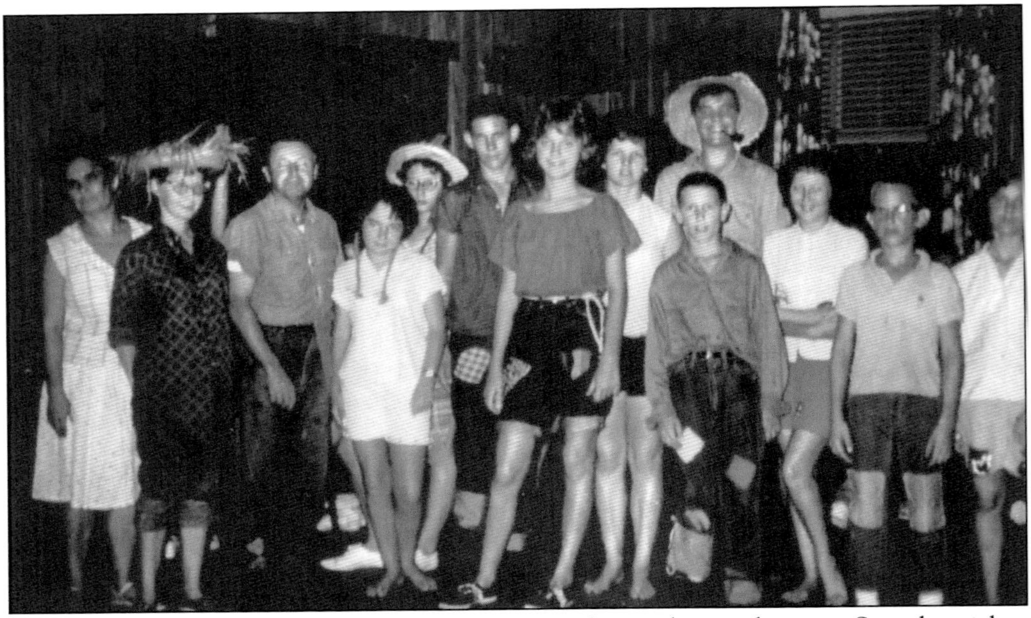

The Teenway Club of the 1950s and 1960s was more than a place to dance on Saturday nights. It was a rite of passage. Girls and boys looked forward to their 12th birthdays when they could get their Teenway cards and attend dances at the Lake David community building, such as this 1960s crowd dressed up for a Sadie Hawkins dance with chaperones Bob and Marion Baysinger. (Courtesy of Ric Baysinger.)

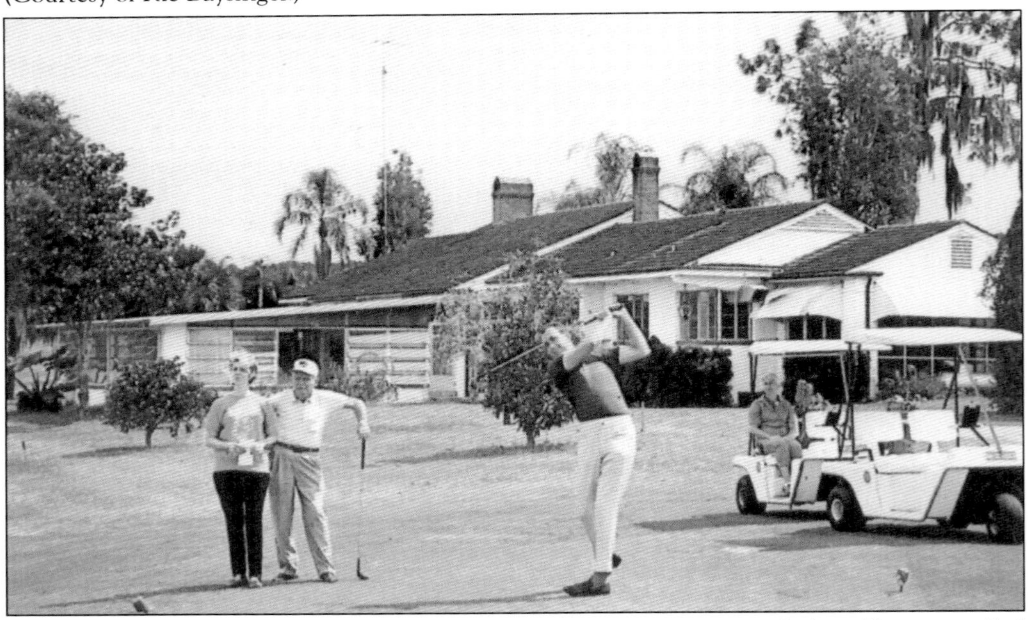

In January 1966, Groveland and Clermont joined forces to start a nine-hole golf course called Green Valley Country Club. The closing for the 107-acre property formerly owned by Ed Burke was held at People's State Bank in Groveland. Charter officers and board members included Howard Kurfiss, Arthur Roberts, L. Day Edge, Graham Payne, and Norton Wilkins. (Courtesy of the Marion Baysinger Memorial Library.)

Four

Business
Lumber Barons and Citrus Kings

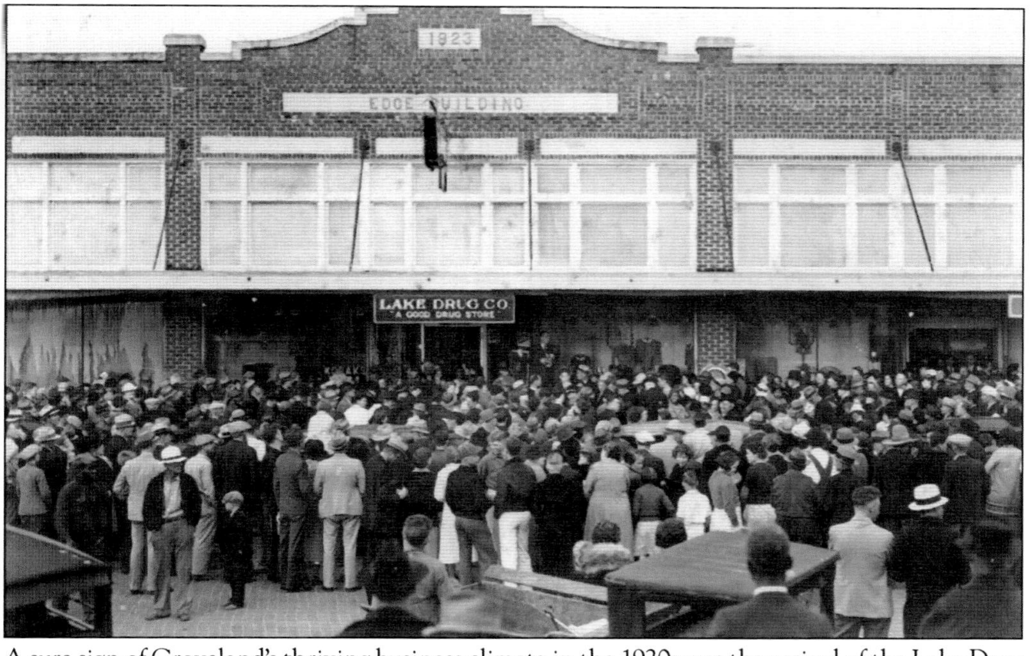

A sure sign of Groveland's thriving business climate in the 1920s was the arrival of the Lake Drug Company, "A Good Drug Store," captured here at its grand opening. Dr. T. Grady McFadden, seen with a megaphone in hand, was a highly regarded figure. His drugstore and soda fountain, in the Edge Building on Broad Street, became a popular place for residents to seek medical advice and to socialize. "Dr. Mac" was part of the Groveland Board of Trade, which promoted commerce of "The Progressive Town." The town's first physician was Dr. Samuel Register, who became the first resident to own an automobile. (Courtesy of Mary Nell McFadden Arnold.)

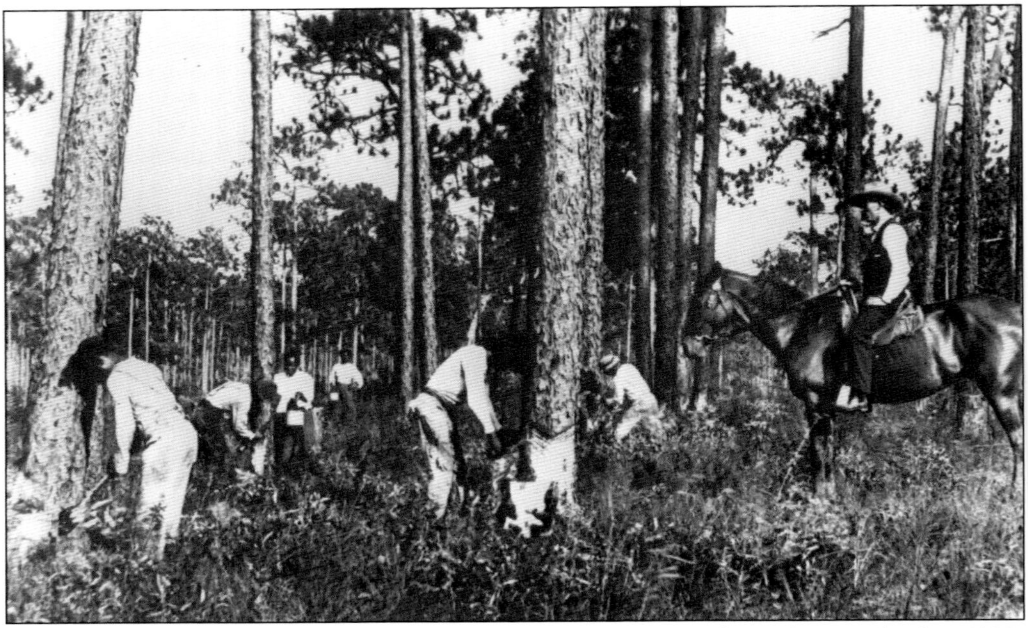

One of the first businesses in Groveland was turpentine farming, shown here in this late-1890s photograph taken near the Green Swamp. Workers cut cavities in the trunk where the sap could drip into clay pots. The pitch was taken by mules to the distilleries. The turpentine business flourished until a severe drought in 1907 killed the longleaf pines. (Courtesy of State Archives of Florida.)

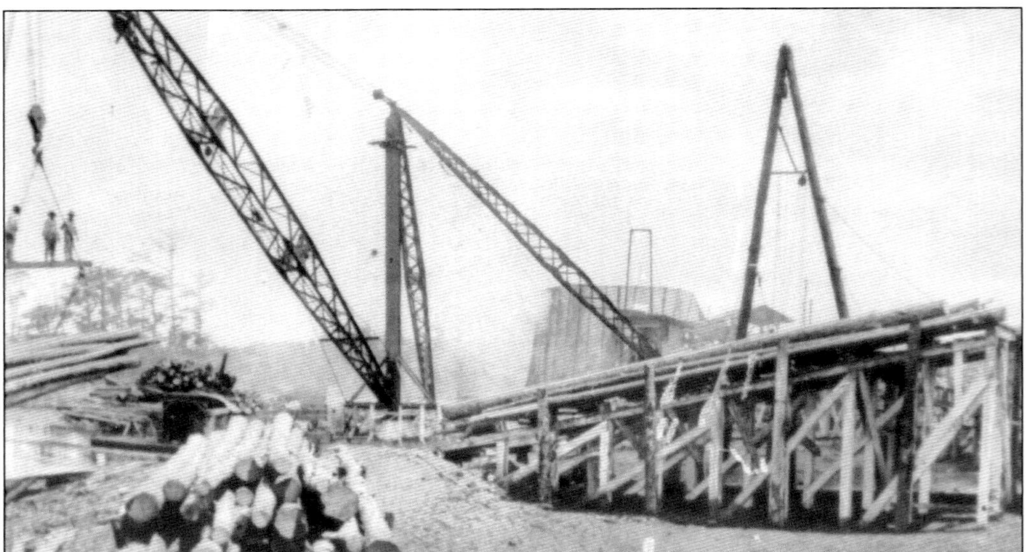

When a drought ended the turpentine business, E. E. Edge built a sawmill to harvest the lumber. J. Ray Arnold bought the mill and turned it into the Southeast's largest. At its peak, the mill owned six locomotives and 100 logging cars. The Arnold lumber company was the largest lumber shipper on the Atlantic Coastline Railroad and was Lake County's largest employer. (Courtesy of the Lake County Historical Society.)

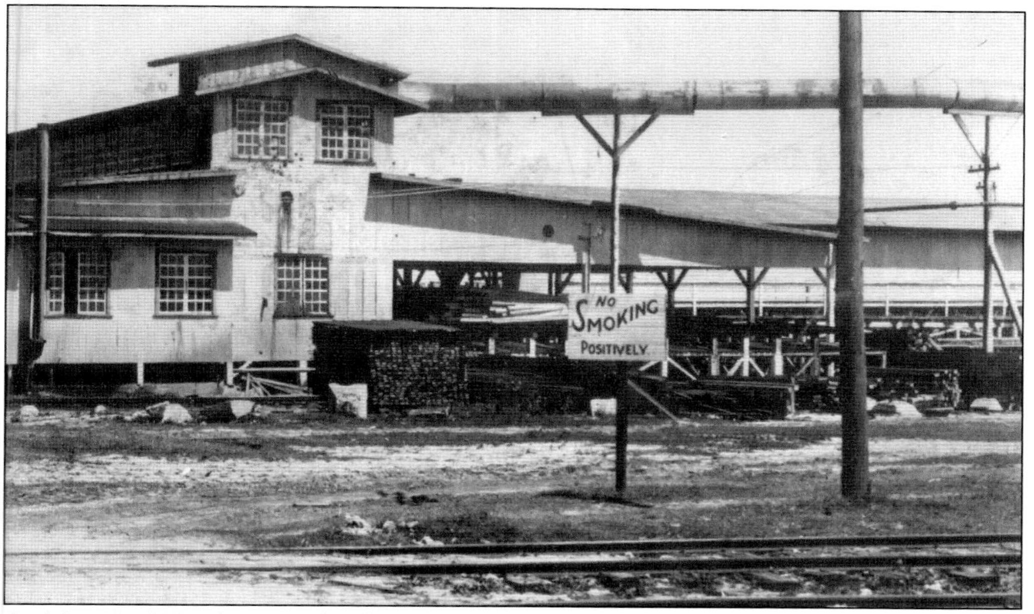

On May 19, 1925, a ferocious fire destroyed the Arnold sawmill, eliminating hundreds of jobs. A new $7 million mill was rebuilt, designed with advanced equipment. But the combination of fewer pine forests and the coming Great Depression ended the mill's glory days and crippled Groveland's economy for decades. Note the sign at the new mill: "No Smoking Positively." (Courtesy of the Lake County Historical Society.)

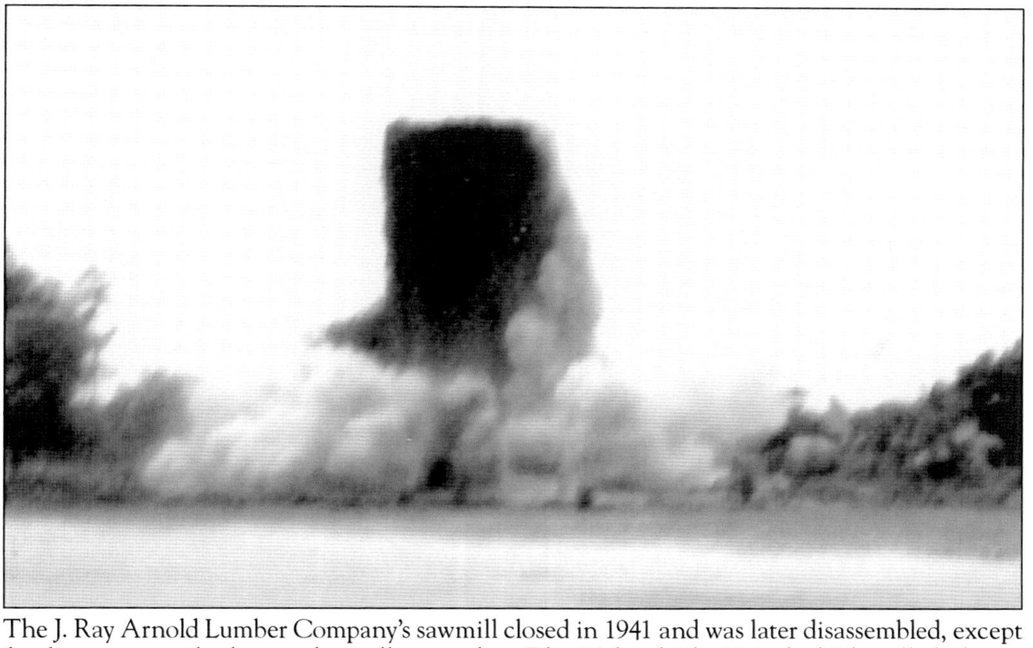

The J. Ray Arnold Lumber Company's sawmill closed in 1941 and was later disassembled, except for the concrete silo that used to collect sawdust. The 35-foot-high, 10-inch-thick walled silo, on the north side of intersecting Highways 33 and 50, became known as "Bat Tower." The steel-and-rail-reinforced structure was dynamited and bulldozed away in May 1979 by Controlled Demolition of Baltimore. (Courtesy of the Lake County Historical Society.)

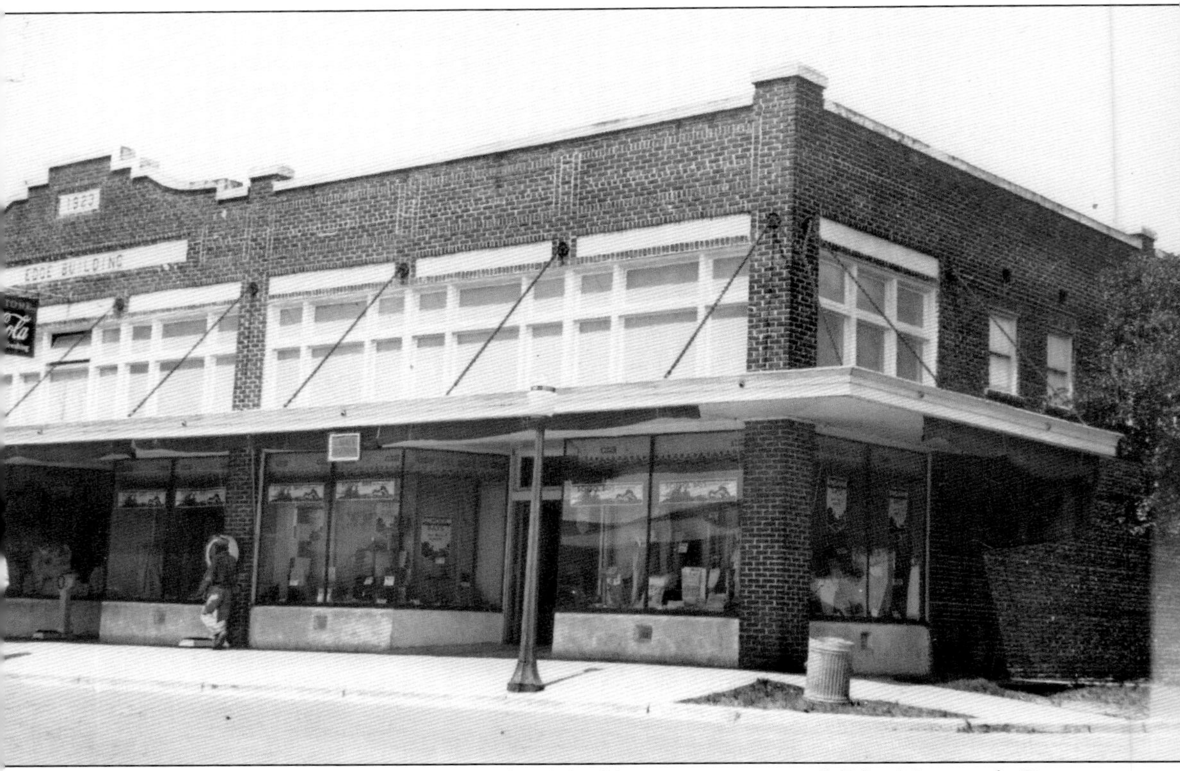

By 1923, when this 12,000-square-foot brick building was constructed, Edge Mercantile Company was one of the largest businesses in the state. The building, on the corner of Broad Street and Main Avenue, was home to Edge's businesses, which included groceries, dry goods, shoes, farm supplies, hardware, furniture, funeral services, and filling station. E. E. Edge ran the businesses until his death in 1934. His son, L. Day Edge, who had been a political star, ran the businesses until his death in 1971. He had helped route Highway 50 through Groveland's downtown in front of the building during his legislative tenure. Edge's daughter and son-in-law, Margie and Kermit Clay, took over the reins until 1979, when the family decided to lease the building. One longtime employee, C. J. Ingalls, had worked for the Edges for 54 years. (Courtesy of Lake Historical Society.)

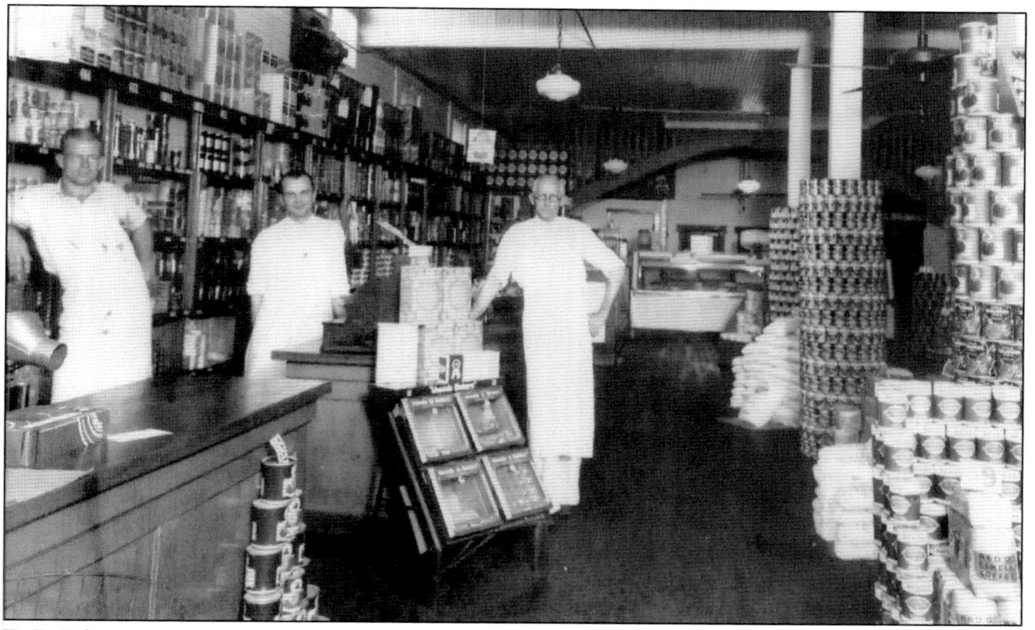

E. E. Edge's commissary evolved into a full-fledged grocery store that became part of the Great Atlantic and Pacific Tea Company (A&P), seen in this 1934 photograph. From left to right are Ralston Holms, manager Charlie Heath, and Bill Pritchett. During the 1960s, Groveland's downtown boasted three grocery stores. (Courtesy of Cyleta Lee Austin.)

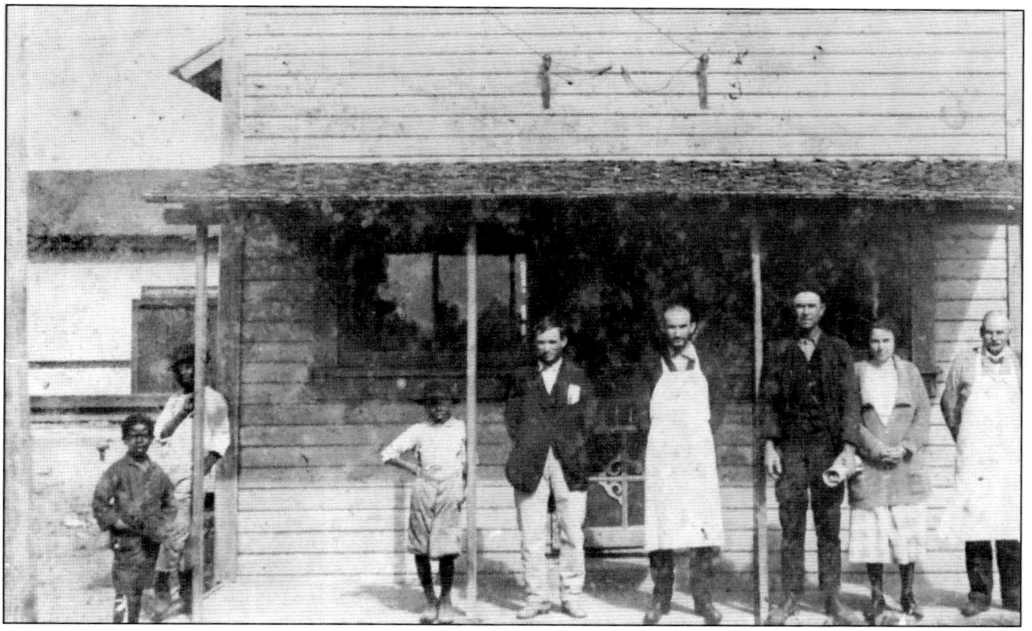

After a near-fatal accident at the Arnold sawmill, Abner Rowe opened the Groveland Meat Market, the first of its type in South Lake. Rowe's store on Broad Street included a refrigerator that was cooled by 5,000 pounds of ice brought by train. Pictured here in 1914 from left to right are three unidentified children, ? Martin, Abner Rowe, Jim Pate, Ollie Sloan, and ? Bowen. (Courtesy of Julian Rowe.)

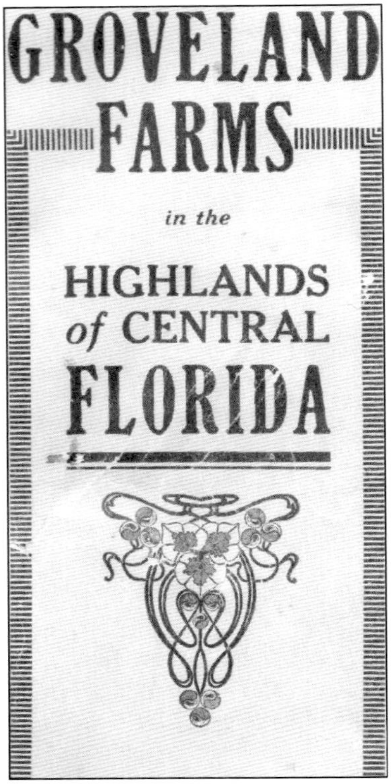
GROVELAND FARMS

in the

HIGHLANDS of CENTRAL FLORIDA

From about 1911 through the 1920s, Groveland Farms, the name given to the thousands of acres purchased and platted by developer John W. Beach, was heavily promoted to Northerners, especially those in Beach's native Rockford, Illinois. Brochures, such as the one pictured here, raved about then Taylorville's attributes, including its rich farmland and location between the Atlantic Ocean and Gulf of Mexico. Beach called Groveland Farms "the greatest produce-raising section of the state." His brochure claimed that practically every purchaser intending to buy 10-acre tracts bought twice the number. Beach was not the only promoter. Charles Anderson, whose real estate company is pictured at the corner of Broad Street and Lake Avenue (below), also touted the city's charms for decades and helped draw many new families, especially those of Swedish heritage. (Both courtesy of the Lake County Historical Society.)

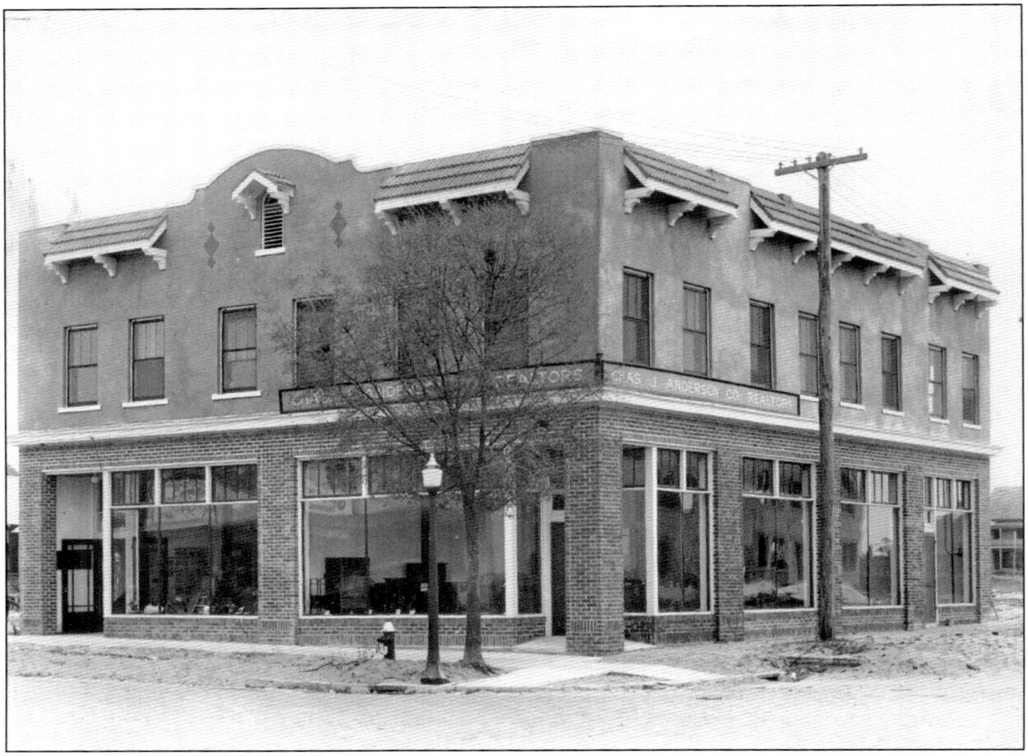

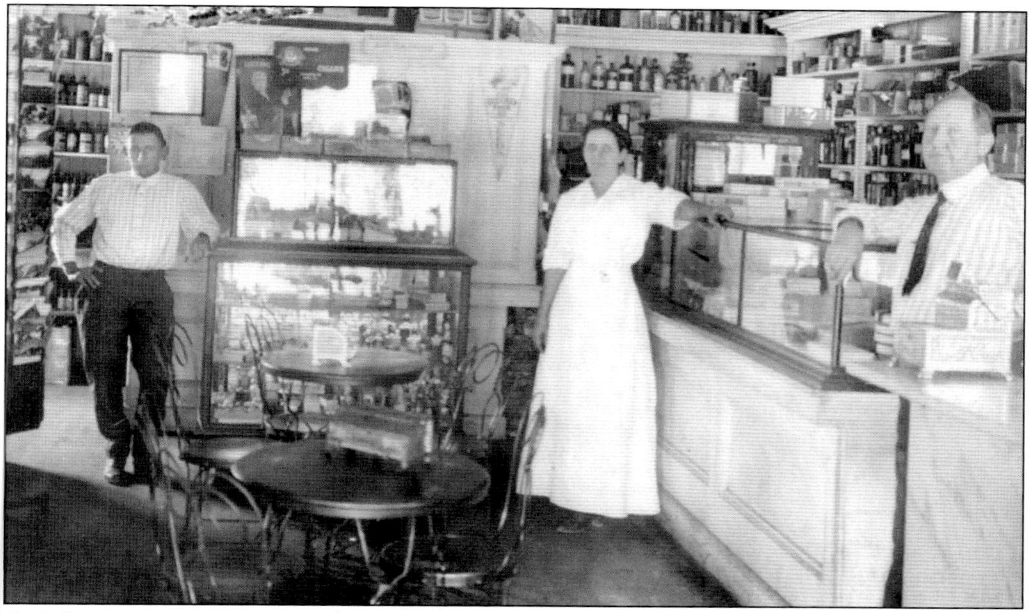

At left is accountant Henry Sheppard standing in Sheppard's Drug Store in the early 1900s. The store was on the northeast corner of Broad Street and Main Avenue. Dr. William DeVane, one of the town's early physicians, bought the pharmacy. During the Depression, downtown merchants showed free movies on the side of the bank across the street to draw customers into town. (Courtesy of Peggy Parrish Sloan.)

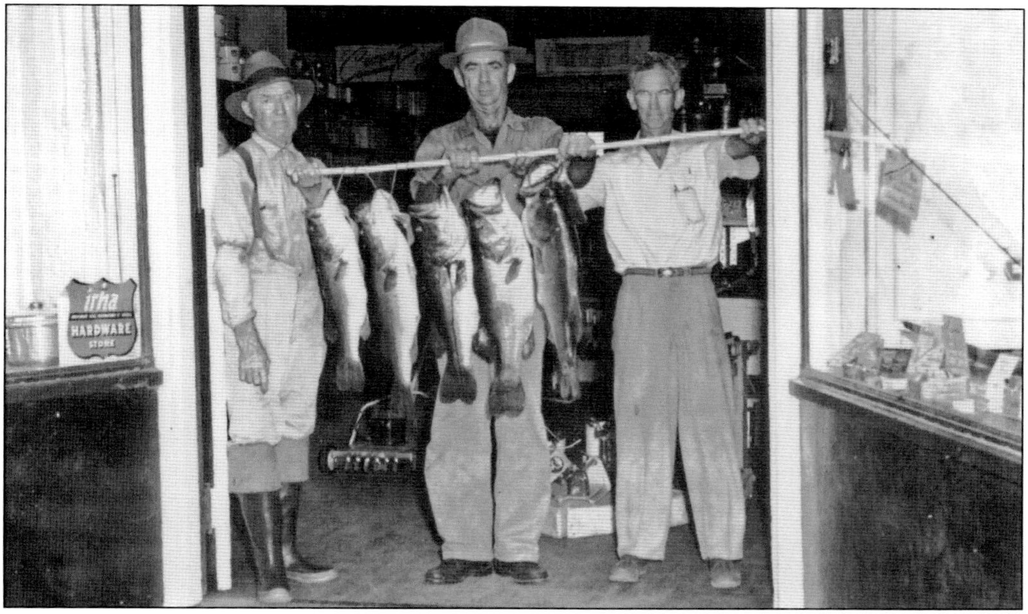

Uhland McKinney (right) ran Edge's Hardware Store for many years. McKinney was born in 1903 and died in 1982. McKinney, Clyde Plowden, Lyda Smith, and Katie Stewart graduated May 12, 1922, from Groveland High School, becoming the school's first graduates. McKinney married Bonnie Revels, and the couple had a son, Wendell McKinney. Uhland McKinney was an active member of Edge Memorial United Methodist Church. (Courtesy of Mandy McKinney.)

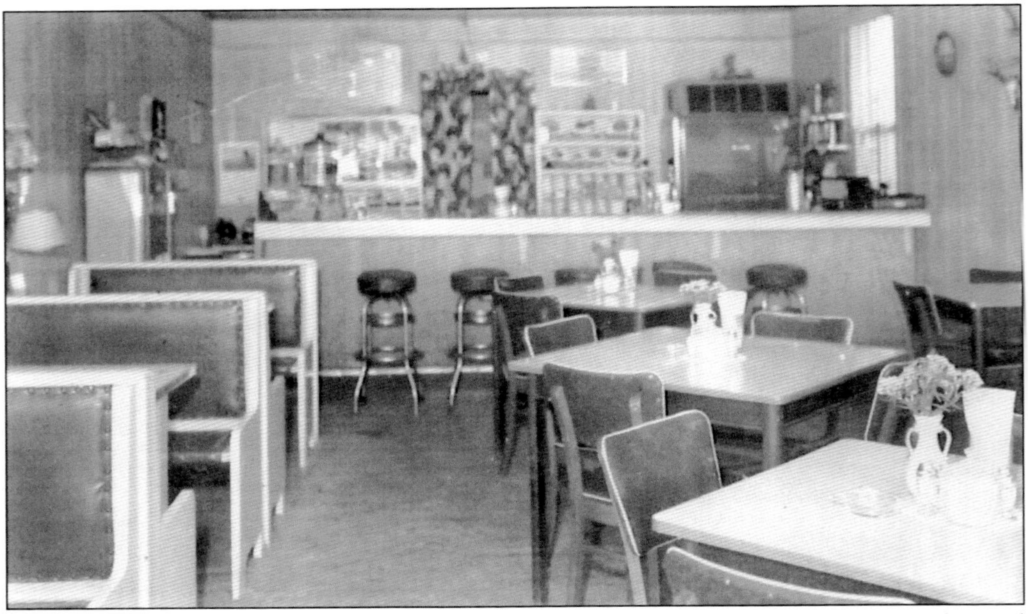

The Palm Restaurant was one of the longest-running diners in Groveland. The restaurant featured German-American food and was run by the Toth family. Joseph Toth, the head proprietor, moved from Kentucky to Groveland in 1962. He died in 1986. The restaurant was located on Broad Street and was popular among families and downtown business diners. In more recent years, it was frequented by retirees. (Courtesy of the Marion Baysinger Memorial Library.)

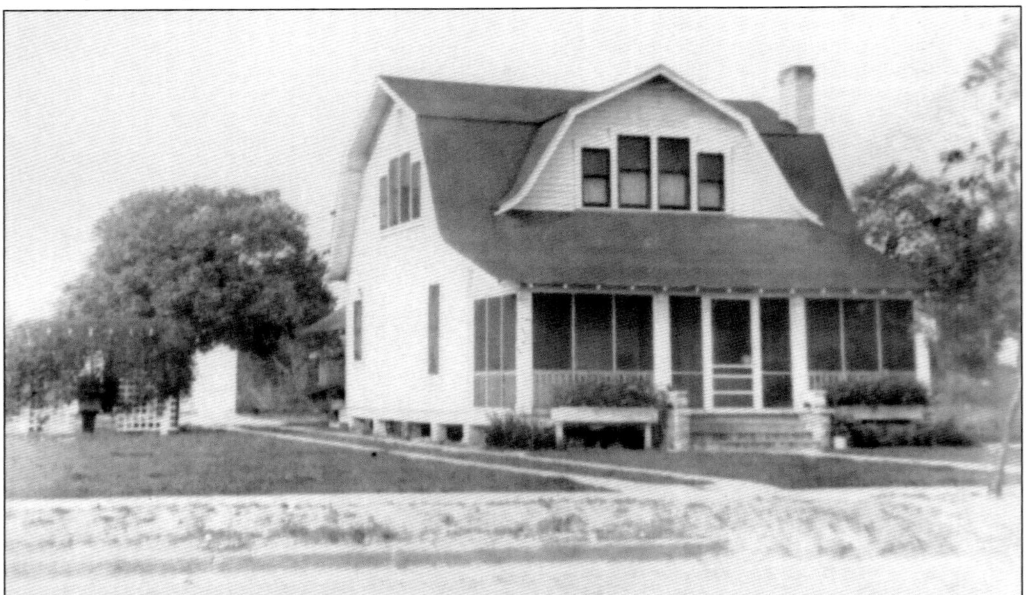

The Hawkins home, near the present-day corner of Magnolia Street and Main Avenue, became the Kurfiss Funeral Home. Groveland's funeral services from the 1920s through 1947 were handled by Edge Funeral Home. Services included a hearse and a parlor upstairs in Edge's Hardware Store. In 1947, Howard Kurfiss bought the business and moved it to Lake Avenue. His family ran the funeral home for three generations. (Courtesy of Cyleta Lee Austin.)

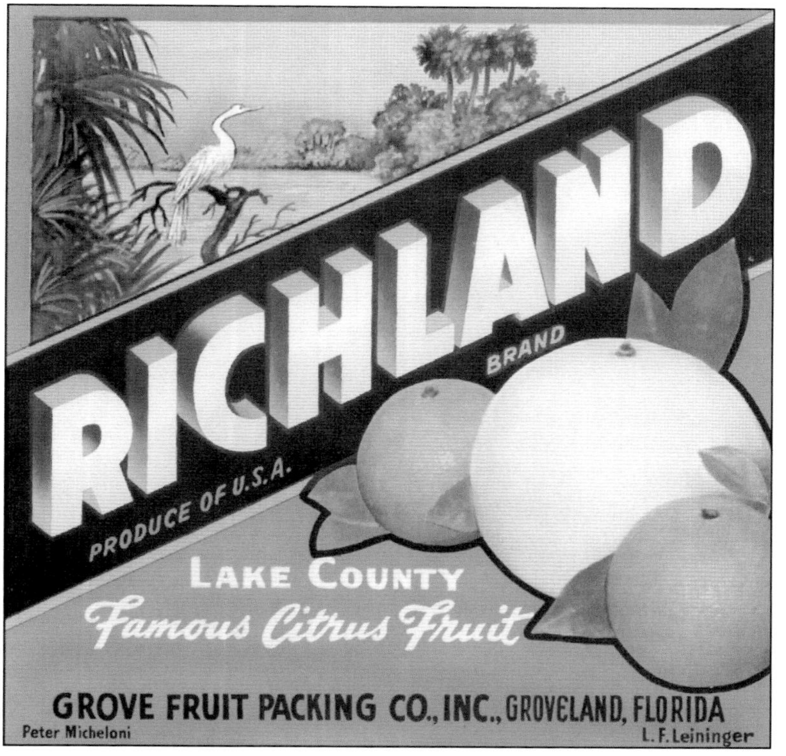

From the 1940s through the 1980s, citrus became king in Groveland as groves and packinghouses flourished. Citrus labels, such as the one pictured here for Richland, owned by Peter Micheloni and L. F. Leininger, became collectible art. The colorful labels decorated wooden citrus crates until the industry shifted to cardboard and pre-printed labels during World War II. Florida birds and plants were common themes. (Courtesy of the Groveland Historical Museum.)

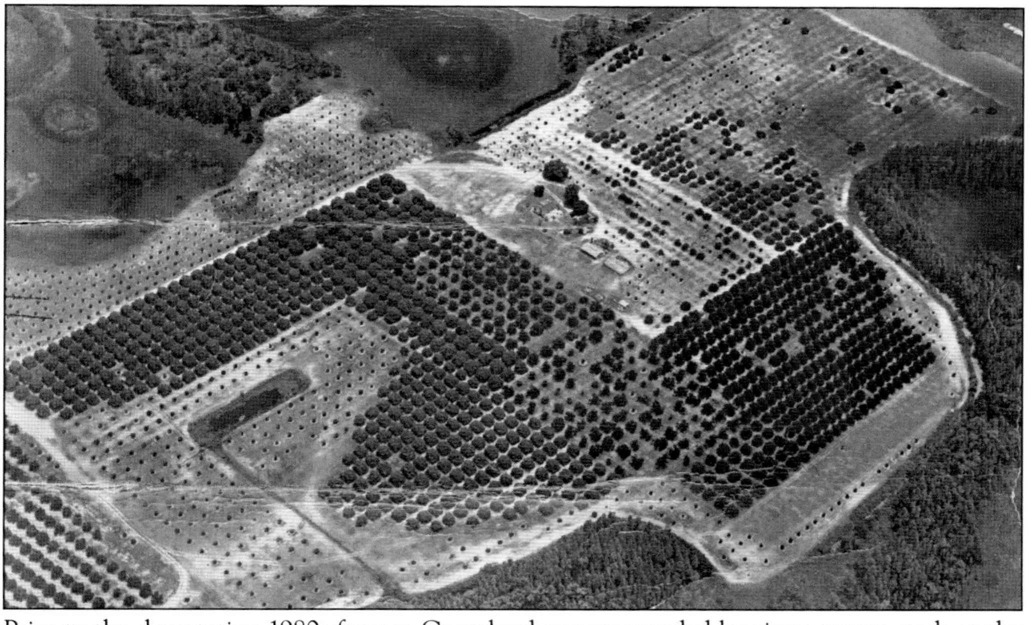

Prior to the devastating 1980s freezes, Groveland was surrounded by citrus groves, such as the ones shown in this 1959 aerial view three miles south of Groveland along Highway 33. The groves pictured here belonged to Basilio and Leo Mussatto. They were part of a group of Italian families in 1924 who established groves, vineyards, and farms in rural Groveland. (Courtesy of the State Archives of Florida.)

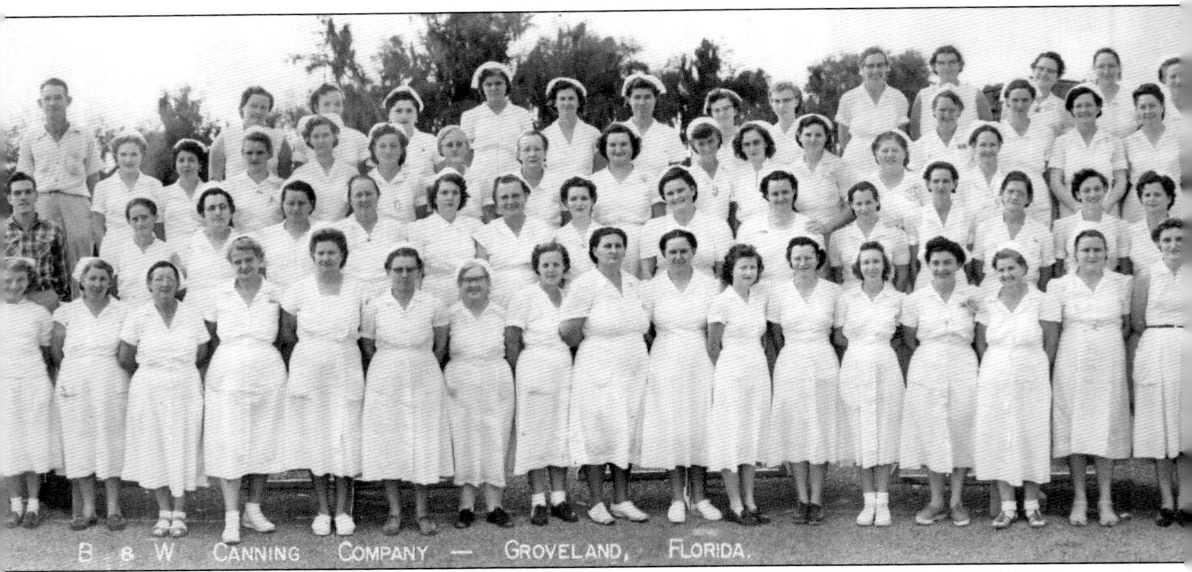

In 1946, two visionary fruit inspectors, Eugene Busbee of Tampa and William "Norton" Wilkins of Mount Dora, founded the B&W Fruit Company in Groveland and incorporated two years later. In 1948, the company shipped almost a million cases of canned fruit and 250,000 boxes of fresh fruit. By the following year, B&W had become the largest employer of any canning plant in Florida with peak payrolls at $23,000 a week. By 1954, women had become an important part of Groveland's

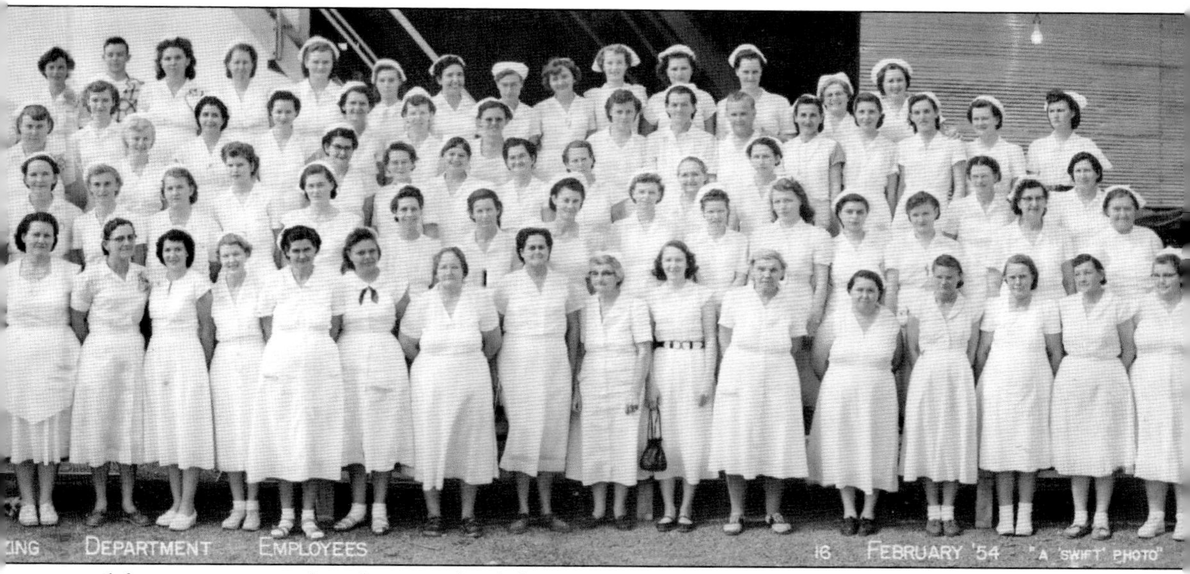

workforce, as seen in this photograph of about 140 workers in the Sectionizing Department. A series of severe freezes in 1983, 1985, and 1989 destroyed nine out of 10 citrus trees in Lake County, crippling the citrus-processing industry. Family members carry on the company under the name Busbee, Wilkins, and Sealy, Inc. (Courtesy of the Groveland Historical Museum.)

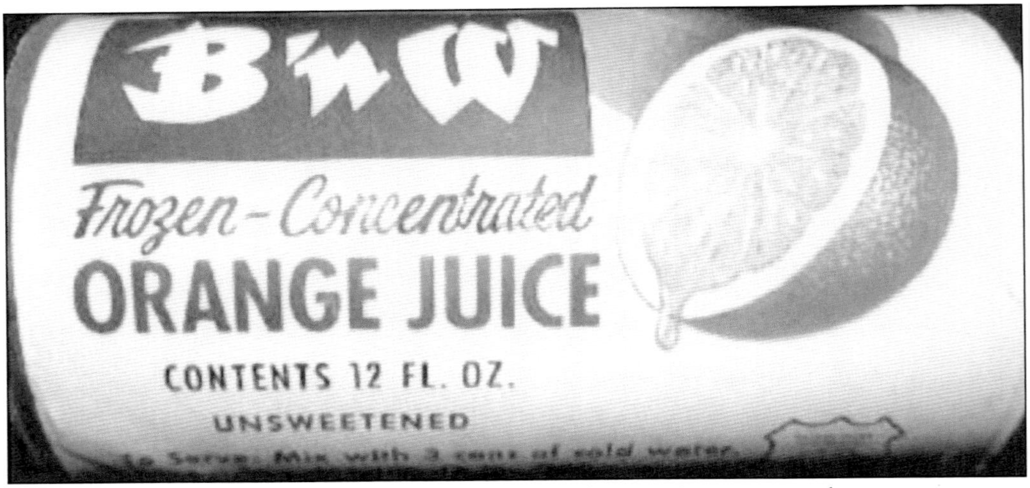

After the frozen concentrate process was developed in 1946, growers and citrus processors suddenly had a new market. Consumers liked the convenience and time-saving qualities of frozen concentrate, which preserved 98 percent of Vitamin C. B&W cofounder Gene Wilkins told a reporter in 1949, "With frozen concentrates taking any crop surpluses, the time has passed when you could have too many oranges." (Courtesy of the Groveland Historical Museum.)

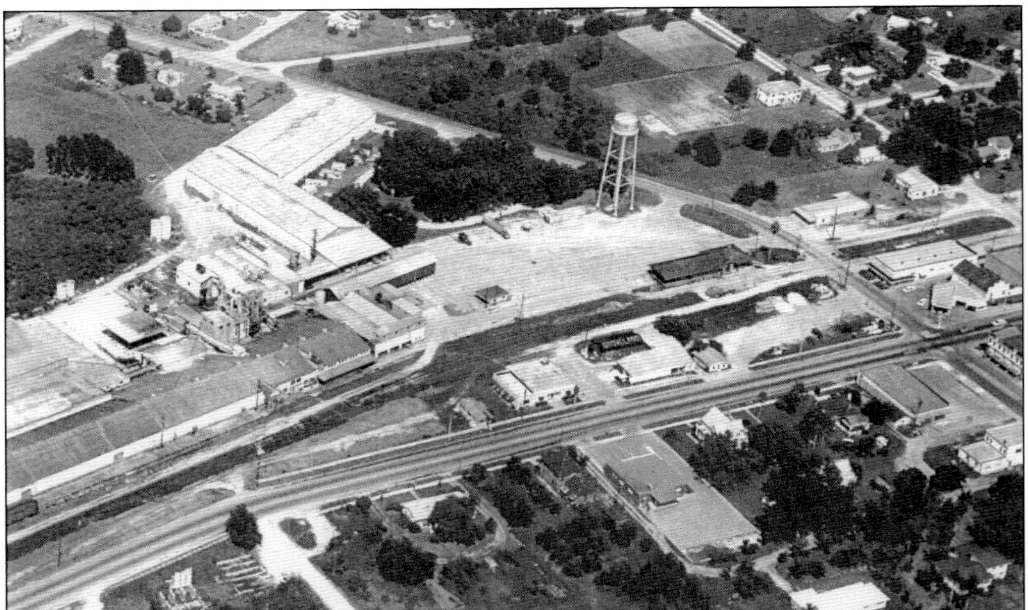

This aerial view of the B&W citrus processing plant shows what a large operation it was, extending from the corner of Highways 19 and 50 westward. The signature feature of the plant during its heyday, from the 1950s through 1980s, was the water tower with the B&W logo. In the 1990s, the plant operated under the name Florida Select Citrus. (Courtesy of the Marion Baysinger Memorial Library.)

In 1936, lumber baron J. Ray Arnold spent a fortune drilling for oil. He hired experts from the Carnegie Institute who determined the best place to drill was about 12 miles south of Groveland near Highway 33. The drilling gave hope to Groveland residents whose economy had been devastated by the Great Depression, but only cupfuls of oil were found. (Courtesy of Kathryn Arnold Herzog.)

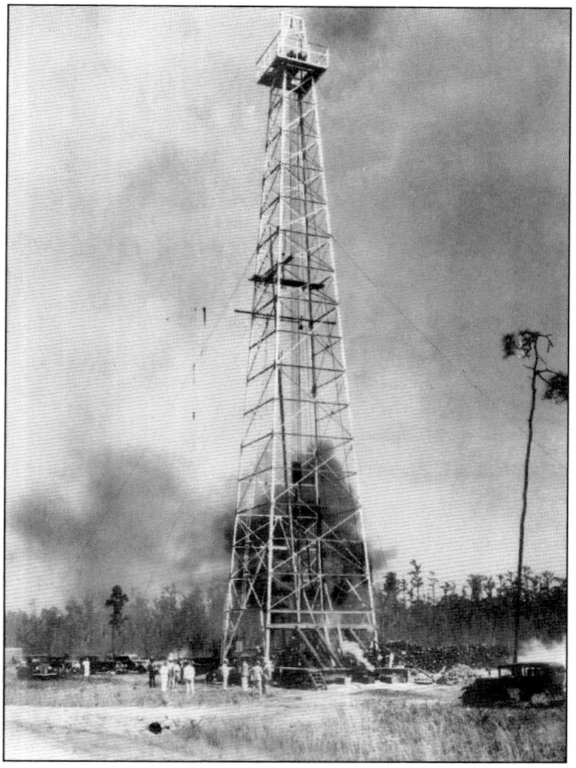

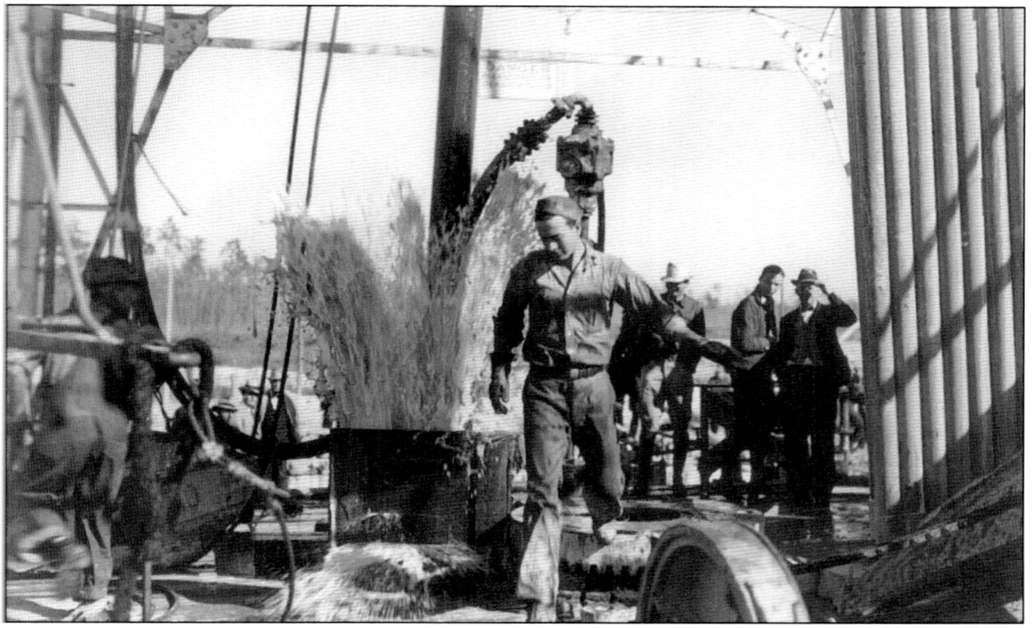

J. Ray Arnold's crews drilled more than 6,000 feet below the surface looking for oil—farther than the height of the tallest mountain in the Eastern United States. Influenced by his early years in Oklahoma and Louisiana, Arnold was convinced until his death in 1957 that Florida had oil in the state and the Gulf of Mexico. (Courtesy of Kathryn Arnold Herzog.)

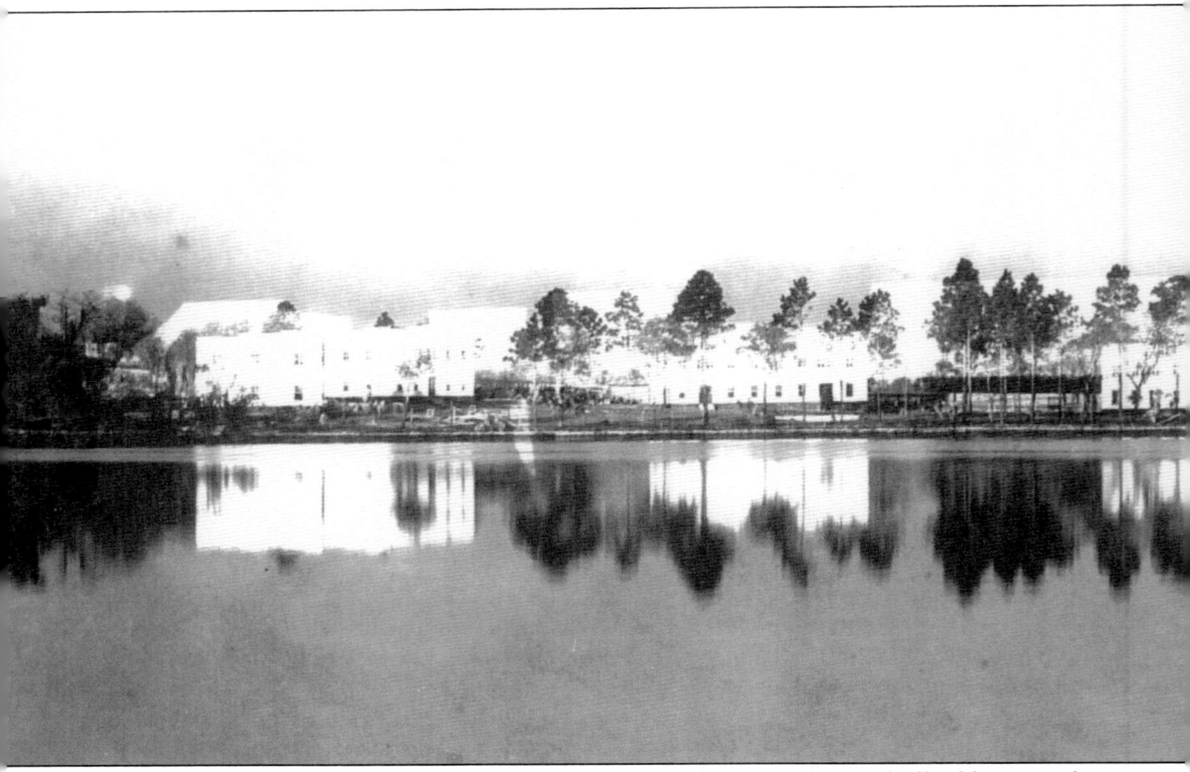

J. W. Beach, a successful business and civic leader during the 1920s, dreamed of building a perfume factory that would rival foreign producers. He created a manufacturing operation on the south side of Lake David under the name Essential Oil Company of America. The plant included five two-story buildings, an ornamental fountain, water tower, and the largest private garden in the world with acres of roses, heliotrope, lilies, geraniums, orchids, violets, and orange trees. But Beach, a city council member who had been successful selling tracts of land to Northerners, failed at producing perfume. The plant closed in 1926, as did another of his ventures in the silkworm industry. Beach eventually moved to Tampa but not before generously donating land for a park, church, and school. No signs of the perfume plant remain. (Courtesy of Rebecca Winn Best.)

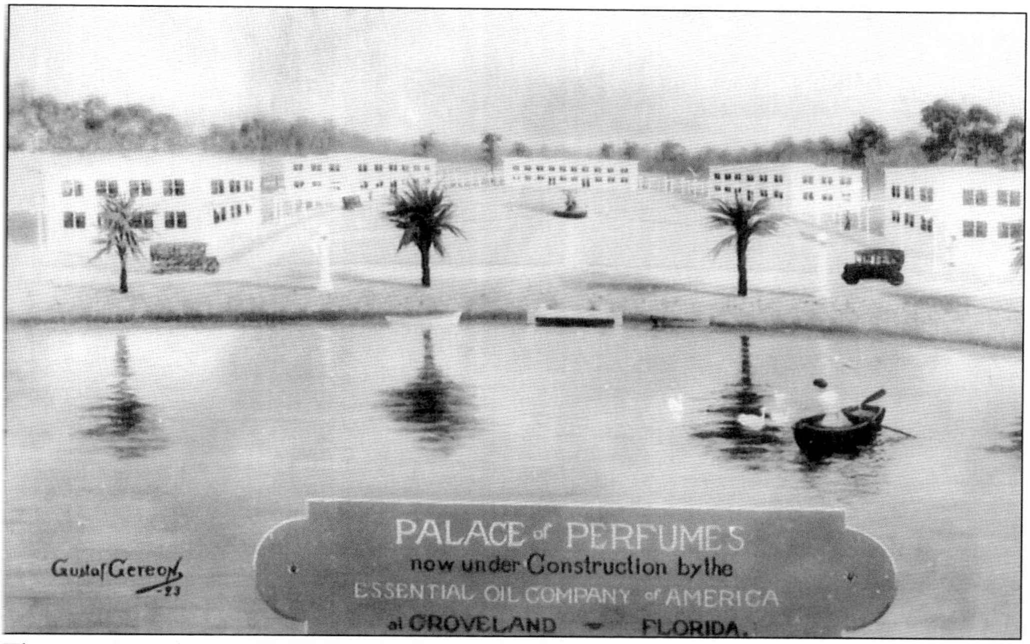

This artist's rendering of J. W. Beach's Essential Oil Company of America's "Palace of Perfumes" shows he had a grand vision in mind. Perfume bottles from the ill-fated venture were unearthed in 2007 from the J. W. Beach estate, which has been restored by its current owner. (Courtesy of the Marion Baysinger Memorial Library.)

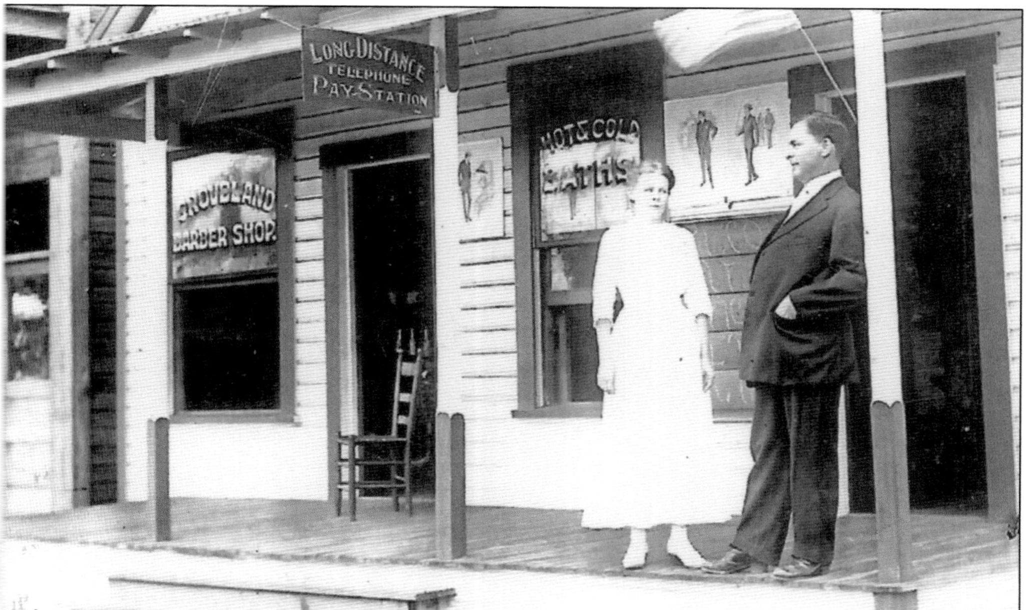

Hilda and Gary Linton are standing in front of the Groveland Barber Shop on the south side of Broad Street. The shop offered weary travelers hot and cold baths. He was one of the town's first barbers. The Lintons also reserved their spot in the town's history by being the first to have residential phone service. (Courtesy of the Marion Baysinger Memorial Library.)

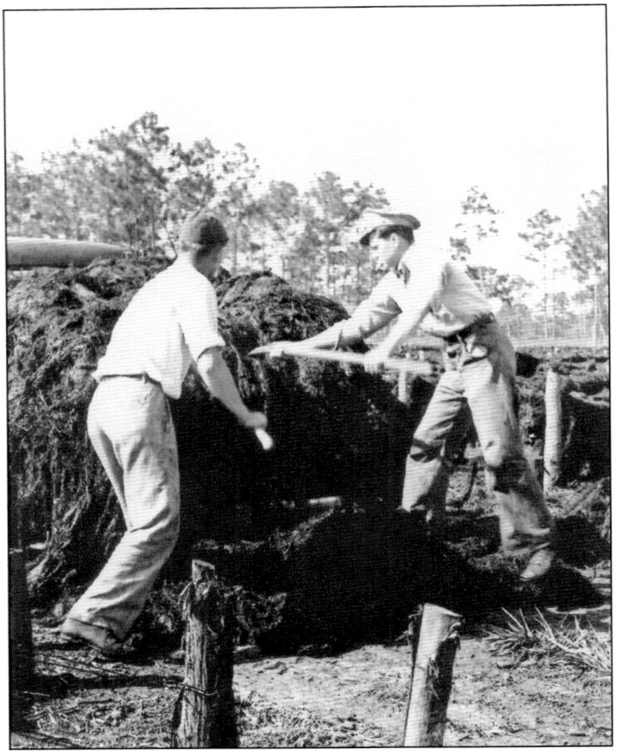

In the 1930s and 1940s, Groveland's economy struggled in the aftermath of the sawmill's closure, bank failures, and the Great Depression. One of the new, short-lived ventures was the Groveland Moss Yard, pictured in this 1946 photograph. The unidentified workers are loading Spanish moss that will be dried and sold to upholstery companies for stuffing. (Courtesy of the State Archives of Florida.)

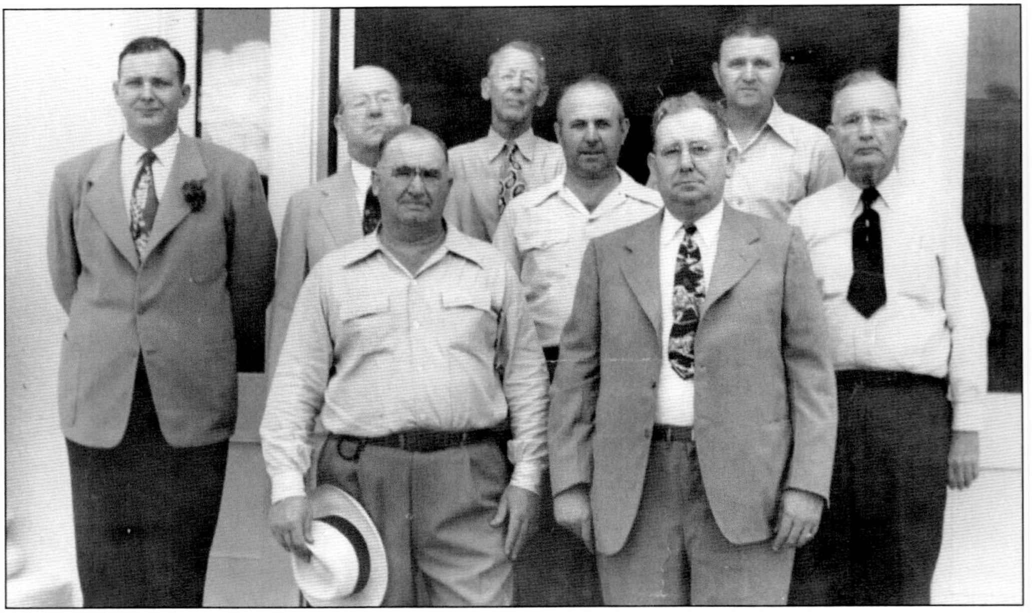

After back-to-back bank failures, Groveland residents went 20 years without a secure place to save and borrow money. In 1949, town leaders organized a bank under the leadership of visionary Joe Fairchild. The first bank directors from left to right are (first row) Bill Sheets and J. S. Fairchild; (second row) Joe Fairchild, George White Sr., Charles Anderson, Pete Micheloni, Gene Busbee, and L. Day Edge. (Courtesy of June Fairchild.)

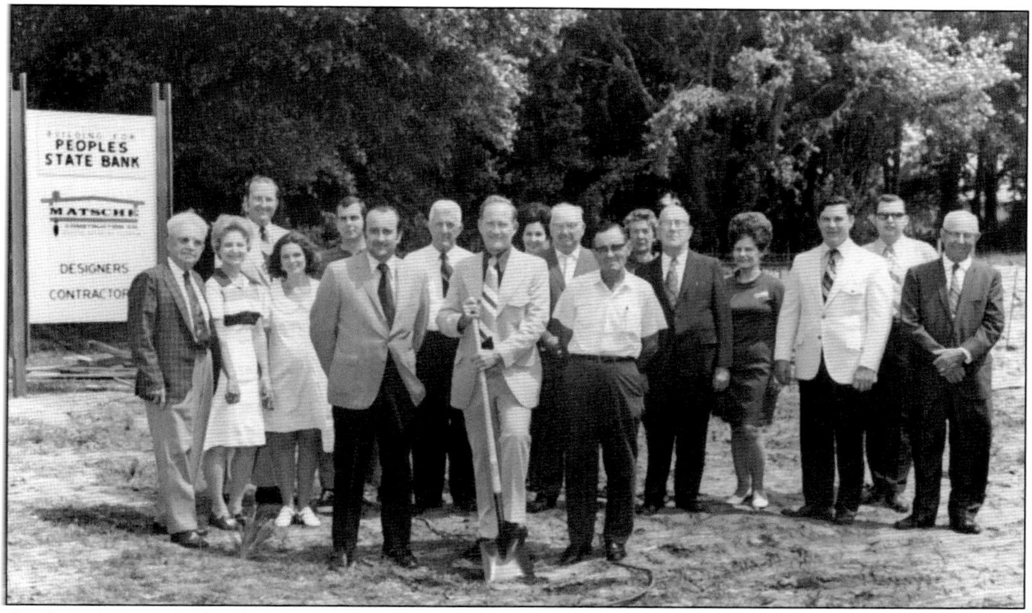

Graham Payne, who became president of People's State Bank after the untimely death of Joe Fairchild, breaks ground for the newly constructed bank. Attending the ceremony are members of Fairchild's family. In the second row, second and third from left are his wife, June Fairchild, and daughter, Clemie Fairchild; in the third row, second from left, is son Joe Fairchild Jr. (Courtesy of June Fairchild.)

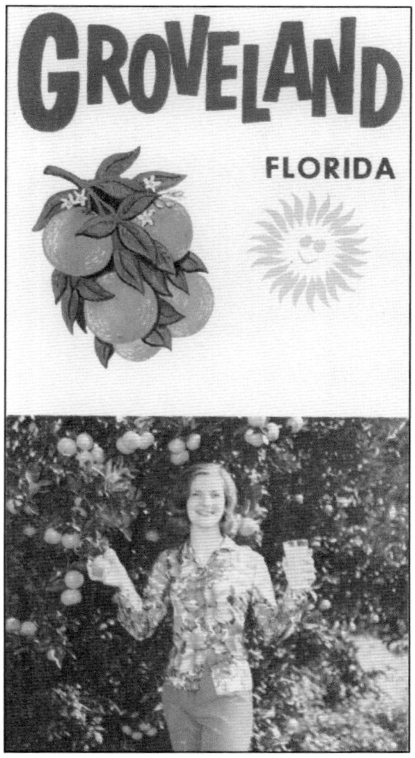

Groveland's glossy brochures of the mid-1960s were a far cry from the early Taylorville versions. This chamber of commerce brochure featured Carol Speer, Miss Groveland of 1965, in front of one of the area's lush orange groves. Speer's grandfather Atticus Carter had worked at the sawmill, and her mother had been part of Groveland High School's championship girls' basketball team. (Courtesy of the Groveland Historical Museum.)

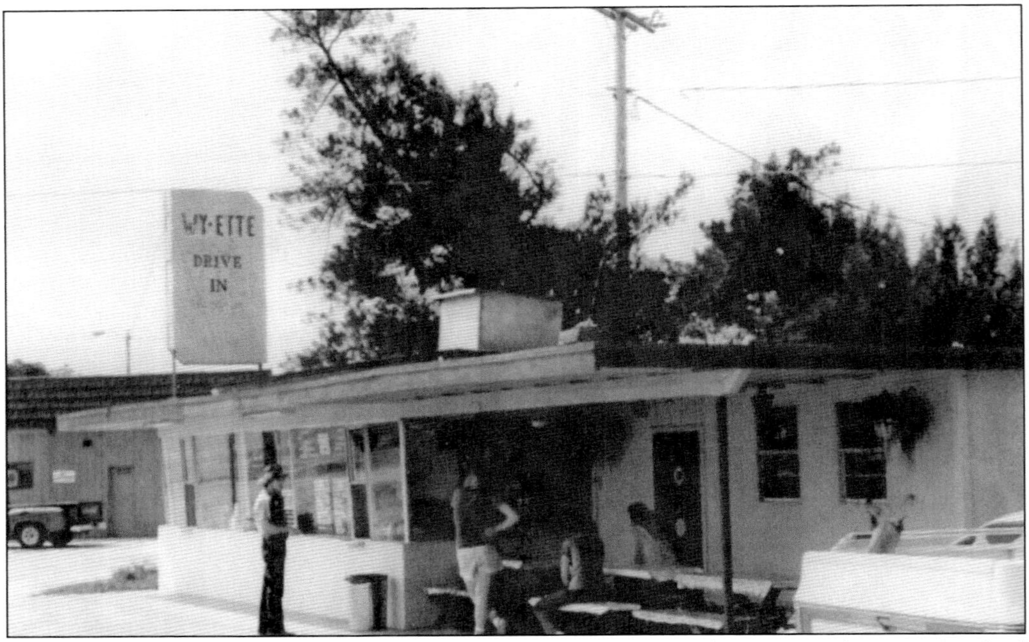

One of Groveland's most popular eateries and teen hangouts was the Y-Ette, a drive-up, fast-food restaurant at the intersection of Highways 33 and 50. In the 1980s, the restaurant was bought by Teddy Wyatt, who changed the name to the Wy-Ette, a word play of his name. It has since been converted to a florist shop. (Courtesy of the Groveland Historical Museum.)

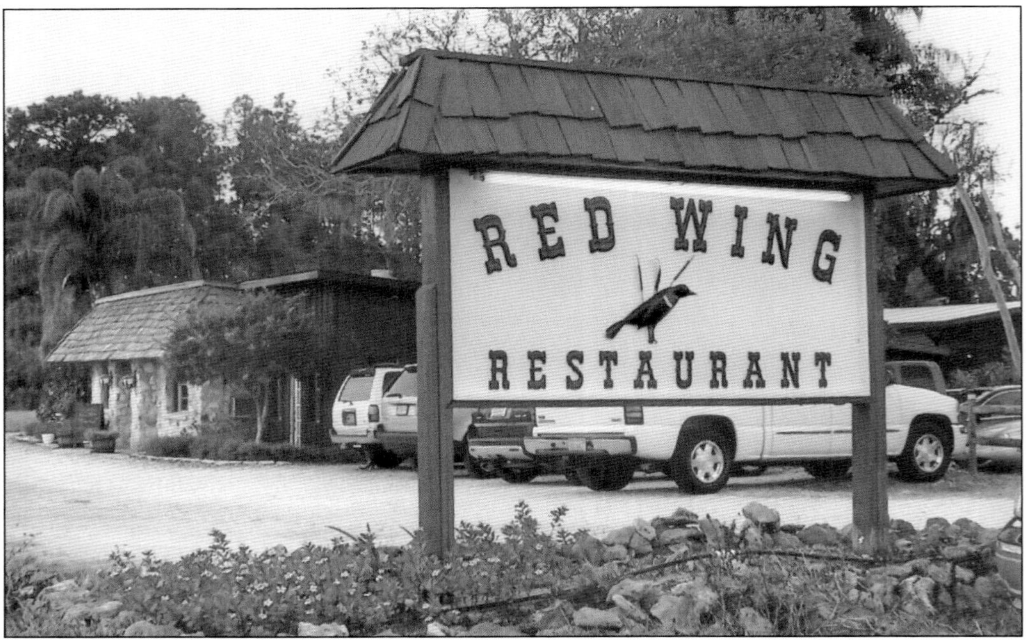

An enduring Groveland fixture is the Red Wing Restaurant on south Highway 33. The restaurant recently celebrated its 60th anniversary. The unique menu offers a variety of items that bring back memories of the town's pioneer days, such as venison, quail, alligator tail, and frog legs. (Courtesy of the Groveland Historical Museum.)

Five

Schools
Pride and Achievement

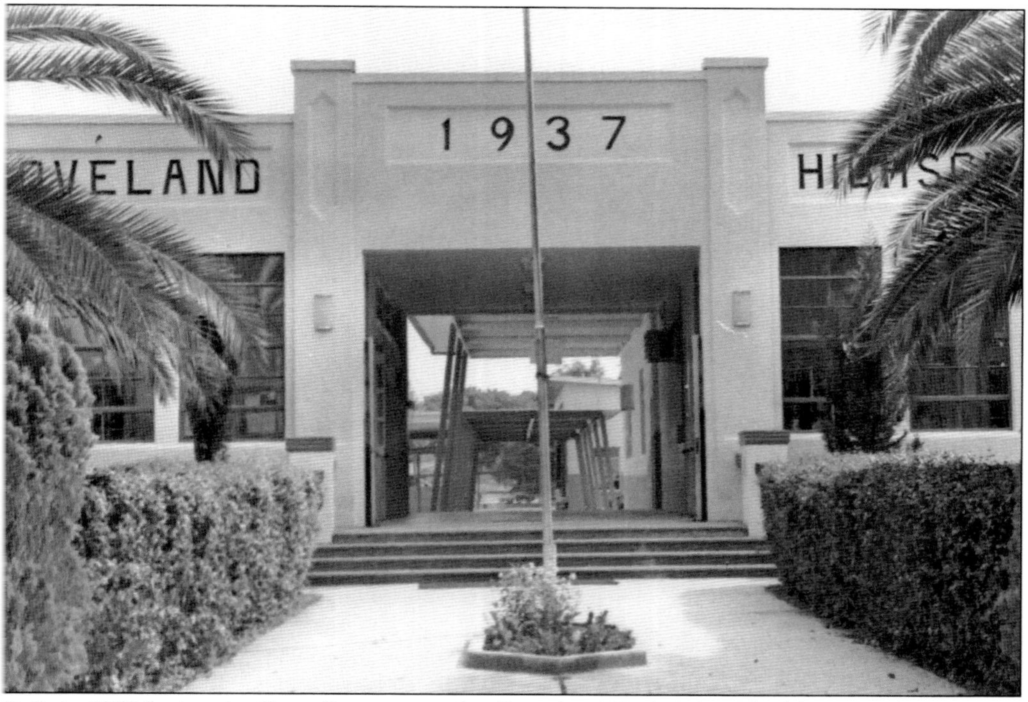

Built in 1937 during the Great Depression, the Groveland High School building on Cherry Street has become an icon for the city's optimism and close ties. It was in these hallowed halls that friendships were made, life lessons were learned, careers were started, romances were sparked, and the meanings of community and patriotism were taught. It was one of the first fully accredited high school in Lake County. And it was here that young people of different races and nationalities learned mutual respect. It offered protection from hurricanes. Even a fire in the 1980s could not destroy the alma mater. When the school became a middle school, it was fitting that it took its name from one of the most dedicated of Groveland High's teachers and principals, Cecil Gray. GHS, all hail! (Courtesy of the Lake County Historical Society.)

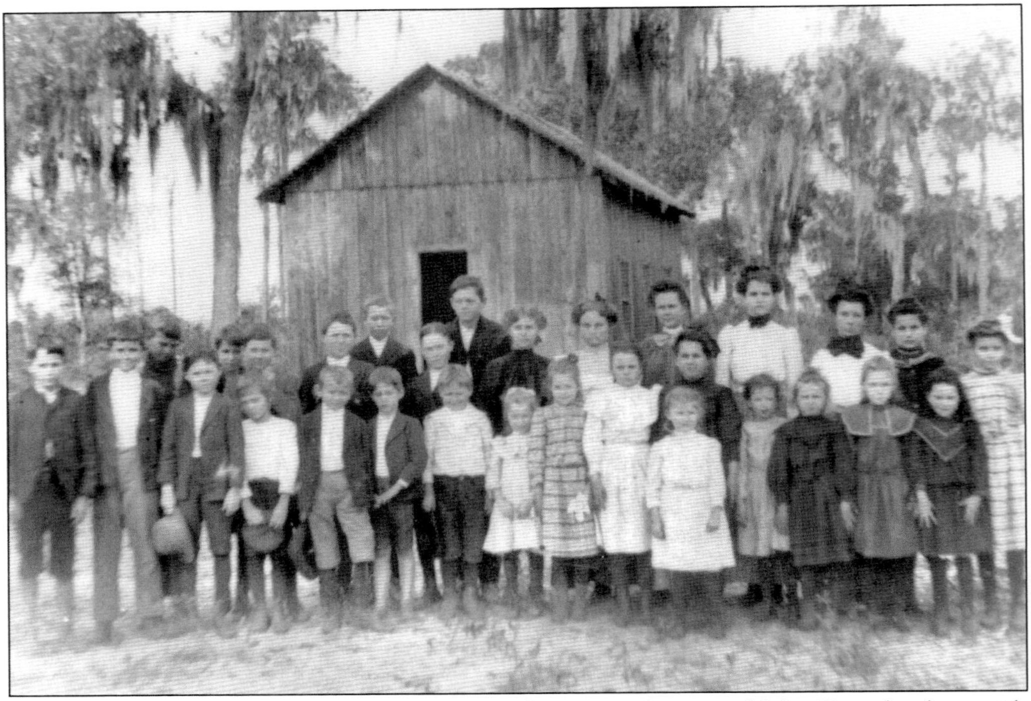

Brown's Ford School was Groveland's first school. In 1899, Cassie and John Daniels, along with the Brown family, gathered signatures on a petition requesting a school. The following year, the Lake County School Board agreed and paid $3 for the labor to build the one-room, 26-by-18-foot schoolhouse. The first teacher was R. B. Ervin. Two of the Danielses' five children became teachers. (Courtesy of Peggy Parrish Sloan.)

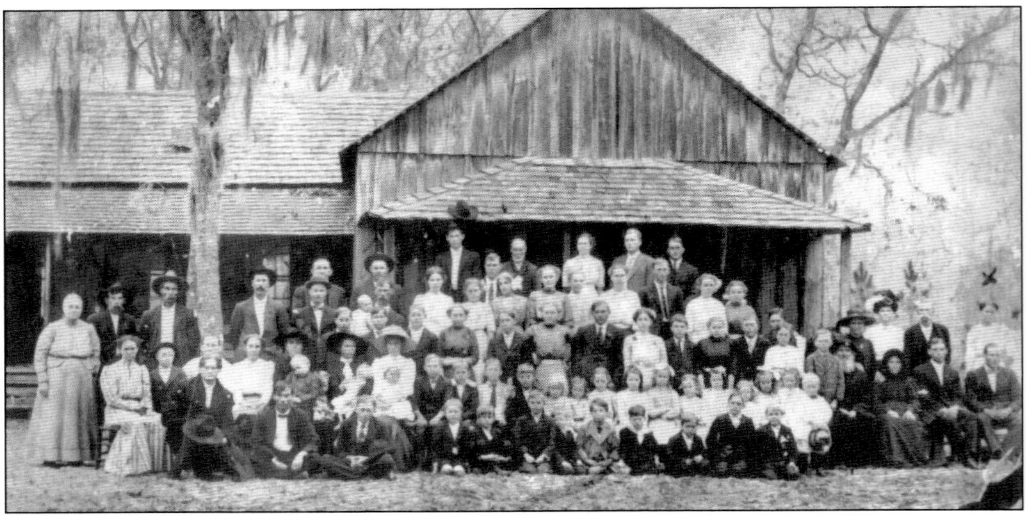

Many Bay Lake families with long ties to the area are shown here with their children in front of Bay Lake's school, originally called Bay Root at the time of this 1912 photograph. Some of the families include the Browns, Storys, and Sloans. The teachers were Edwina Griffin and Robert Giles, pictured in the last row, sixth and seventh from left. (Courtesy of Peggy Parrish Sloan.)

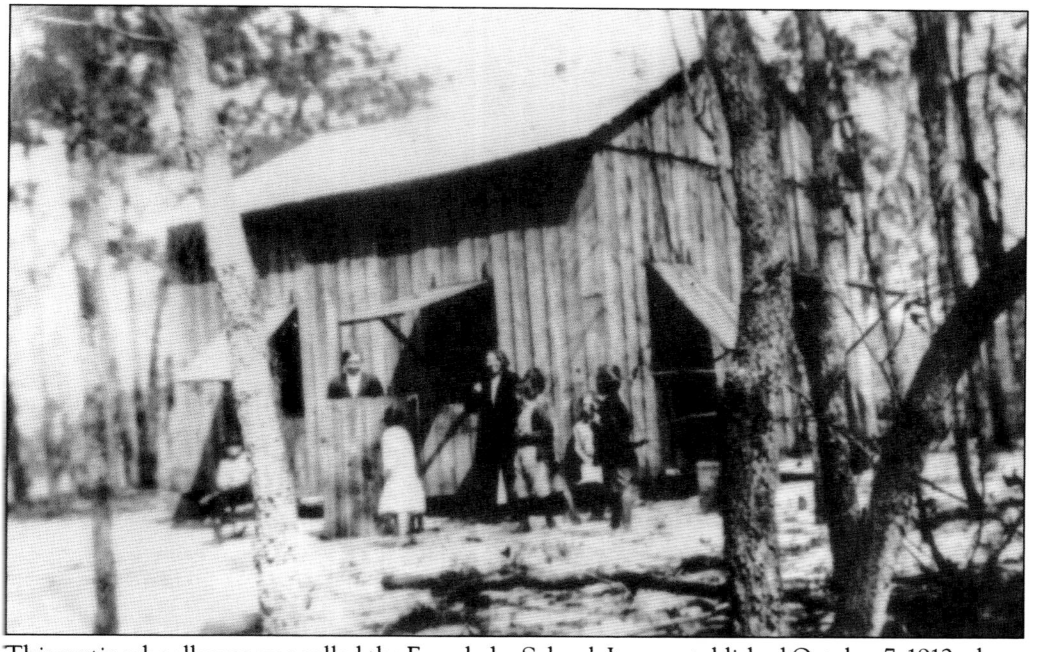

This rustic schoolhouse was called the Everglades School. It was established October 7, 1912, about seven miles north of Groveland near Highway 19. The school was surrounded by longleaf pines. The early schools often followed a schedule that was dictated by the seasonal crops, which required the help of some of the older children. (Courtesy of the Lake County Historical Society.)

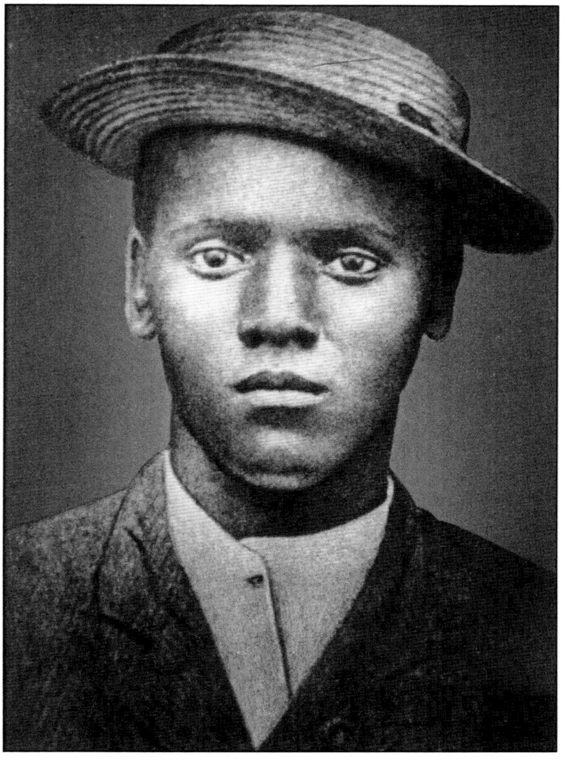

Albert S. Blue walked from the Groveland-Mascotte area to Tavares to petition the school board to build a school for African American children. He pledged $50 toward the construction. The first African American school served children from Groveland and Mascotte. A street in Groveland was named after Blue to honor his efforts. Several of his descendants became teachers. (Courtesy of Emma Sullivan.)

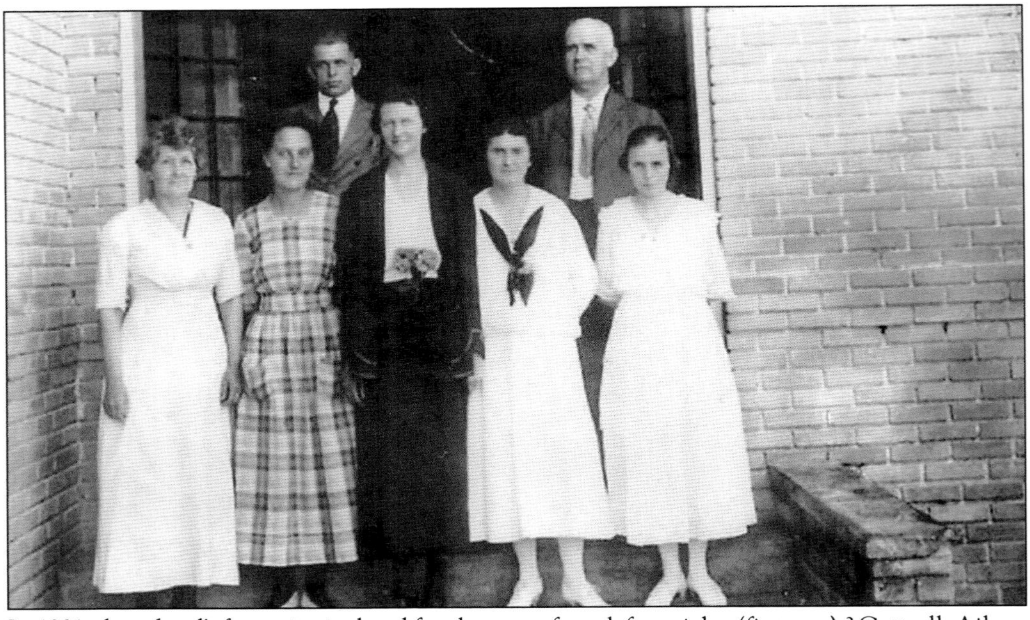

In 1921, the school's first principal and faculty were, from left to right, (first row) ? Cottrell, Aileen Surrency, Mill Lilla Gilbert, Lillian Marshall, and ? Carlson; (second row) Lacy Thomas (principal) and George DeWeese. Sawmill owner J. Ray Arnold had gone to the University of Florida to seek the best educator he could find from his friend and future university president John Tigert. Tigert recommended Thomas. (Courtesy of Marilyn Gammon Smith.)

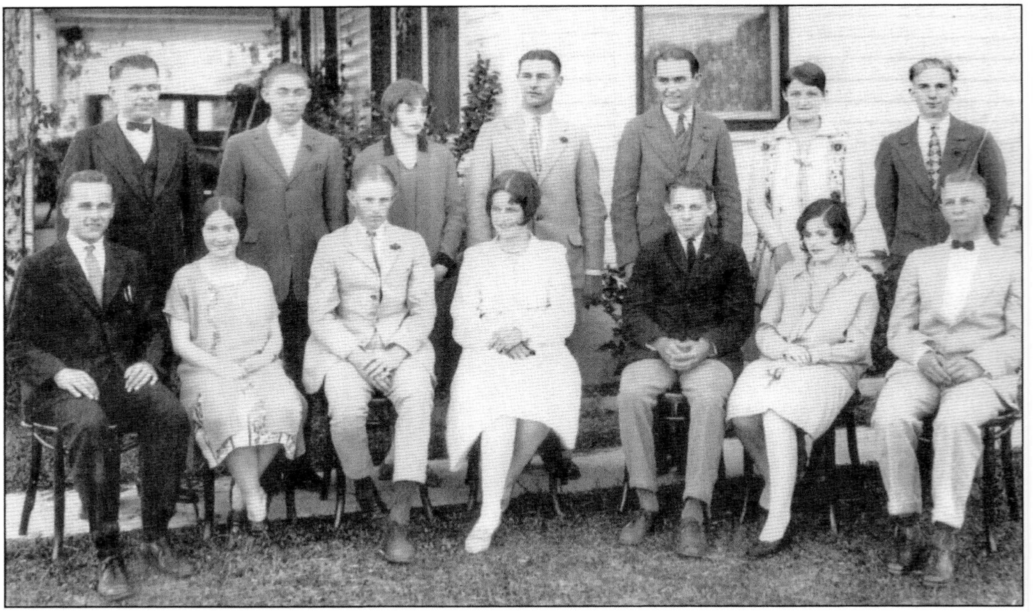

One of Groveland High School's first graduating classes is pictured in front of the "teacherage," a boardinghouse built for single teachers. From left to right are (first row) Bob Bradley, unidentified, Gordie Weir, Camille Beach, Joel Walberg, Louise Morris, and Ted Averitt; (second row) Principal Lacy Thomas, unidentified, Elizabeth Register, Albert Bauer, Guy Smith, Helen Emergy, and Pearlie Brown. (Courtesy of the Groveland Historical Museum.)

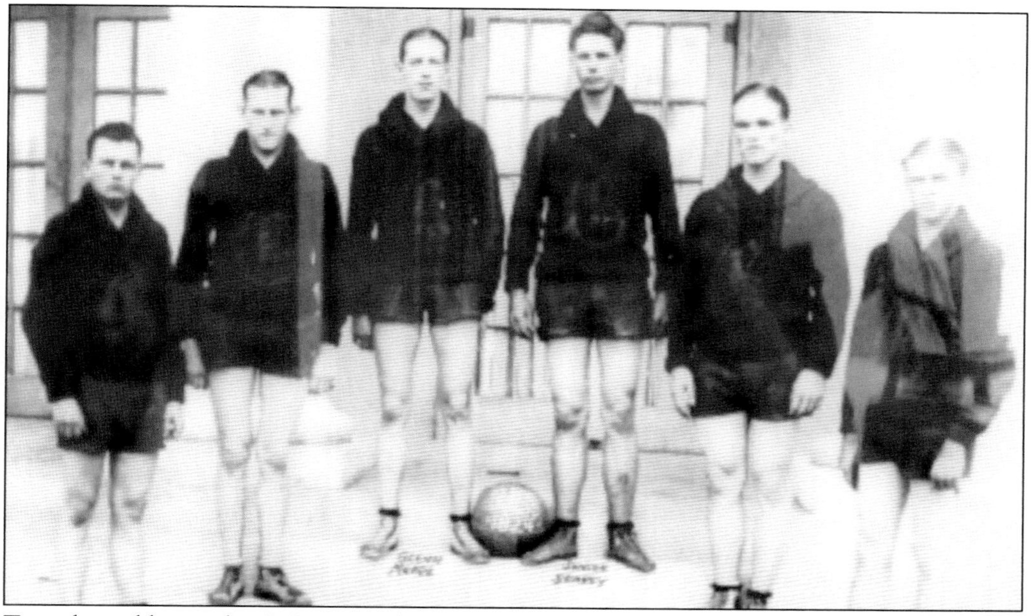

Town legend has it that J. Ray Arnold came up with the idea of having the Greenbacks as the high school mascot. "There's nothing stronger than the U.S. Greenback," he said. Pictured here is the 1924 basketball team that claimed the title "the First Greenbacks." From left to right are Conrad Williams, Raymond Anderson, Glenn Meade, Junior Sampey, Garland Rice, and Ken Hawkins. (Courtesy of the Groveland Historical Museum.)

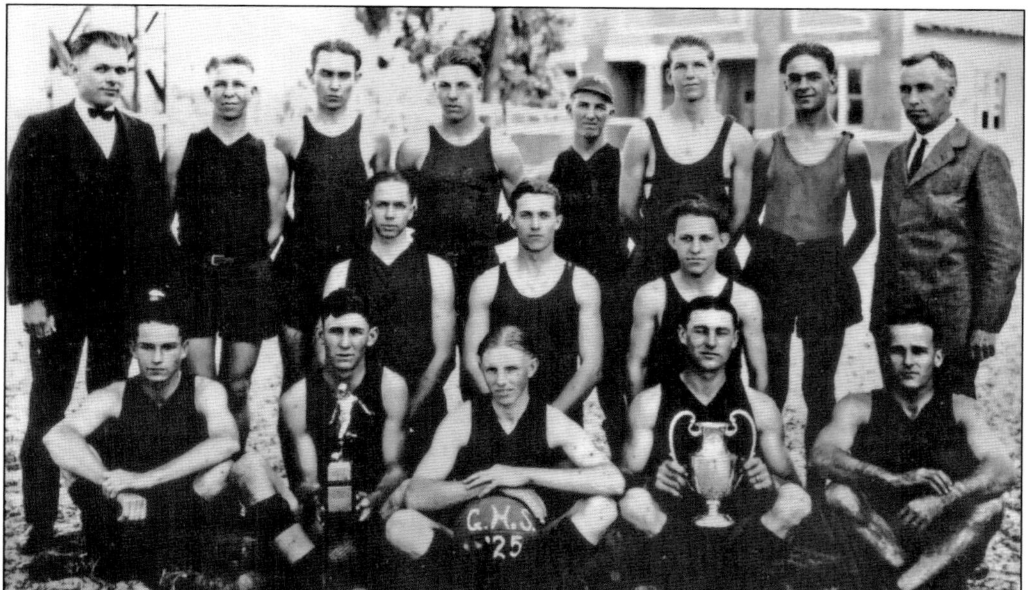

Winning traditions started early among Groveland High School's athletes. Pictured here proudly showing their trophies are the 1925 high school's championship soccer team with principal Lacy Thomas (second row, left). In the 1930s, football replaced soccer in the school's athletic program. In the background is the school's gymnasium built in 1923. (Courtesy of the Groveland Historical Museum.)

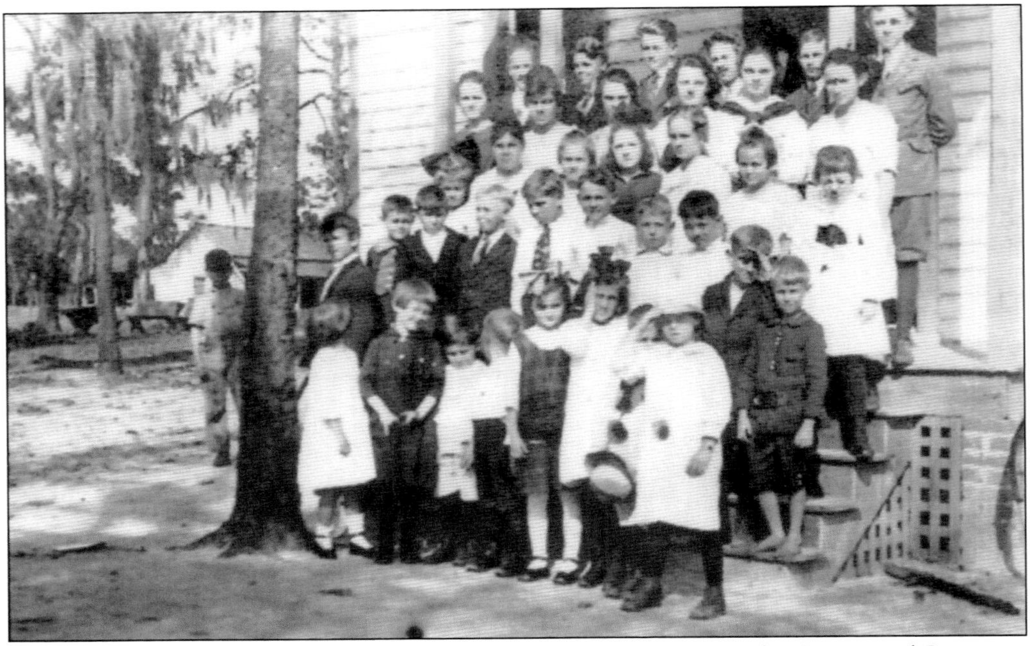

Around 1905, Groveland gained its second school, built near the present-day Greenwood Cemetery. The two-story school had two classrooms downstairs and an auditorium upstairs. Two teachers taught grades one through eight. Students encountered snakes and an occasional alligator on their way to school. (Courtesy of Imogene Weir Tallant.)

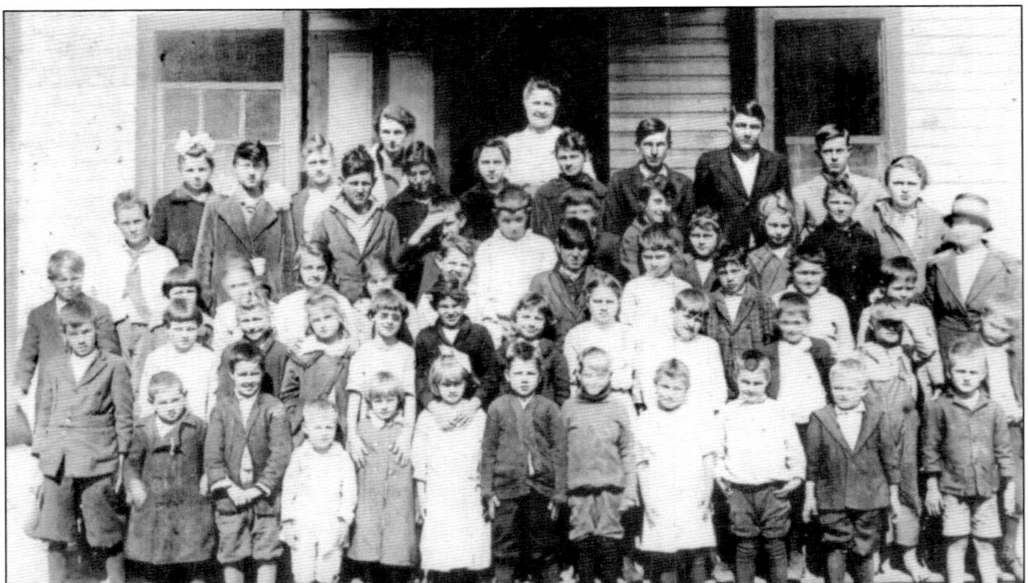

Between 1900 and 1922, students a few miles west attended Mascotte School, a two-story building later used as a store and boardinghouse. The original school had one room. The first teacher was Professor Osterhout from New York. One early teacher escaped through a window after an irate mother, angered that the teacher had spanked her son, came to school with a shotgun. (Courtesy of Cyleta Lee Austin.)

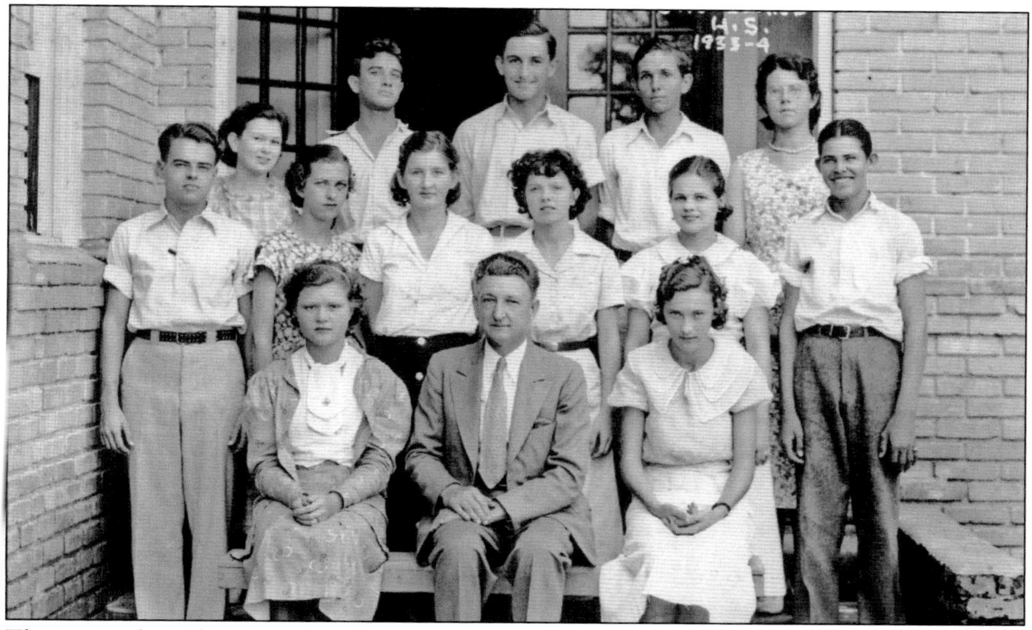

The senior class of 1934 is shown on the steps of Groveland's yellow-brick high school. The town and country were in the throes of the Great Depression. Some families had moved away. Those who stayed sacrificed so that their children could attend school. Seniors (above) are pictured from left to right (first row) Vera Sloan, E. L. Beeson, and Jewell Wagner; (second row) W. W. Arnold, Louise McFadden, Martha Harris, Grace Partridge, Beatrice Bradley, and B. J. Merritt; (third row) Dorothy Menendez, A. P. Rowe Jr., Charlie Arnold, Ray Robbins, and Helen Hamilton. The 1934 Greenback basketball team are, from left to right, (first row) Charlie Arnold, Bob Arnold, Harry Cashwell, and Darrell Cashwell; (second row) Coach Wade Weaver; (third row) H. C. Cash, J. W. Martin, Bradford Williams, Chris Martin, Clyde Sandefur. (Both courtesy of Charles Arnold.)

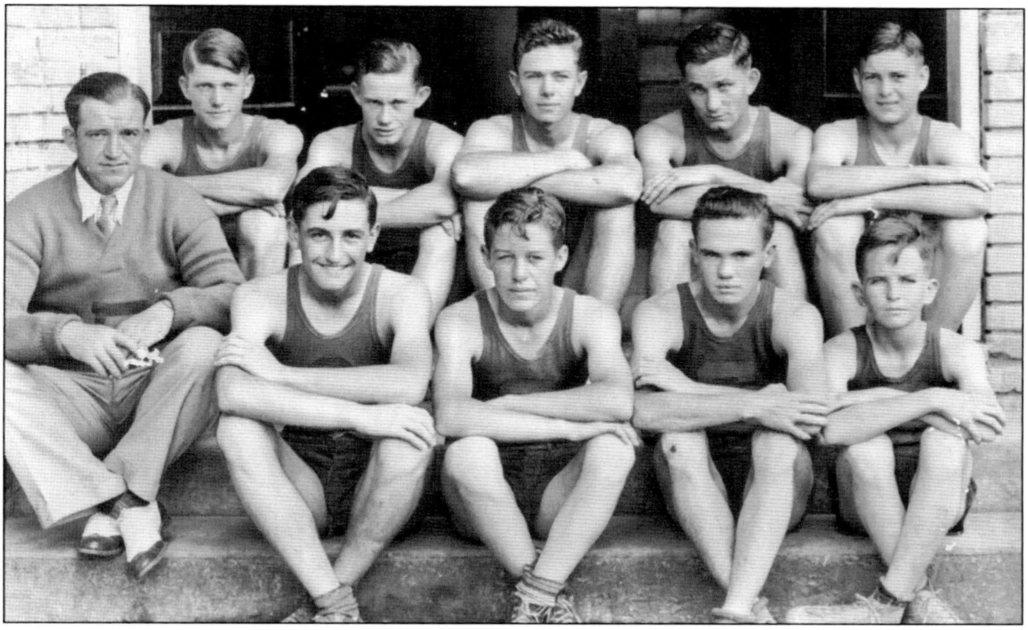

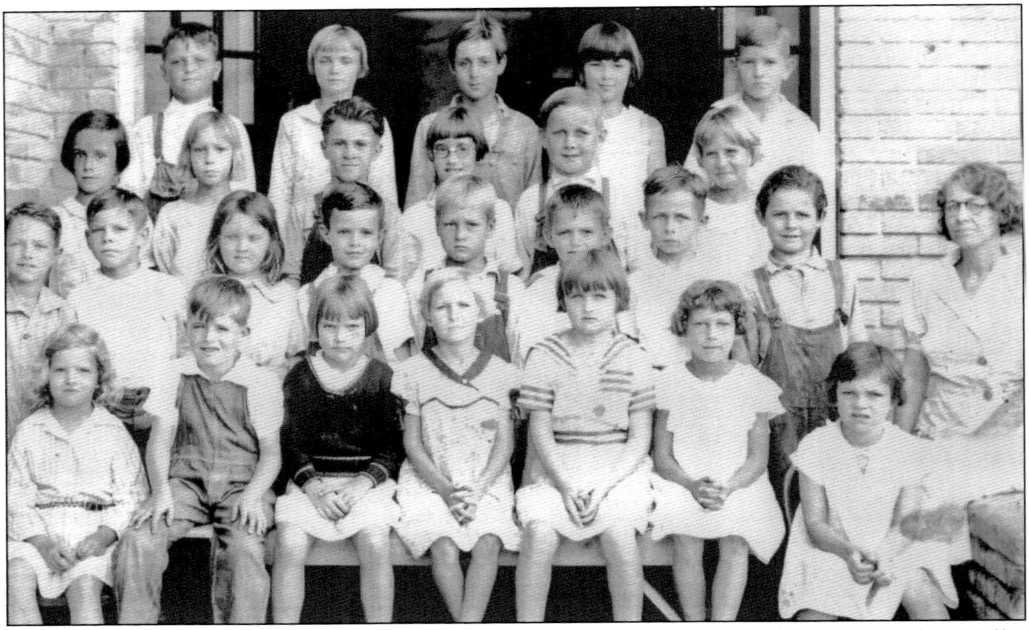

These younger students from the same 1934 school year are pictured with their teacher Nellie Smith sitting on the steps of the Cherry Street school. Some students, such as Imogene Weir (first row, right), were second-generation natives, symbolizing the town's growth from a settlement of transplants to a town of permanent residents. (Courtesy of Imogene Weir Tallant.)

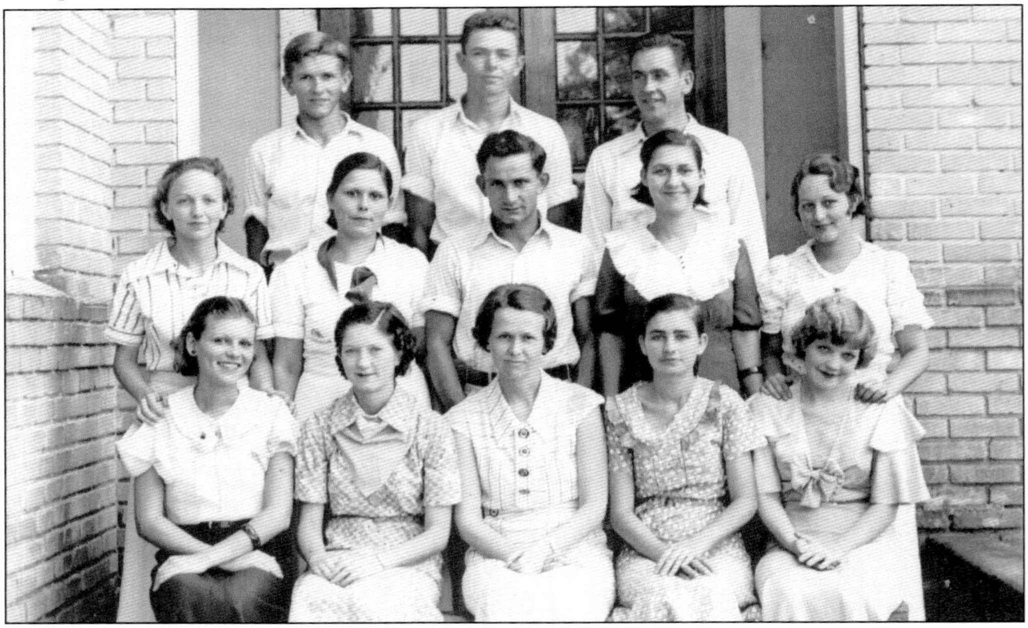

The senior class of 1935 included descendants of some of Groveland's founding families, such as Cyleta Lee (first row, right) Louise Sloan (second row, fourth from left), and Doris Brown (second row, second from left). Lee's family settled Carter's Island. Sloan's great-grandfather was one of the earliest settlers, Daniel Sloan. Brown's family came to the area in the 1870's. (Courtesy of Cyleta Lee Austin.)

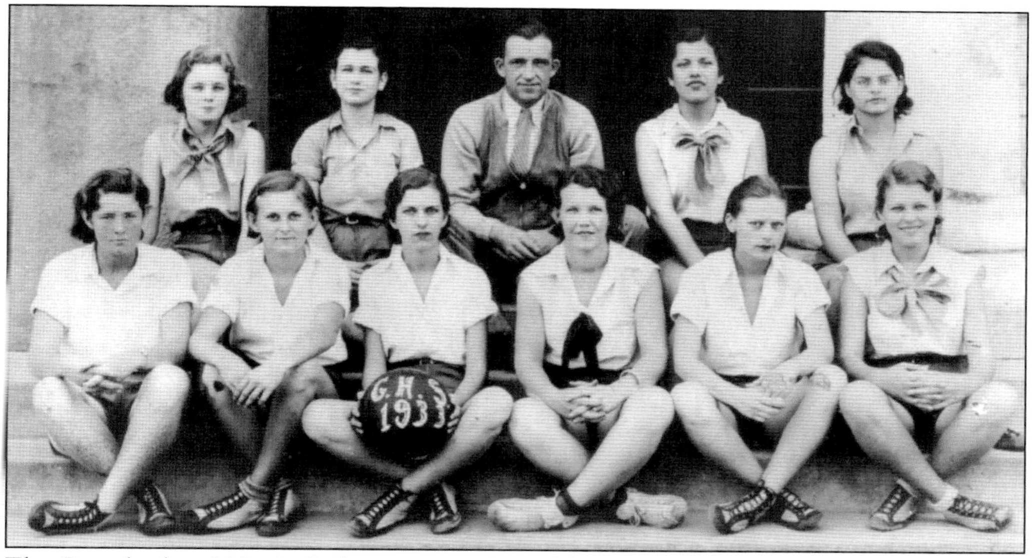

The Greenback girls' basketball teams were formidable. Their crowning achievement came in 1940 when they won the state championship (below). Principal Leo Bolles, holding the winning banner with then mayor Clayton Weir, taught the girls to be as aggressive as the boys' team. At the time, Groveland had one of the only gyms in the county. The Greenback girls played the South Carolina girls' state champions and split the two-game series. The 1940s team roster included Kathryn "Kitty" Arnold, Joycelen Carter, Leila Marjorie Edge, Pauline Griffin, Daisy Hart, Wilma and Mary Hendry, Cynthia and Doris Hogan, Estelle Hill, Iris McFarland, Eva Lee Morgan, Emily and Norma Nuttall, Eddie Frances Pritchett, Verna Tomlinson, and Sara Tuten. (Above courtesy Cyleta Lee Austin; below courtesy of Imogene Weir Tallant.)

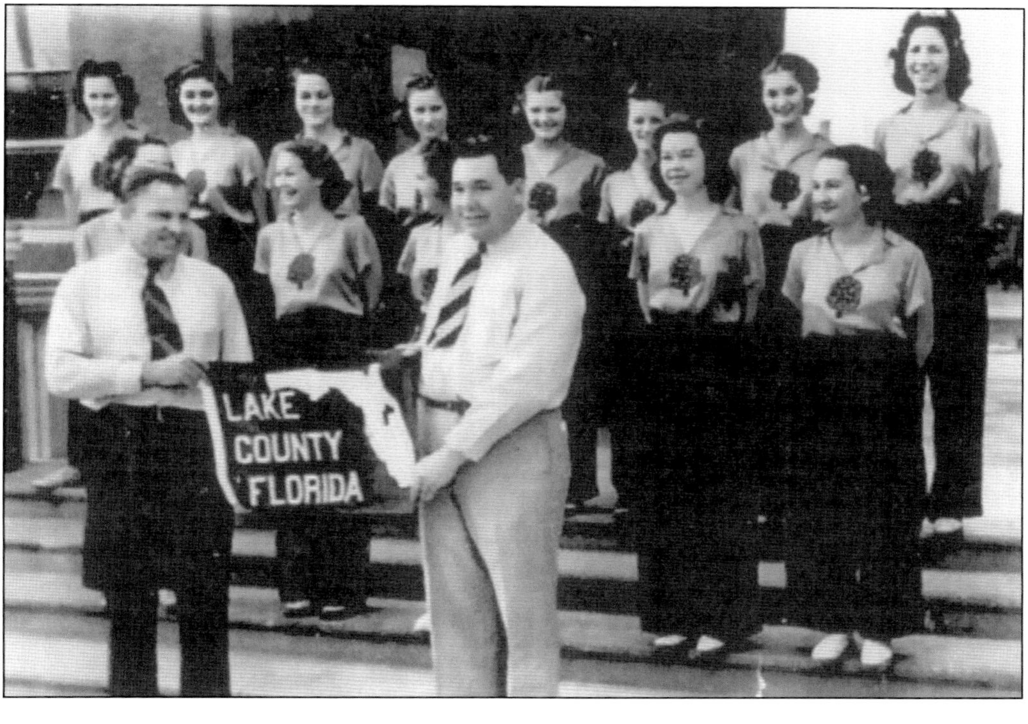

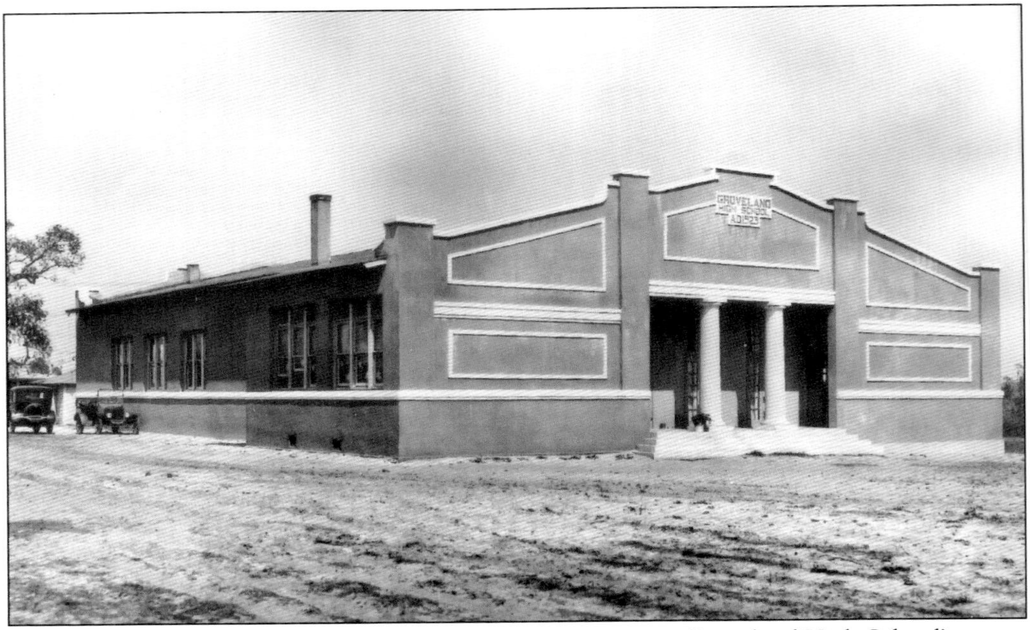

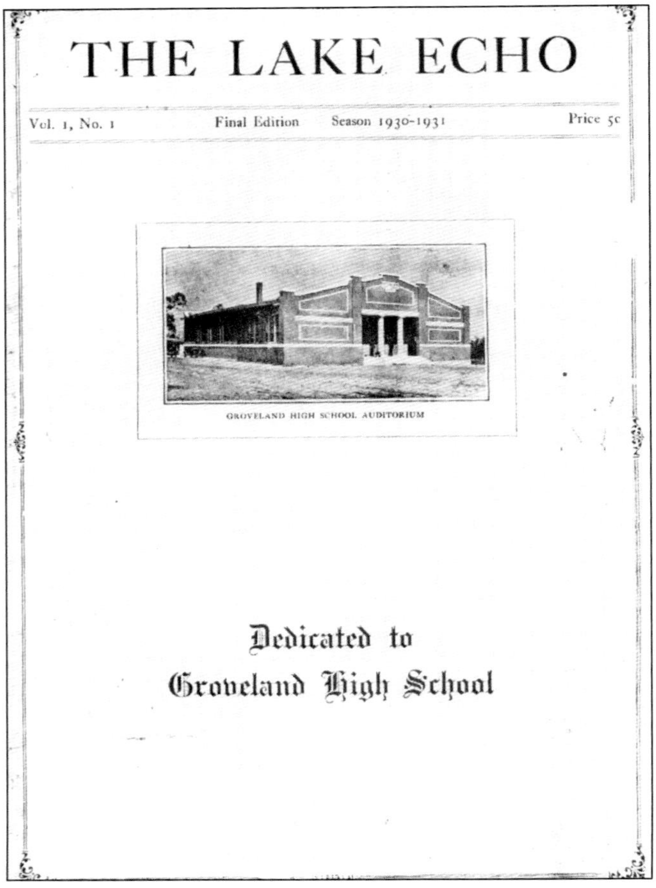

THE LAKE ECHO

Vol. 1, No. 1 | Final Edition | Season 1930–1931 | Price 5c

GROVELAND HIGH SCHOOL AUDITORIUM

Dedicated to
Groveland High School

Groveland High School's gymnasium, built in 1923, was a source of great pride. Constructed during the prosperous 1920s, it was the first high school gym in Lake County. The gym was featured on the front of the final 1931-school-year edition of the *Lake Echo*, which was published by A. W. Newett as part of the town's paper, the *Groveland Graphic*. This edition included news about the boys' state championship basketball team, a feature profiling principal T. J. Poppell, sports scores, jokes, poetry, and the senior class will and testament, a tongue-in-cheek tradition that lasted for decades. (Both courtesy of the Groveland Historical Museum.)

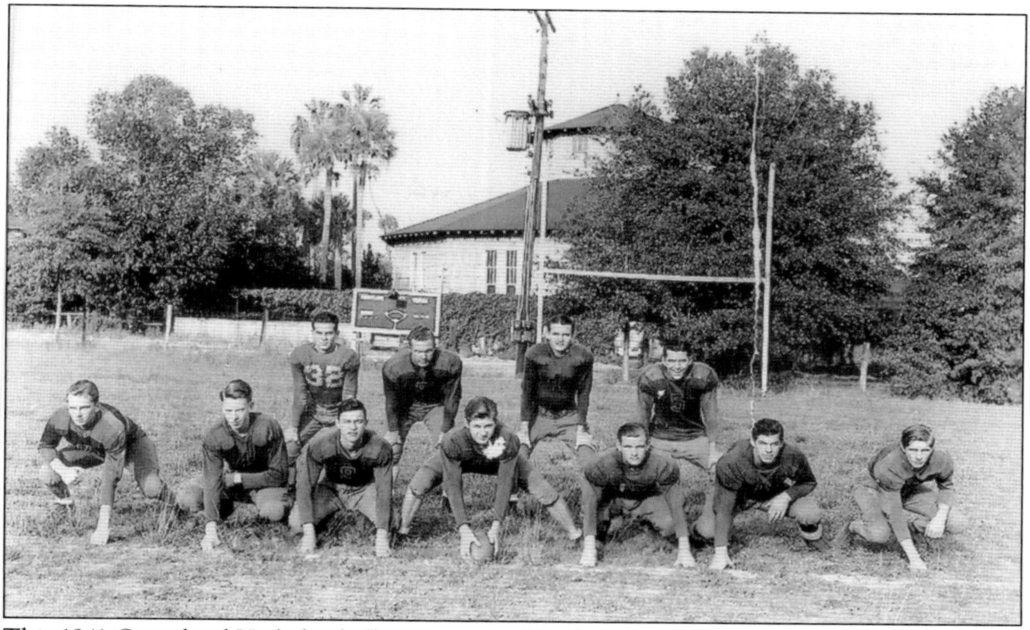

This 1941 Groveland High football team is posed at the school's field that had once been a cow pasture behind the J. Ray Arnold home. The team included cocaptain Sven Pederson (first row, second from left). Behind the team is the recreational gym of the Arnold family that included bowling lanes. (Courtesy of the Groveland Historical Museum.)

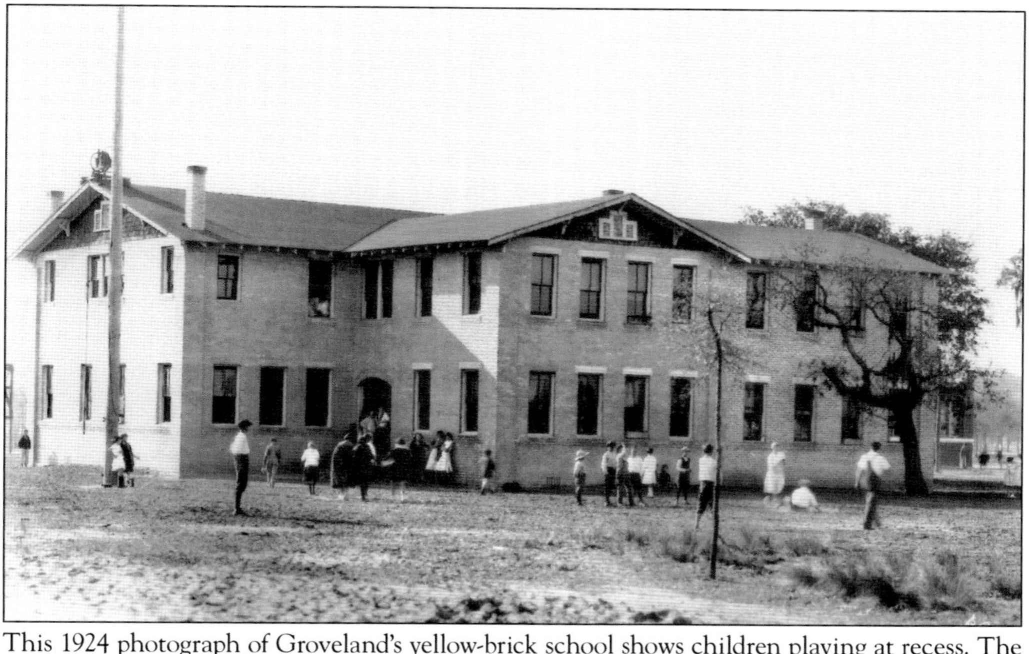

This 1924 photograph of Groveland's yellow-brick school shows children playing at recess. The school had a large school bell on the left side of the roof that was rung to let students know when school started. Some adventurous students once hauled a desk to the top of the roof, which did not amuse the school principal. (Courtesy of the Tampa-Hillsborough Public Library System.)

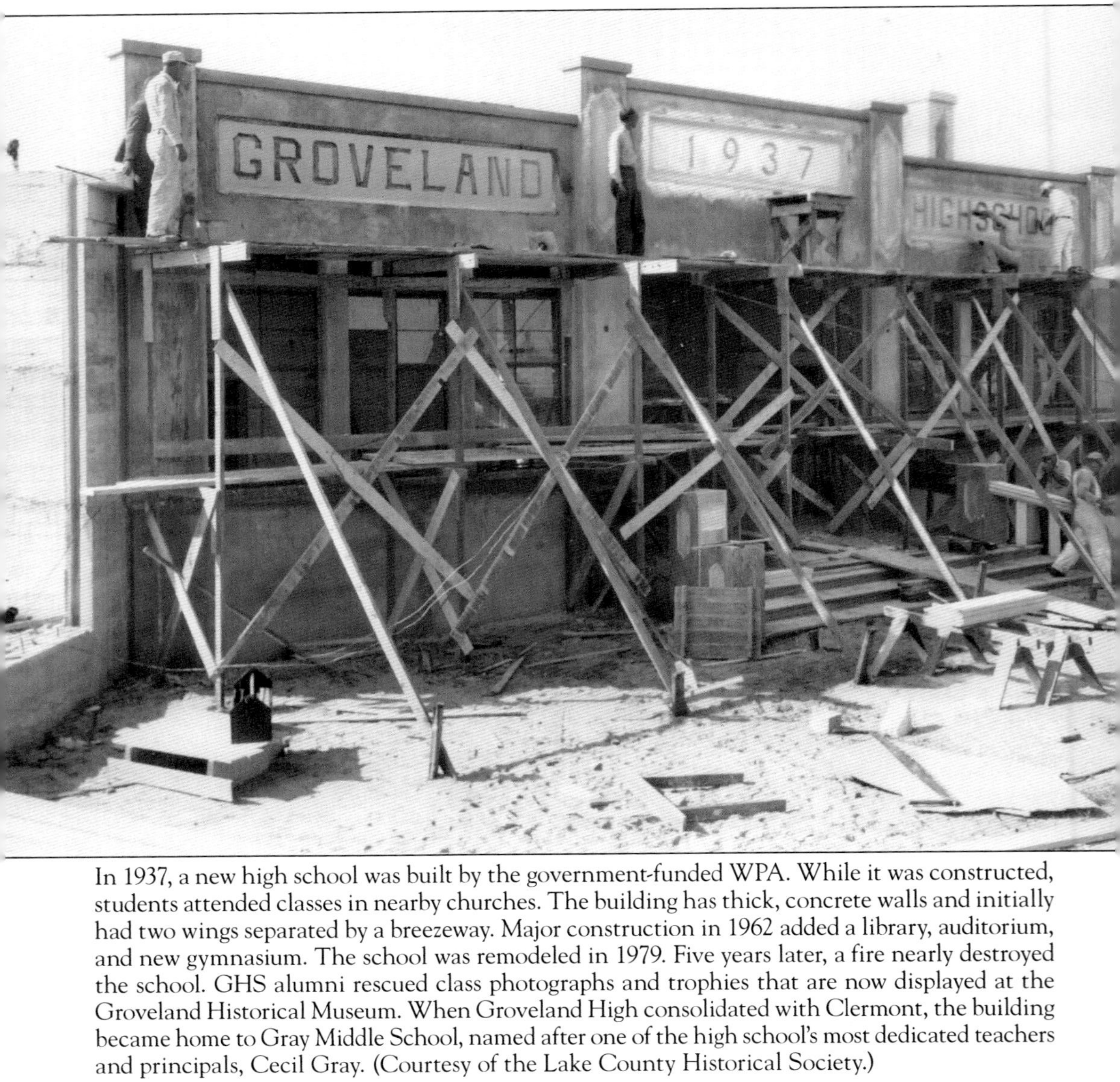

In 1937, a new high school was built by the government-funded WPA. While it was constructed, students attended classes in nearby churches. The building has thick, concrete walls and initially had two wings separated by a breezeway. Major construction in 1962 added a library, auditorium, and new gymnasium. The school was remodeled in 1979. Five years later, a fire nearly destroyed the school. GHS alumni rescued class photographs and trophies that are now displayed at the Groveland Historical Museum. When Groveland High consolidated with Clermont, the building became home to Gray Middle School, named after one of the high school's most dedicated teachers and principals, Cecil Gray. (Courtesy of the Lake County Historical Society.)

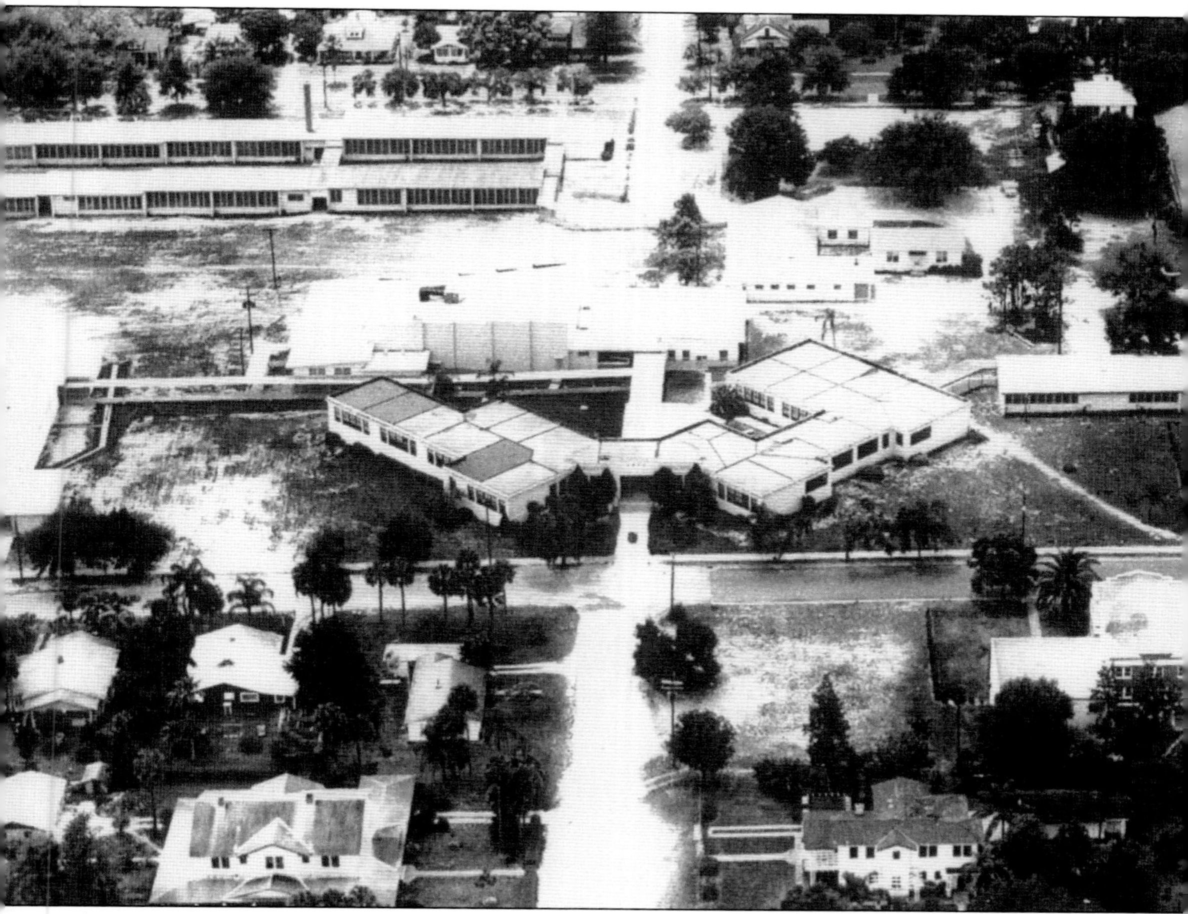

This 1965 aerial view shows the connected campuses of Davis Elementary and Groveland Junior High and High School. The land for the elementary school, seen at the top, was donated by a former mayor. Davis Elementary included first through sixth grades. Groveland Junior High School classes were held mostly in the left wing of the high school building (center). Most high-school classes were held in the right wing and in the science annex extending to the right. All campuses shared the same lunchroom and auditorium. Many students went through all 12 years of school with the same classmates, which is one of the reasons that many alumni are lifelong friends. The annual GHS Alumni Reunions draw hundreds from across the United States. (Courtesy of the Groveland Historical Museum.)

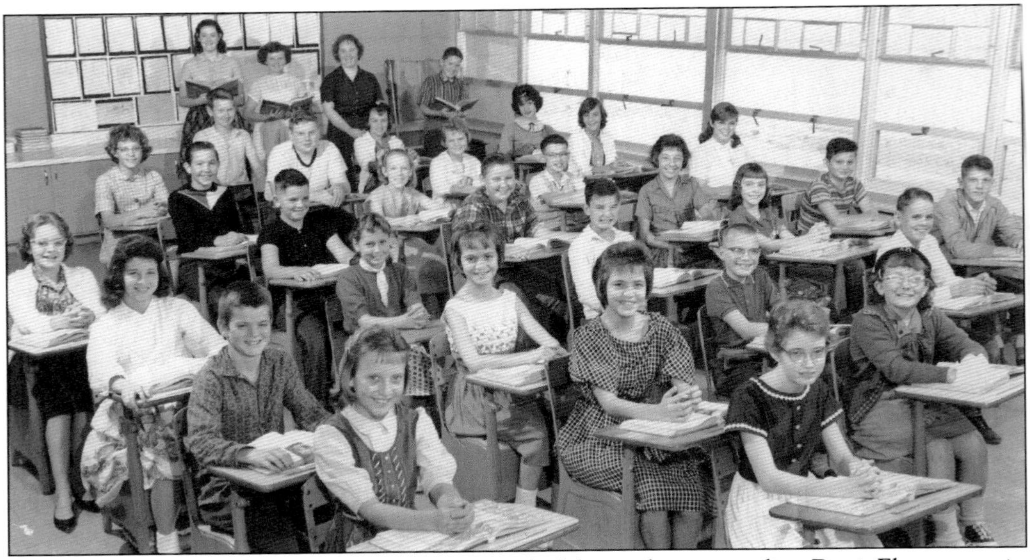

Miss Patricia Kell's 1962 sixth graders were typical of the students attending Davis Elementary in the 1950s and 1960s. The end-of-the-year party included a twist dance contest. Close friendships also began at Mascotte Elementary School, where students would later attend Groveland Junior High and High School. In 1932, students participated in a Tom Thumb wedding (below). From left to right are (first row) Cleo Skelton, Ray Raines, Maud Rice, Charlotte Crawley, Willie Ruth Conley, Dorothy Rose Link, J. Harris Poppell, Bobby Sutton, and June Crawley; (second row) Imogene Weir, Viola Sheppard, Bobby Cox, Nancy Carolyn Poppell, Glen Thomas, Mary Stone, Mary Nell McFadden, and Aline Ogden; (third row) Marlow Link, Herbert Crawley, Jimmy Westfall, Frank Williams, George Long, Junior Reed, Carl Acree, and Dick Kurfiss. (Above courtesy of the Groveland Historical Museum; below courtesy of Imogene Weir Tallant.)

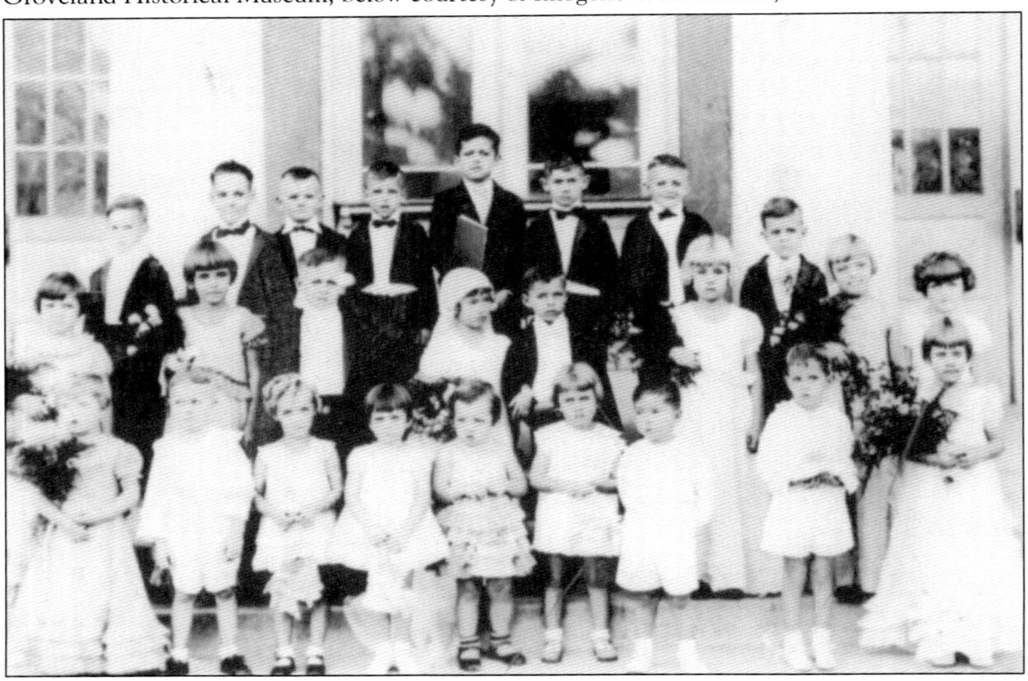

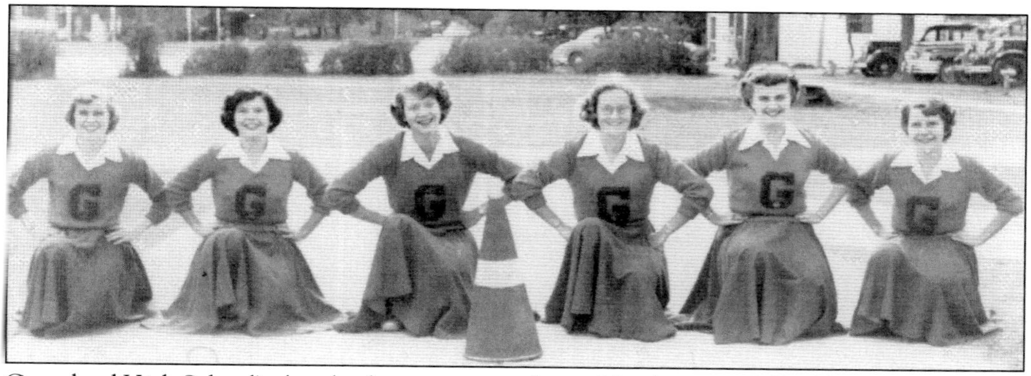

Groveland High School's cheerleaders were a proud—and loud—part of all athletic events. While the uniforms changed over time, the chenille letter "G" remained basically the same. The 1953 squad, from left to right, was Delores Bridges, Jeanette Short, Gerry Sewell, Ann Hendricks, Christine Plowden, and Patsy Short, captain. (Courtesy of the Groveland Historical Museum.)

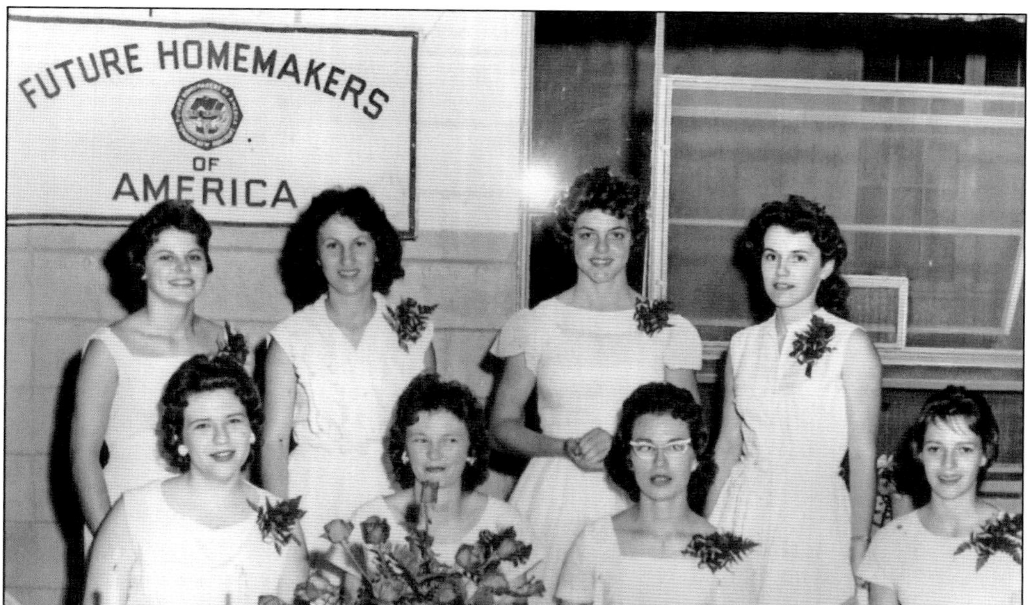

The Future Homemakers of America was one of the largest girls' organizations on campus during the 1960s. Tradition held that the members wore all white during the annual Mother-Daughter banquet. Officers shown in this 1962 photograph from left to right are (first row) Estelle Tyson, Gloria June Varnado, Zelda Brown, and Mary Ellen Tate; (second row) Marie Patterson, Mary Ann Gaudio, Sandy Schoenberger, and Mary Helen Robbins. (Courtesy of the Groveland Historical Museum.)

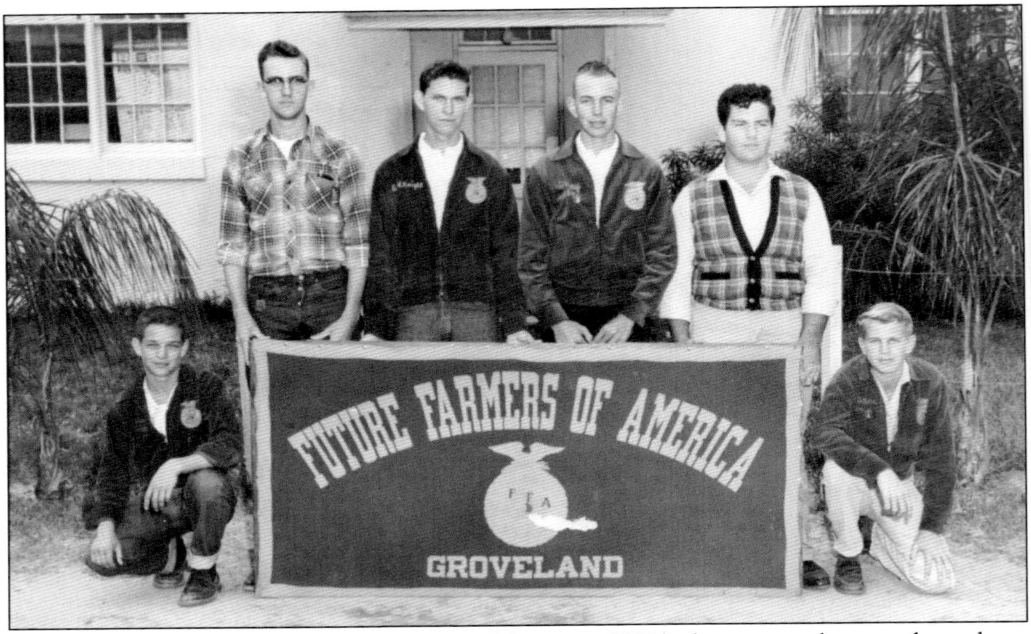

Groveland High School's Future Farmers of America (FFA) chapter was known throughout the state for its excellence. The school had one of the few agricultural farms where students got firsthand experiences in growing produce and livestock. Above, the FFA officers for 1959 are, from left to right, Bernie Merritt, Ronald Story, Pres. William Lee, Pres. Jerry Beard, Jay Stewart, and Henry Lee. In the photograph below, Tommy Watson accepts the Green Star Award from FFA sponsor and teacher Freddie Garner. Under his direction, he led the school's chapter to state and national honors. During the 1970s, the Groveland chapter won the national Gold Emblem Award, the highest honor in FFA. Groveland's chapter produced three state presidents. (Above courtesy of Jerry Beard; below courtesy of the Groveland Historical Museum.)

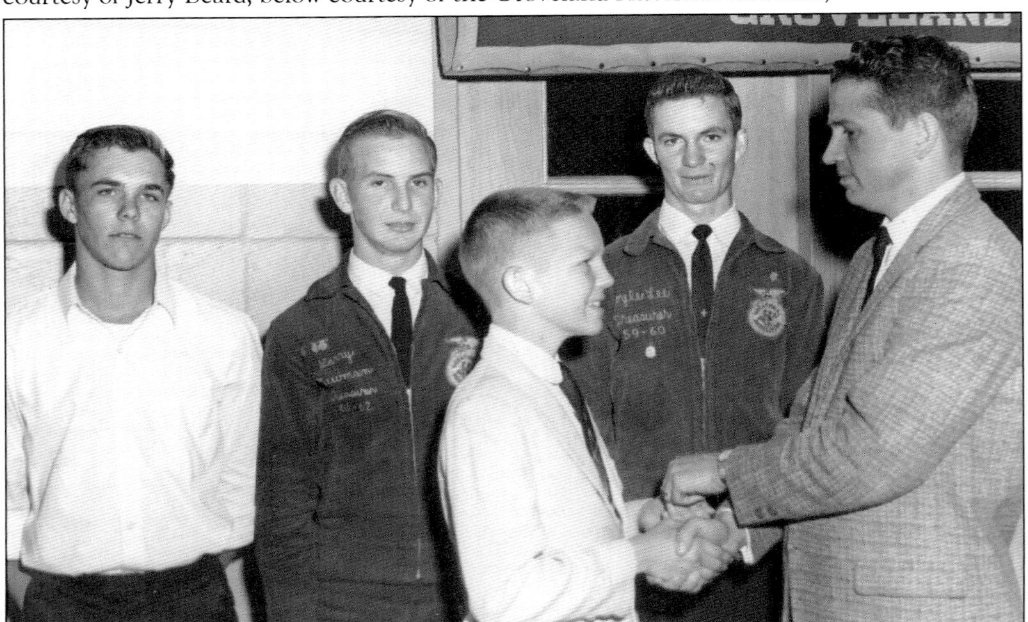

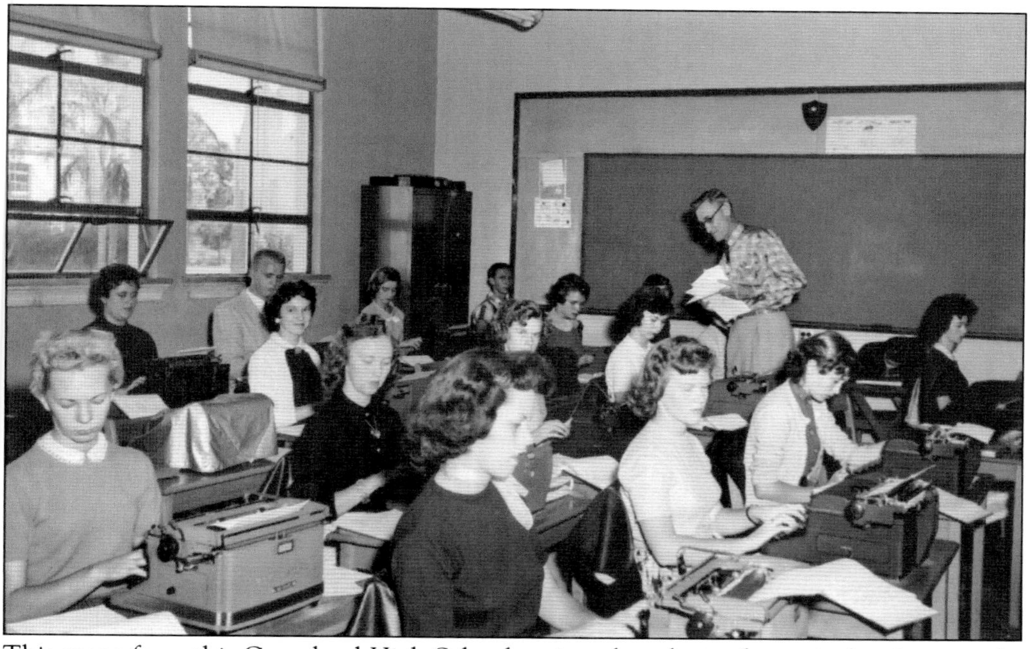

This scene from this Groveland High School typing class shows the typical attire worn by students during the 1950s. Most of the business classes were taught by John Doyle, who was infamous for clapping his hands to the beat of songs to teach typing rhythm. (Courtesy of Cookie Stewart Beard.)

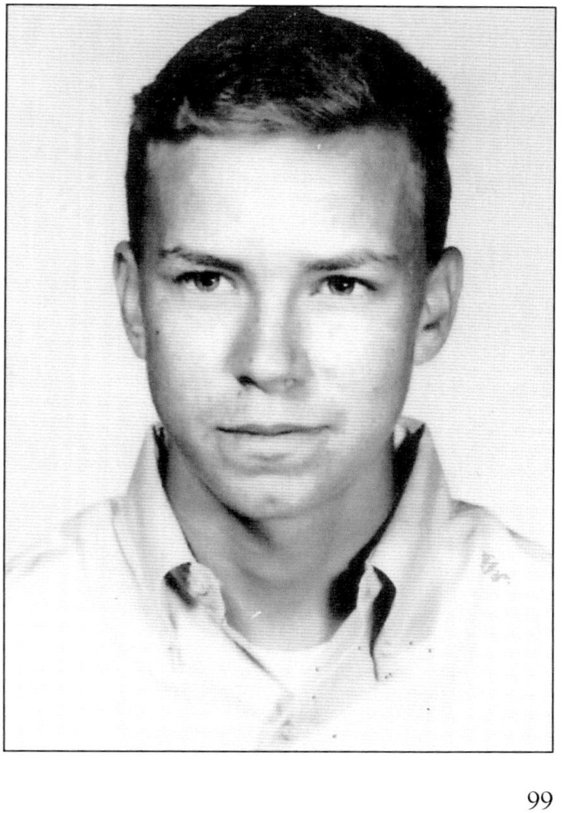

Frank B. Farr Jr. was the only child of Groveland High School principal Frank B. Farr Sr. and math teacher Elizabeth Farr. Frankie Farr, as he was known to friends, had a ready smile but was focused and determined when he ran the mile on the school's track team. In April 1965, he dropped dead while running the final lap at a home event. The football stadium was named in his honor. His father died later the same year. (Courtesy of Linda Stephens Davis.)

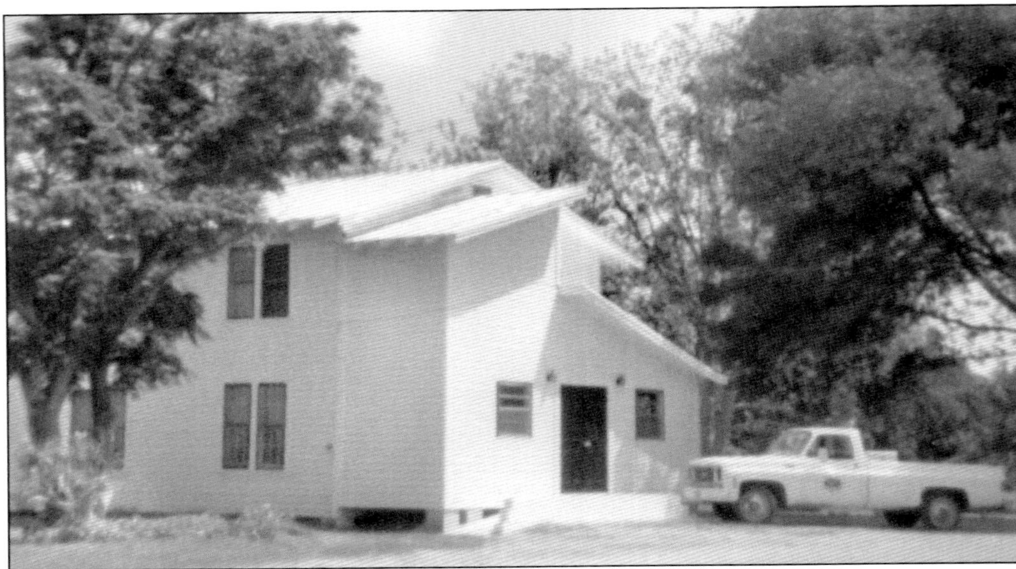

Before integration, Groveland's African American students attended Edgewood Elementary School, a white clapboard school near Mills Avenue. The heart pine lumber came from the nearby Arnold sawmill, where many of the students' fathers worked. From 1949 until 1967, the school was run by beloved husband-and-wife teachers James and Flossie Wyche. She taught first through third grades. He taught fourth through sixth and served as the school's principal. At Christmas, the couple would give the children small gifts paid for out of their teachers' salaries. After integration, the building was used as a community center. Over time, it fell into disrepair and was burned. Memories of the Wyches lived on, however, and in November 2007, Groveland's senior center was named after James Wyche (below, right). He was presented a plaque by Vice Mayor John Griffin in front of a standing-room-only crowd. (Courtesy of the Groveland Historical Museum.)

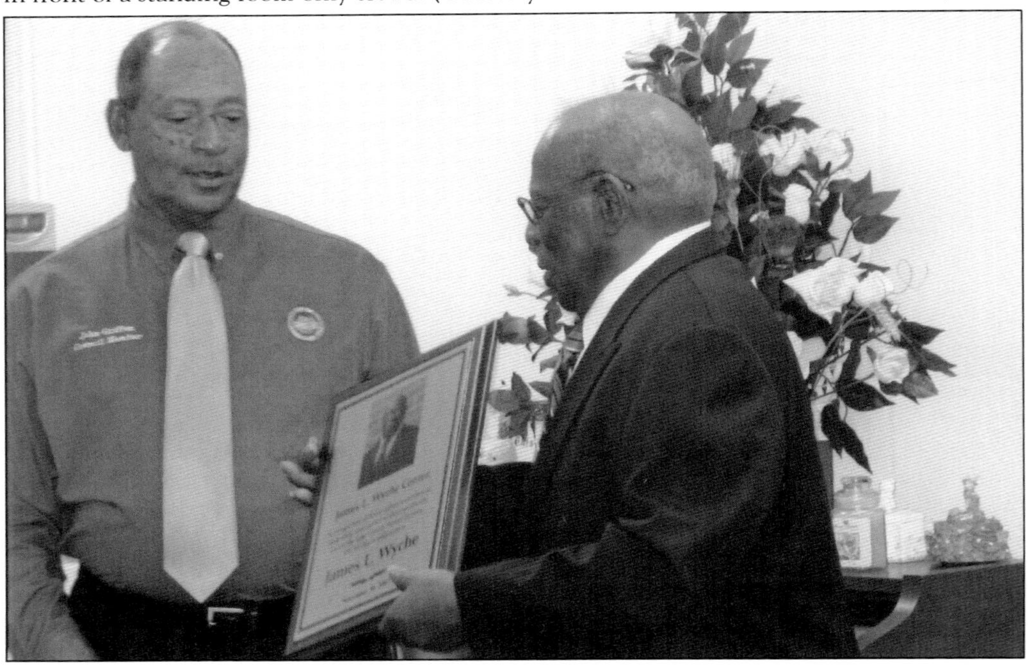

In 1962, Marilyn Gammon wore a crimson gown when she attended the prom with her date, Ken Narehood. The dress symbolized her happy memories of Groveland High. She donated the gown to the Groveland Historical Museum at her death in 2007. (Courtesy of the Groveland Historical Museum.)

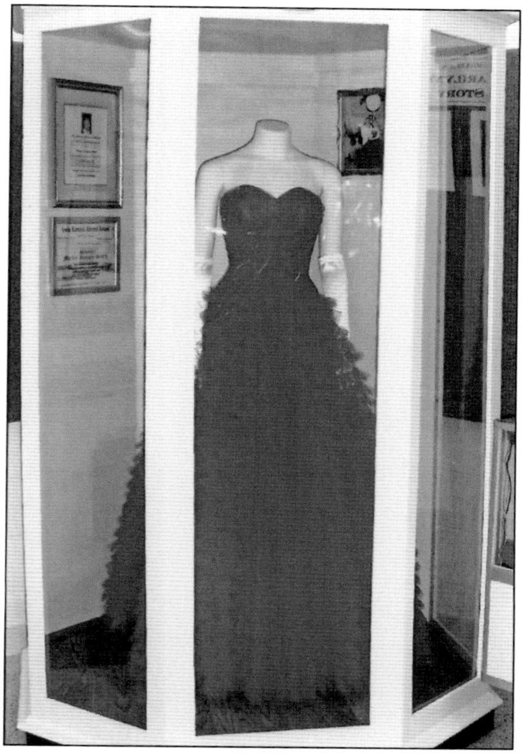

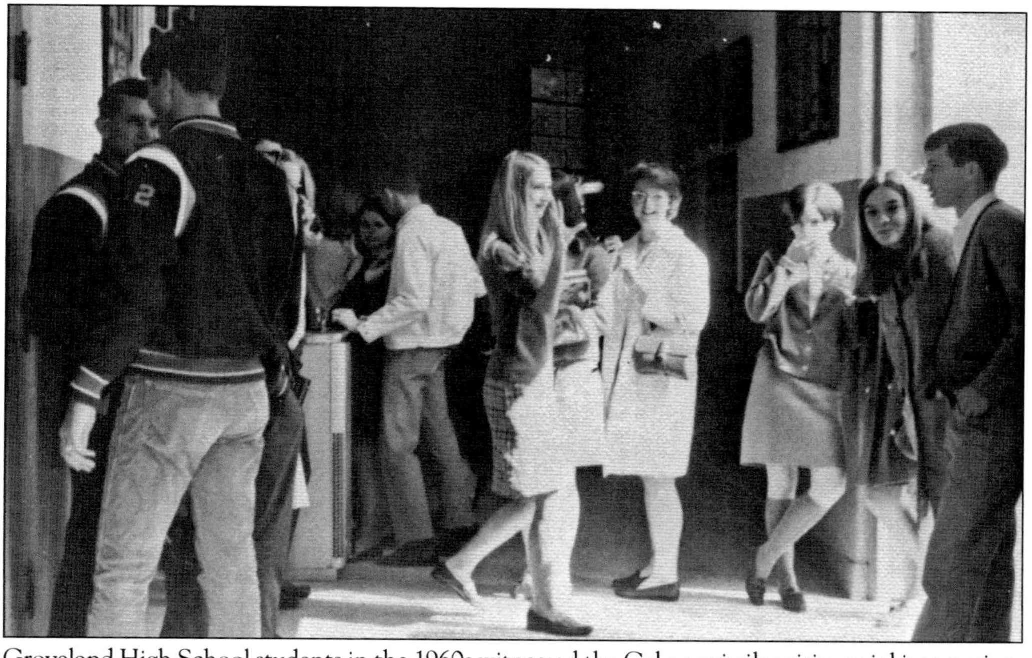

Groveland High School students in the 1960s witnessed the Cuban missile crisis, racial integration, the Vietnam War, assassinations, and the rise of women's rights. The decade started with the Beatles and ended with an American landing on the moon. It was 100 years since the city's first settlers came to start a new life. (Courtesy of the Groveland Historical Museum.)

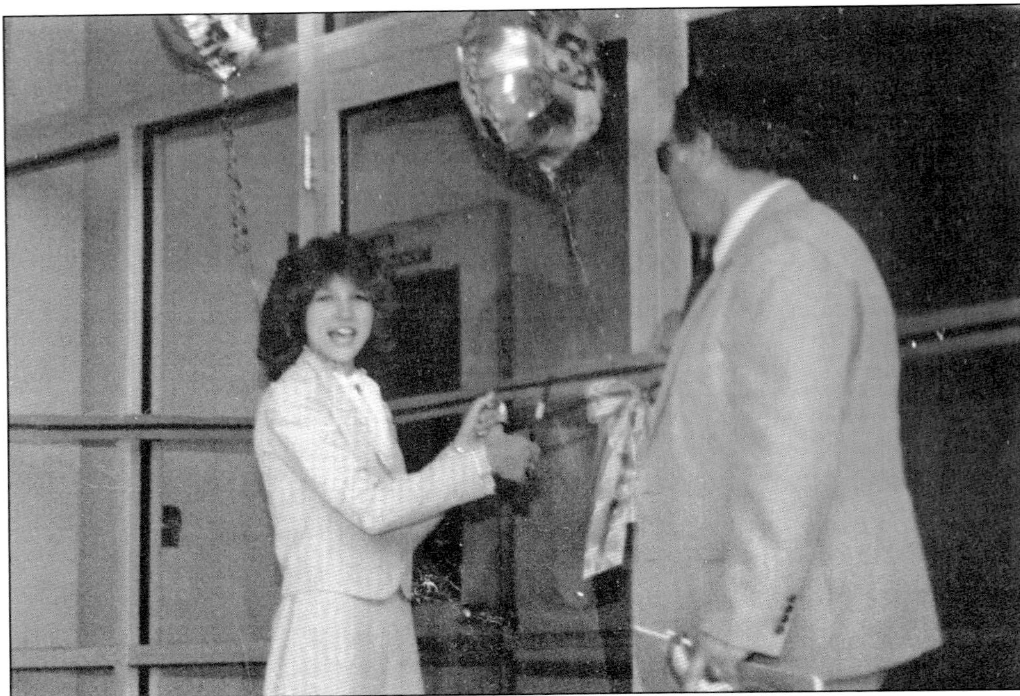

In 1984, an arsonist set a fire that almost destroyed the original Groveland High School buildings. Fifteen classrooms, the guidance office, school records, and memorabilia were badly burned. Graduation class photographs and trophies won from the school's glory days were rescued by caring alumni. After extensive restoration, the school reopened in 1986 amid helium-filled "Greenback" balloons as seen above with Principal Cecil Gray and student Heather Voight. The GHS Alumni Association (below), which began meeting in 1980, held its 2009 reunion at the school shortly before the iconic main building was scheduled for demolition to make way for a new $45 million campus. (Both courtesy of the Groveland Historical Museum.)

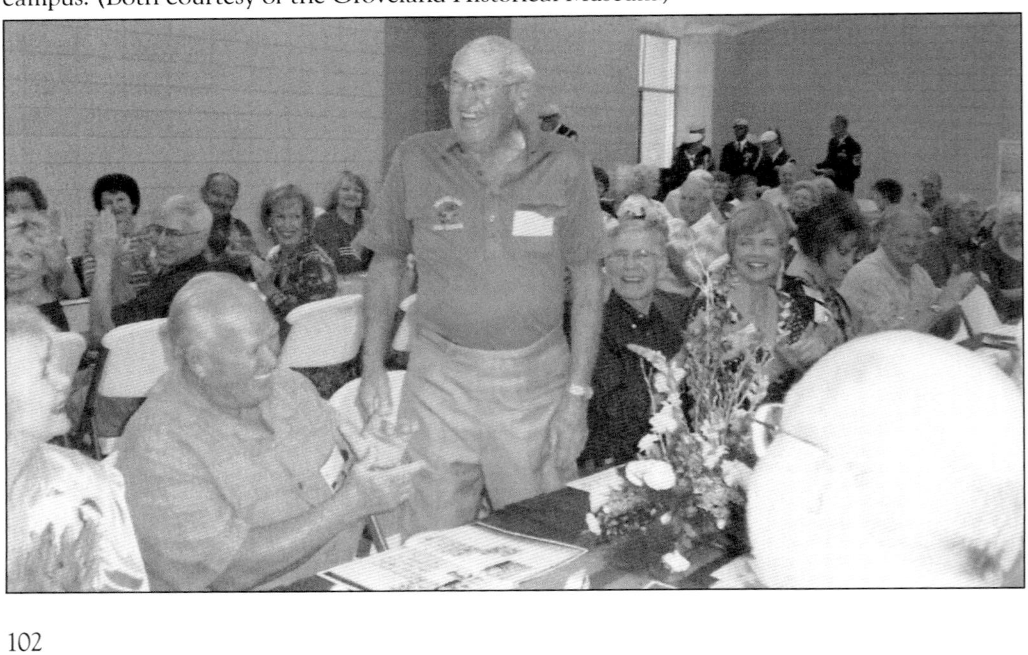

Six

Churches
Heart and Soul

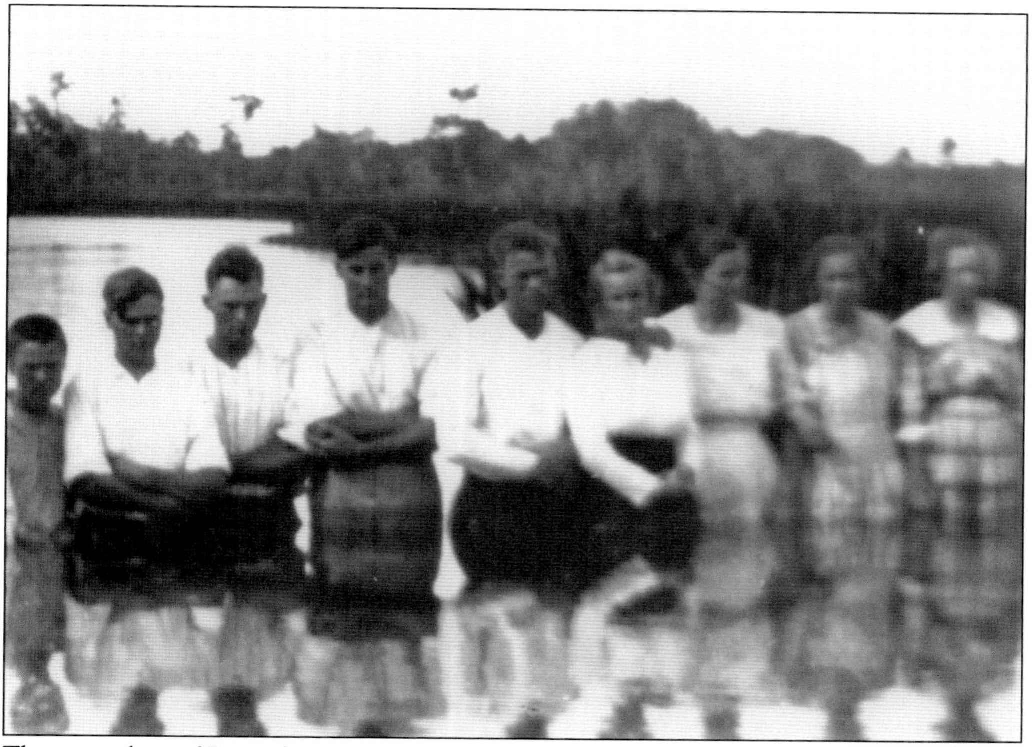

These members of Bay Lake Missionary Baptist Church are being baptized in Bay Lake during the church's first revival, held in 1921. The evangelist was Br. E. L. Gillentine. From left to right are Charles Todd, George Story, William Story, Charlie Rutledge, James Brown, Lydia Brown, Cornelia Bridges Sloan, Mary Jane Henderson, and Edna Tyson. The Bay Lake community sprang up around the lumber and turpentine camps in the heavily wooded longleaf pine forests. In the 1920s, and in the previous years, the weekend of the third Sunday in October was reserved for the annual meeting with dinner on the grounds. These services evolved into revival meetings. Churches were always at the heart of the Groveland community. (Courtesy of Carol Murray Tomlinson.)

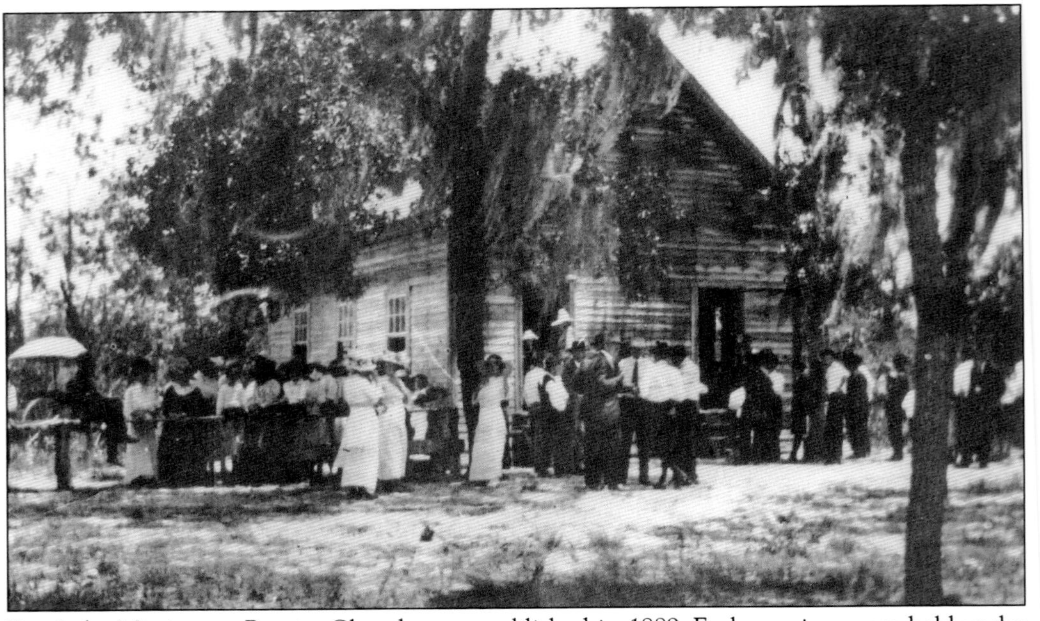

Bay Lake Missionary Baptist Church was established in 1889. Early services were held under an oak tree. The first two churches were wood-frame structures. The second was completed in 1926. Sunday school classes began under the leadership of Br. Charley Gray, who served from 1948 to 1950. From 1958 to 1998, Br. Ray Kirkland served as church pastor. (Courtesy of Carol Murray Tomlinson.)

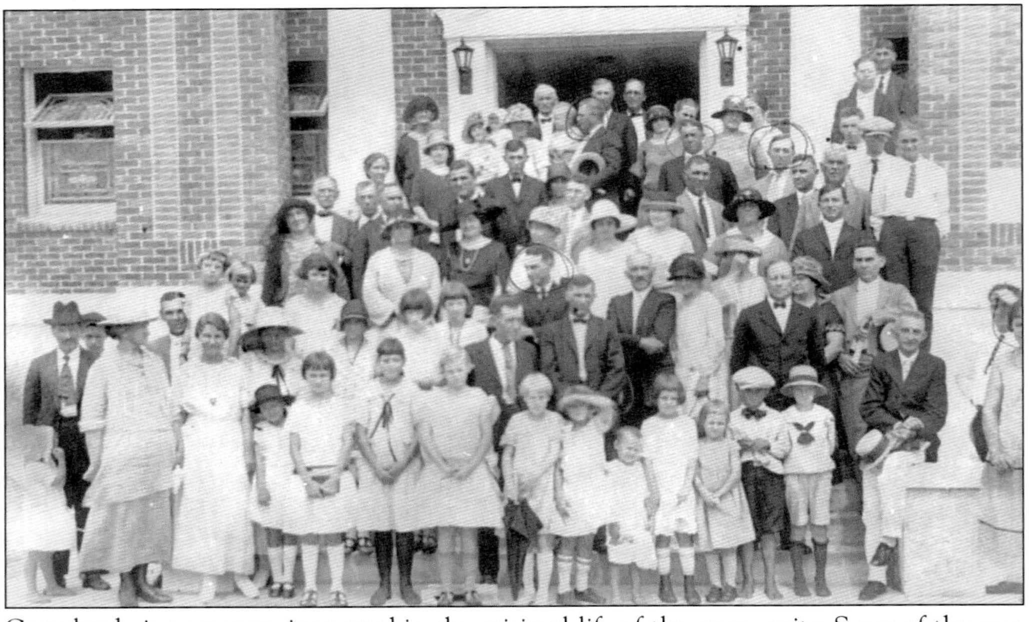

Groveland pioneers were interested in the spiritual life of the community. Some of the core members who helped start First Baptist Church of Groveland include the following families, some of whom are pictured in this 1920s photograph: Anderson, Arnold, Benson, Bradley, Cash, Cashwell, Hawkins, Johnson, Lindell, Lyon, Molin, Nelson, Plowden, Register, Wahlberg, Webb, Williams, and Woodard. (Courtesy of Kathryn Arnold Herzog.)

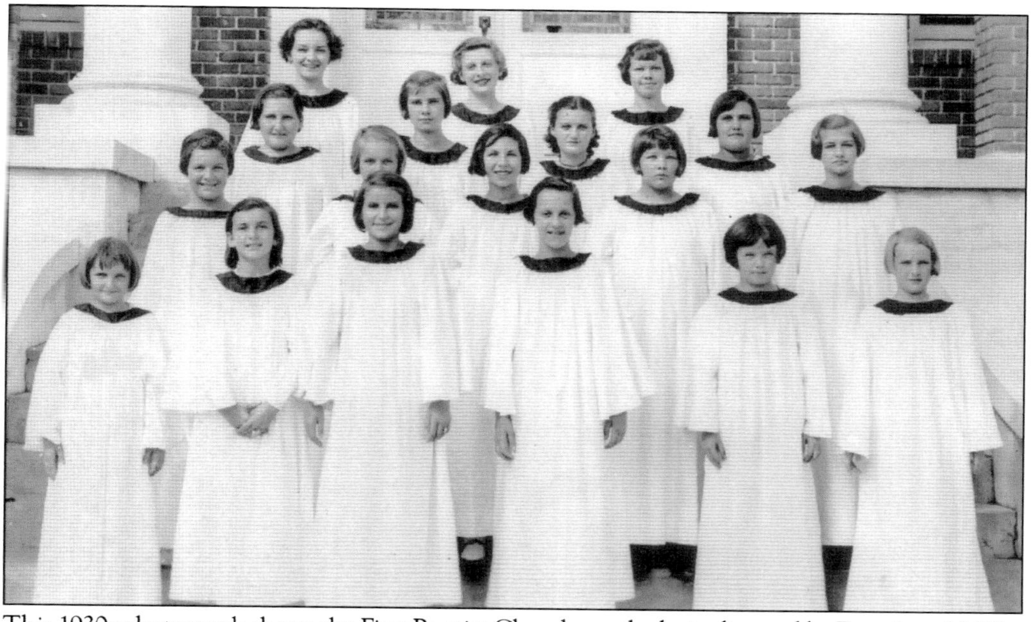

This 1930s photograph shows the First Baptist Church youth choir, directed by Bert Arnold. The choir members would march into the sanctuary on Sunday morning singing, "Holy, Holy, Holy." The choir was a tight-knit group that included two Arnold sisters, Kathryn "Kitty" Arnold and Lucile Arnold, and four of their cousins, Justine and Aline Ogden, and Cynthia and Doris Hogan. (Courtesy of Kathryn Arnold Herzog.)

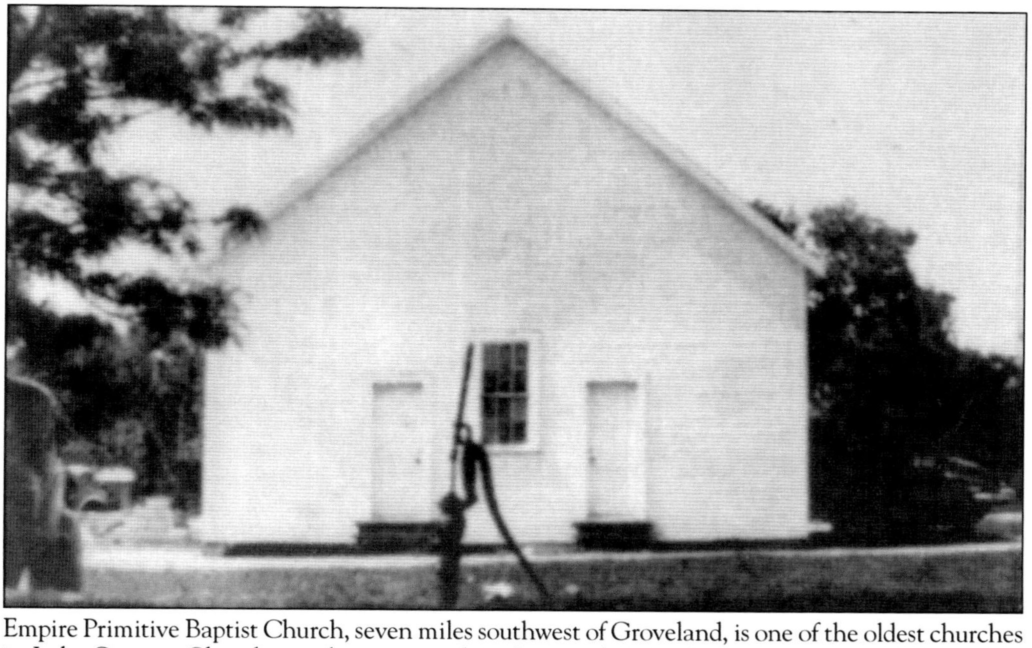

Empire Primitive Baptist Church, seven miles southwest of Groveland, is one of the oldest churches in Lake County. Church members met under a large oak tree when the church was established in 1871. The following year, a log cabin was erected. In 1890, the present white frame building was erected. The first pastor was Elder Joel Swain, who served from 1871 until 1876. (Courtesy of the Lake County Historical Society.)

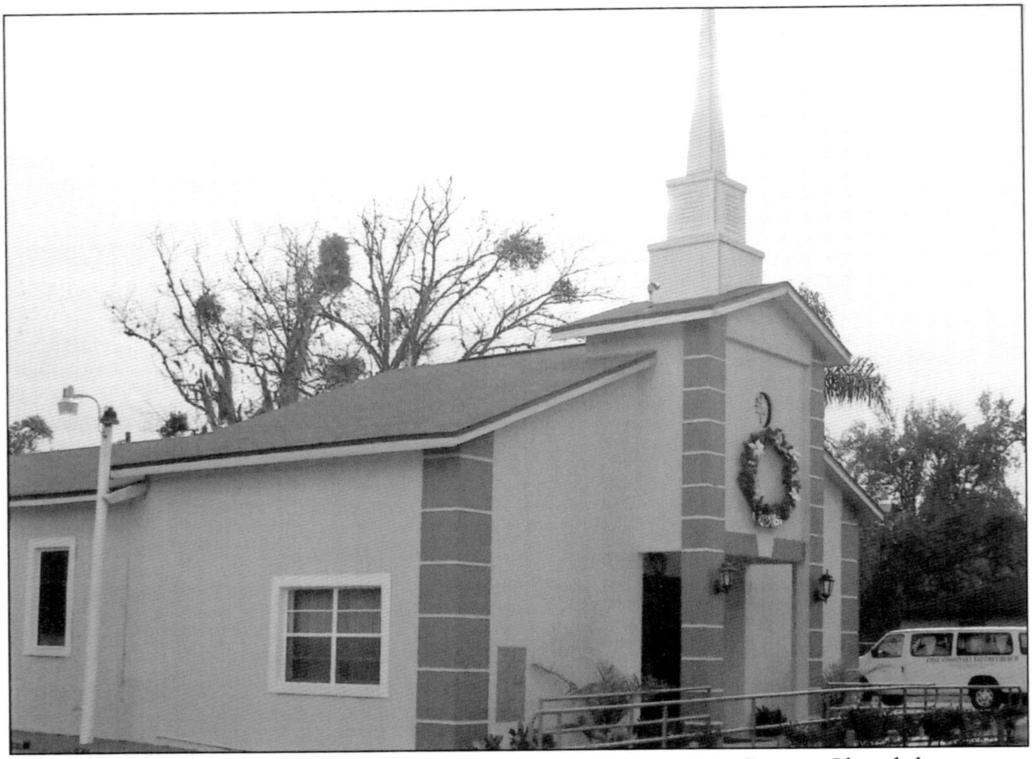

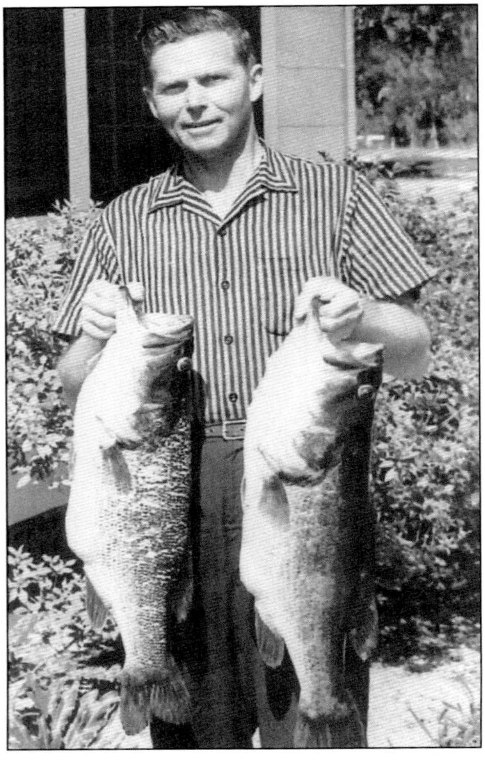

The First Missionary Baptist Church began in 1895 as Oak Hill Baptist Church under the leadership of Pastor Robert J. Boone. The church gave birth to the Greater Harmony Baptist Church. Olea Mitchell, born in 1911, united with the church in 1924. Her sister, Florence Bryant, was the church's first secretary. Bishop Isaac D. Wilkes Sr. began serving as pastor in 1995. (Courtesy of the Groveland Historical Museum.)

The Reverend Wallace Register shows a catch of bass he caught after fishing with one of the members of his congregation. Register was pastor in the 1960s at First Baptist Church. His wife, Delva, was a music teacher at Davis Elementary School. His oldest daughter, Debby, graduated from Groveland High School in 1968. (Courtesy of Rev. Wallace Register.)

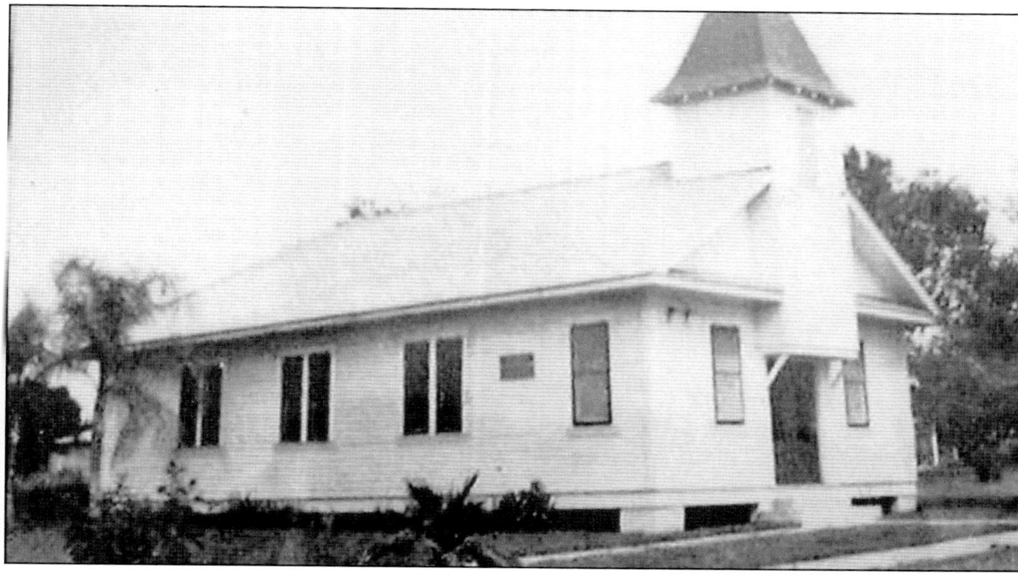

In 1904, pioneers built the Union Church, which served three denominations for 15 years. Zion Lutheran Church was founded in 1919 by families who moved here from the North. The first pastor was the Reverend J. E. Swanborn from Pierson, Florida. The first church (pictured above) was built in 1923 and was replaced in 1954 with the church pictured below at the corner of Main Avenue and Waldo Street. The church helped start two other parishes and a retirement center. (Above courtesy of the Groveland Historical Museum; below courtesy of the Marion Baysinger Memorial Library.)

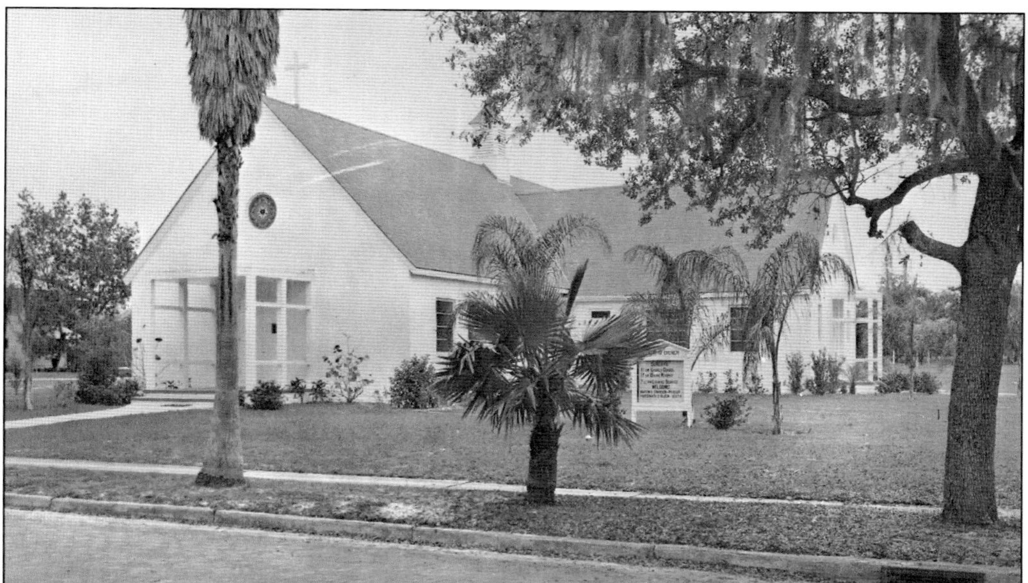

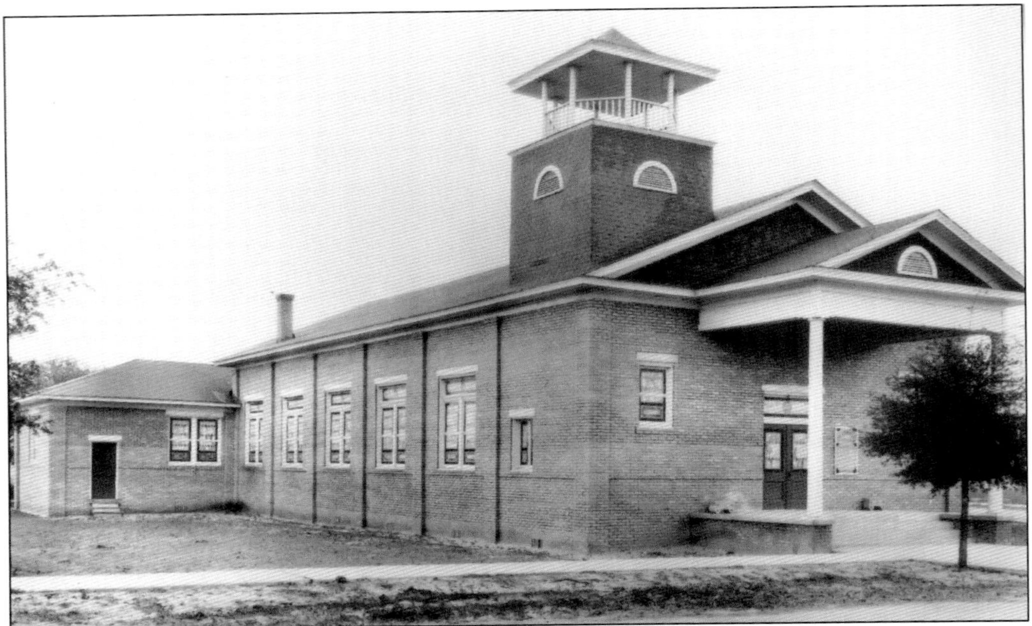

Edge Memorial United Methodist Church was founded in 1909. Before that, members worshipped with other religions at the Union Church. The Methodist church pictured here was constructed in 1920 and rebuilt in 1962. Charter members included the Edge, Sampey, Averitt, and Rice families. The church was named Edge Memorial after the 1934 death of E. E. Edge to honor his devotion to the church. (Courtesy of the Marion Baysinger Memorial Library.)

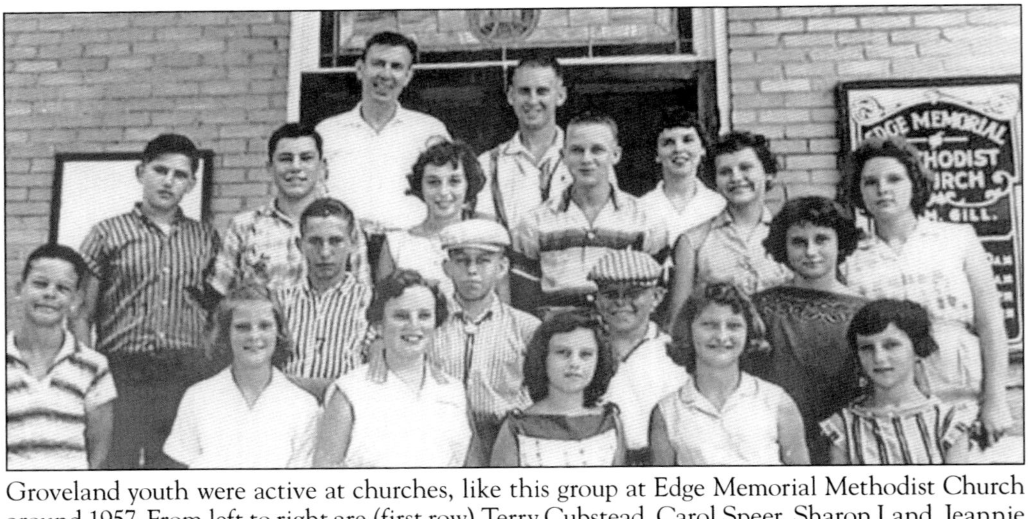

Groveland youth were active at churches, like this group at Edge Memorial Methodist Church around 1957. From left to right are (first row) Terry Cubstead, Carol Speer, Sharon Land, Jeannie Potter, Jane Taylor, and Carol Cressey; (second row) Bobby Boswell, Bobby Campbell, Muggins Willard, and Mary Ruth Rice; (third row) Royce Clousier, Ross Hooks, Becky Vickers, Billy Joe Vans, Mary Boggs, and Clemie Fairchild; (fourth row) the Reverend Dan Gill, Dick Westervelt, and Mickey Westervelt. (Courtesy of the Groveland Historical Museum.)

Seven

Memorable
History Makers and Headliners

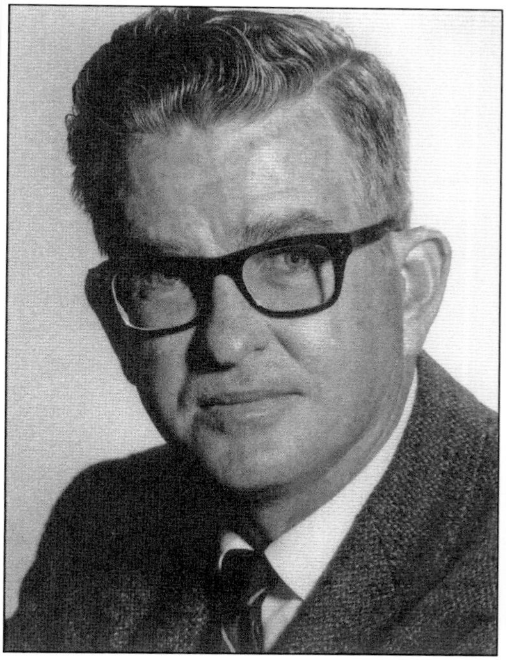
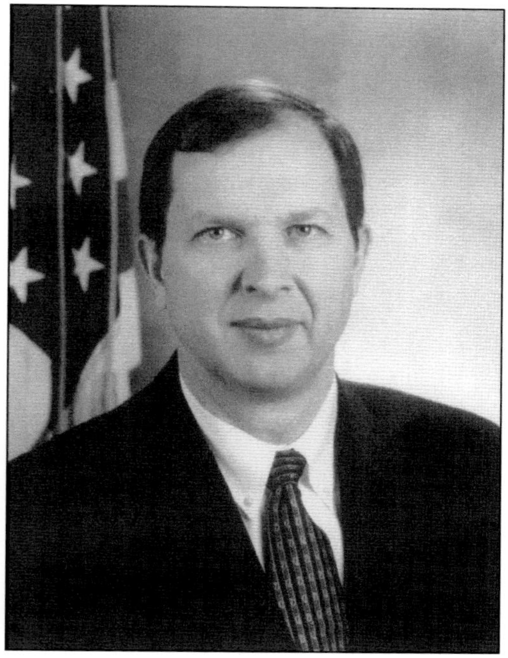

Edmond "Darrel" Cashwell (left) and Dale Watson (right) shared the same hometown and high school. They had significant roles in separate events that changed the course of history. Cashwell, born in 1920, was a brilliant mathematician and physicist who was one of the Manhattan Project scientists who created the atomic bomb. He urged caution about use of the bomb and helped create the Monte Carlo mathematical code. He spent his career at the Los Alamos National Laboratory. Watson, born in 1950, was head of counterterrorism and counterintelligence for the FBI on September 11, 2001. In his 24-year career, he was involved in every major terrorist investigation during the 1990s. He briefed Presidents Clinton and George W. Bush and testified before Congress. He is the sole recipient of the Presidential Rank Award for the FBI. (Left courtesy of Shirley Cashwell; right courtesy of the FBI.)

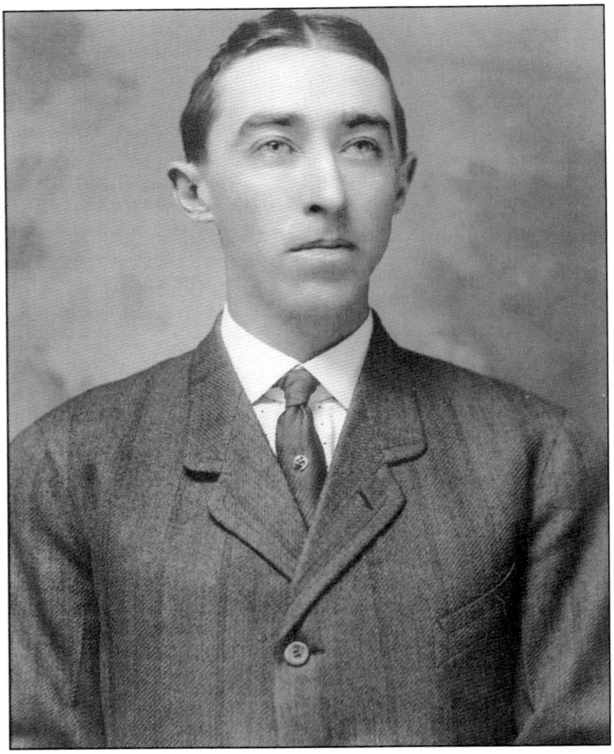

J. Ray Arnold built the J. Ray Arnold Lumber Company into the largest sawmill in the Southeast. He owned vast acreage across the state and was the largest employer in Lake County. He drilled for oil in the 1930s and helped build the First Baptist Church of Groveland. He wore a four-carat diamond stick pin and was known as a sharpshooter, visionary, and genius as well as a devoted husband and father of six children. (Courtesy of Kathryn Arnold Herzog.)

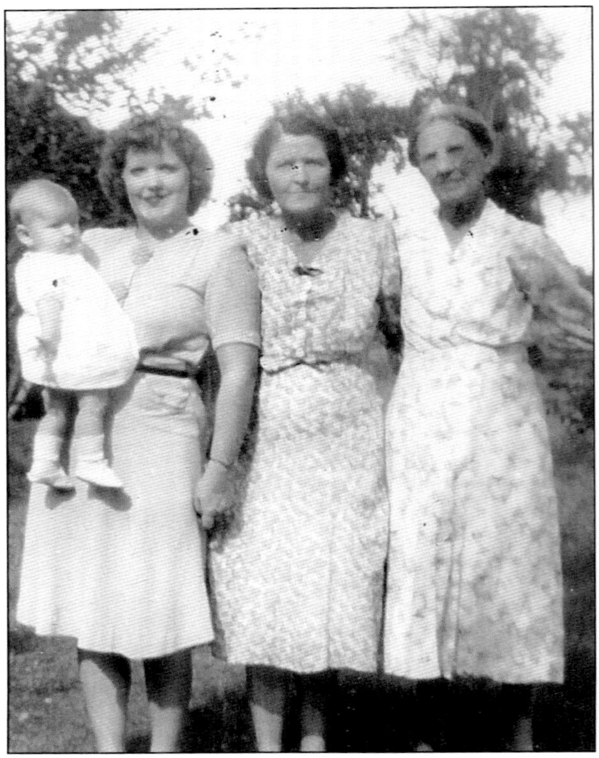

Cyleta Lee Austin is recognized as Groveland's historian emeritus. Her roots go back to early settlers of Carter's Island and Monte Vista. She is shown (left) holding her daughter Diane Austin. In the center of this 1943 photograph is her mother, Bessie Carter Lee, with her grandmother, Matilda Carter (right). She also has another daughter, Valerie Austin Bronson. Austin has researched and recorded South Lake history for numerous publications. (Courtesy of Cyleta Lee Austin.)

Marion Baysinger, for whom Groveland's library was named, was a teacher and librarian and helped run the Teenway Club. Her list of civic achievements is practically unparalleled. The mother of three was president of the Groveland Women's Club and Garden Club and served as secretary of the Groveland-Mascotte Chamber of Commerce and as den mother in addition to singing in the church choir. (Courtesy of the Marion Baysinger Memorial Library.)

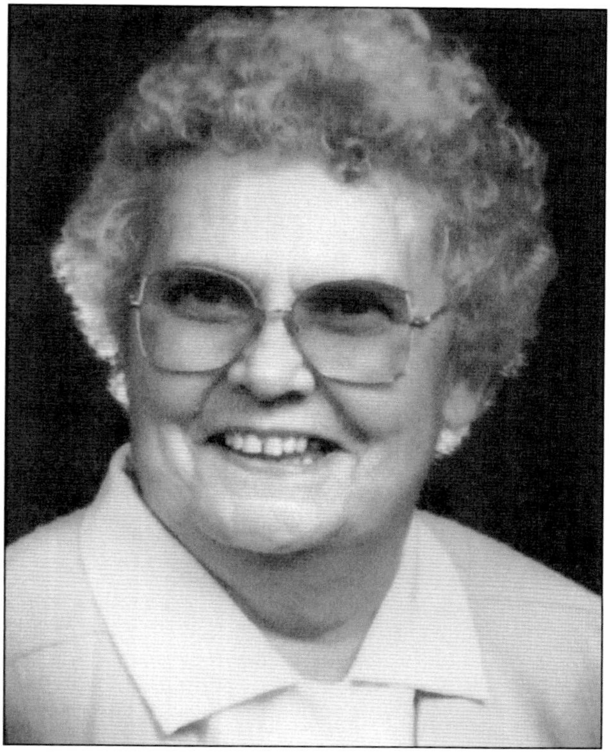

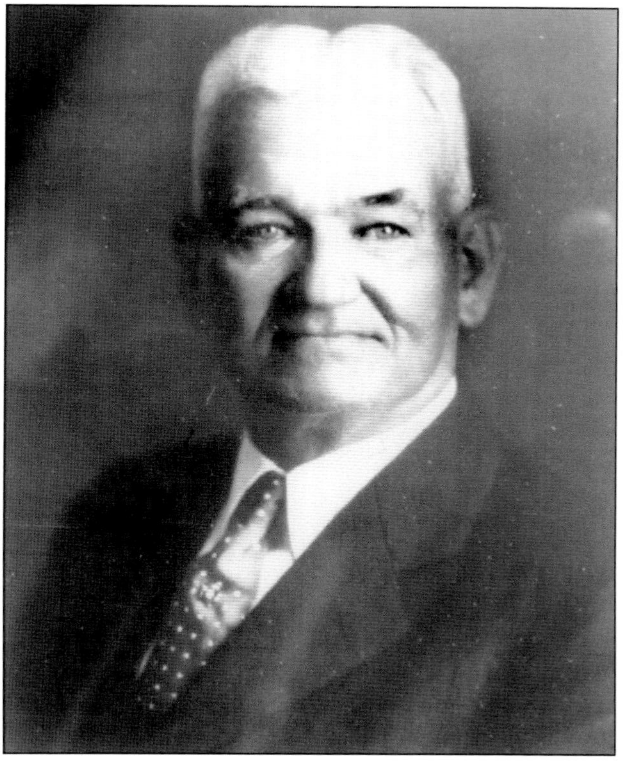

John Washington Beach of Rockford, Illinois, born in 1869, bought 33,000 acres in Taylorville; then he promoted his Groveland Farms to Northerners. He built the Groveland Hotel, named Lake Audrey after his daughter, and served as a city council member. He pushed for the town to be renamed Groveland. He donated land for Lake David Park, the Methodist church, and Groveland's high school. (Courtesy of Lake Historical Society.)

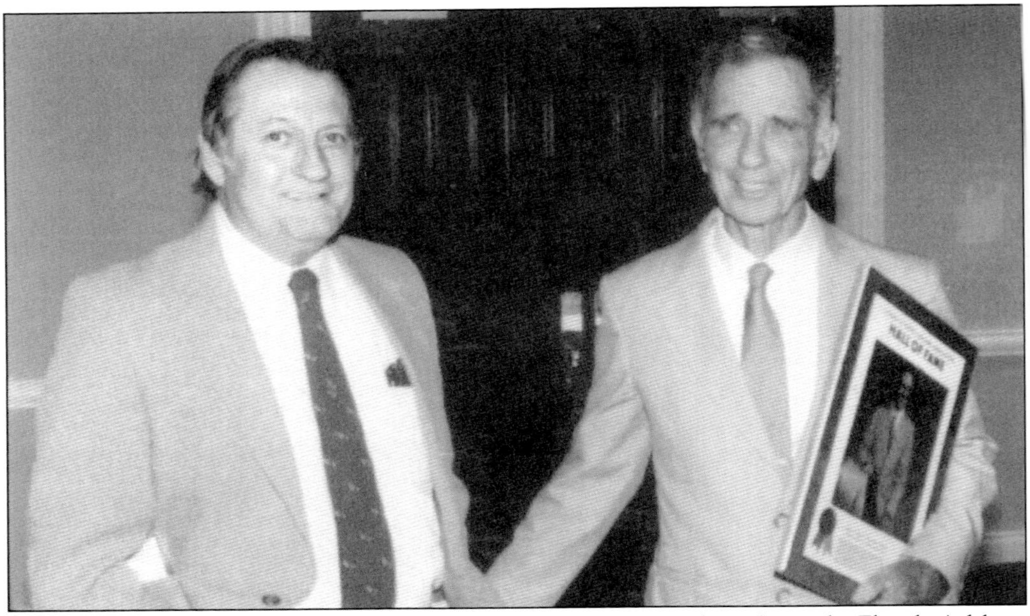

Shaw Buck (right) and Bill Cockcroft are shown after Buck was inducted into the Florida Athletic Coaches Hall of Fame in 1988. Buck played football at the University of Florida and professional baseball. He coached at Groveland High School from 1937 to 1972, stressing character while earning the winningest football record of any school its size in Florida. The football field was named in his honor. (Courtesy of Julian Rowe.)

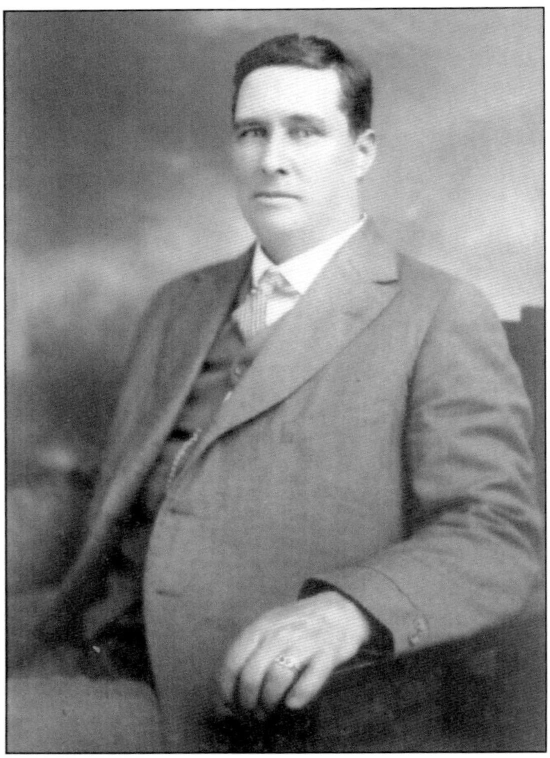

E. E. Edge (left) and L. Day Edge are perhaps one of the most successful father-and-son entrepreneurs in Florida's history. E. E. Edge grew a turpentine and commissary into numerous successful businesses and started what became the Florida Telephone Company. His son became Groveland's first mayor and the youngest state Speaker of the House before expanding the family business and citrus groves. (Courtesy of Lake Historical Society.)

Joe Fairchild was a visionary leader who started People's State Bank in 1949 and served as president and director from then until his untimely death at age 46 in 1964. He was a progressive mayor from 1959 to 1960, pushing for residential mail delivery among other advances. He was an active civic and church leader as well as a devoted husband and father of six. (Courtesy of June Fairchild.)

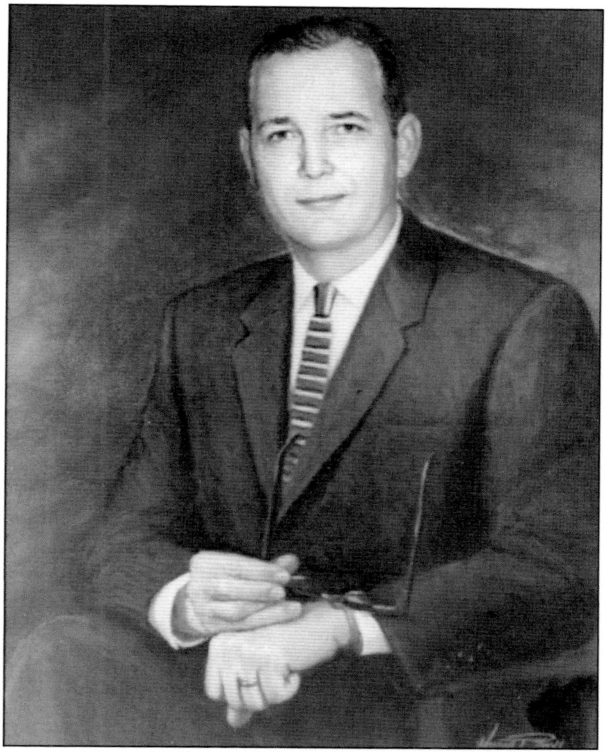

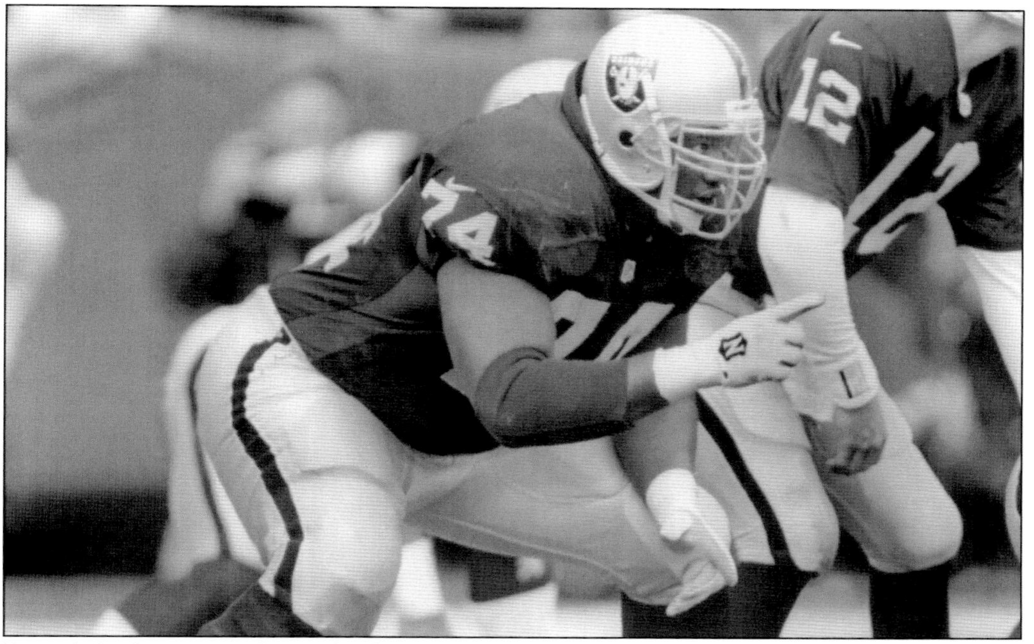

Derrick Graham, seen playing for the NFL Oakland Raiders, was born in 1967 in Groveland. He played football at Groveland High School and Appalachian State University before a professional career that included playing lineman for the Kansas City Chiefs, Carolina Panthers, and Seattle Seahawks in addition to the Raiders. (Courtesy of the Oakland Raiders.)

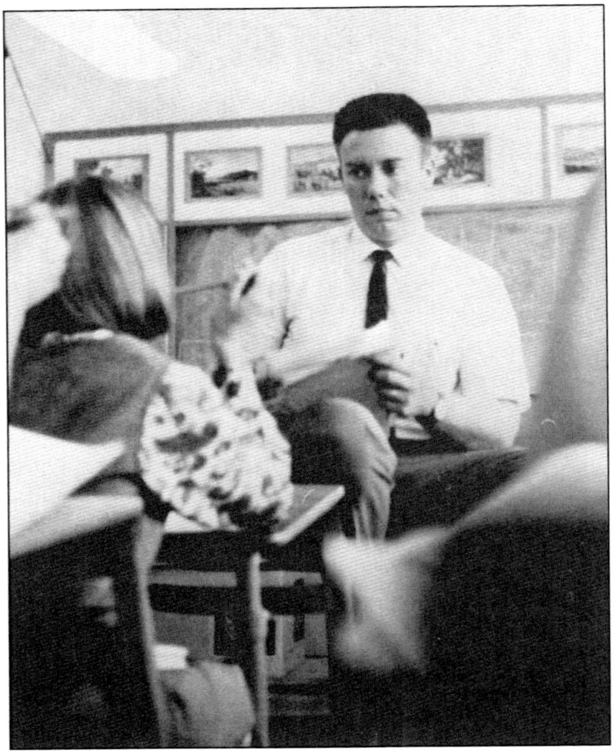

Cecil Gray started teaching English at Groveland High School in 1960. He served as senior class sponsor, assistant principal, and head principal. In 1987, he became principal of the newly formed Groveland Middle School and remained head administrator until his accidental death from a fall in 1997. Parents and teachers sought to have the school named in his honor, which was approved in 1998. (Courtesy of the Groveland Historical Museum.)

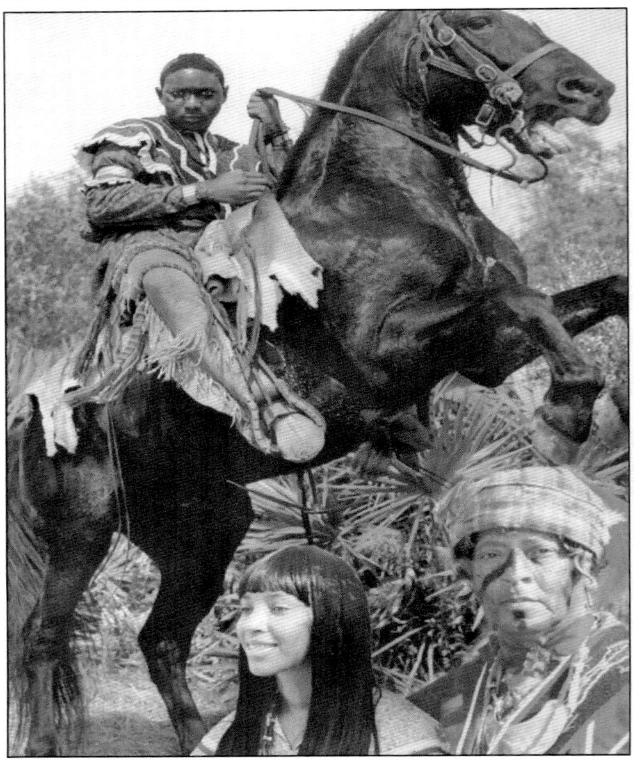

John Griffin (lower right), vice mayor of Groveland, cattle rancher, and business owner, is of Black Seminole heritage and a recognized expert on South Lake and Black Seminole history. He and his daughter, Tamu Griffin (left), and grandnephew Matthew Griffin (top) wear traditional Seminole clothing when they participate in the annual Dade Battlefield Re-enactment each January. (Courtesy of John Griffin.)

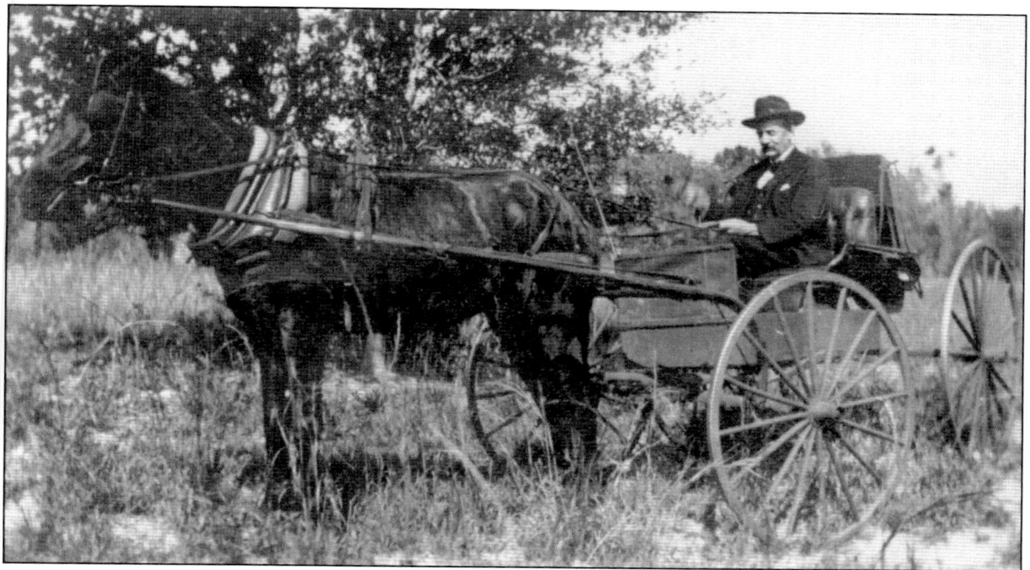

George King, a wealthy Baltimore sales manager for Colgate Company, dreamed of a city of villas. In 1884, King, accompanied by his family, built a grand house and lush gardens and named the new settlement, north of Groveland, Villa City. He was joined by dozens of other affluent Northerners. But they left when the Great Freeze of 1895 turned the paradise into a frozen ghost town. (Courtesy of Howard King.)

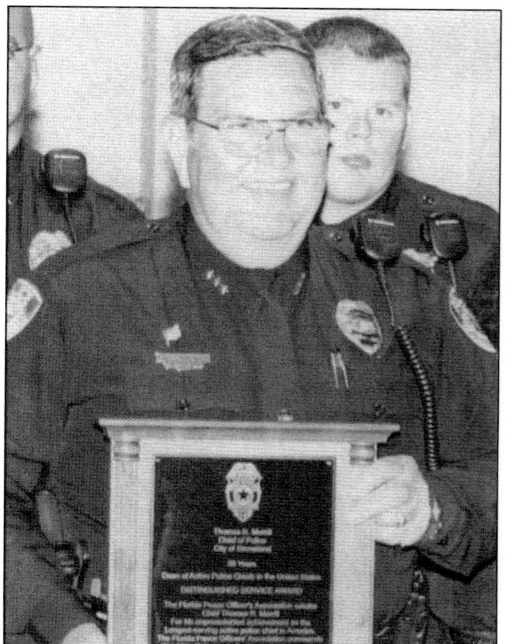

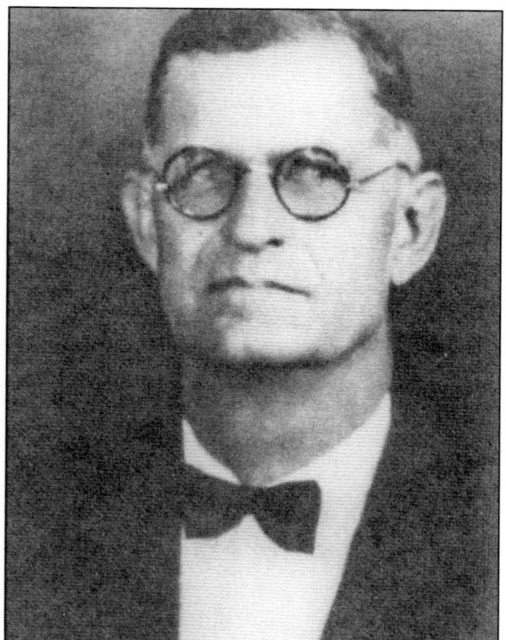

Groveland's police chief Thomas "Tommy" Merrill is recognized as the longest-serving police chief in the United States, celebrating 40 years in 2009 as the city's top cop. George Myers (right), a former Wild West federal marshal, became Groveland's marshal in 1928 and served as Mascotte's first mayor in 1925. Myers Boulevard is named after him. (Left courtesy of the City of Groveland; right courtesy of Dolores Gano Walker.)

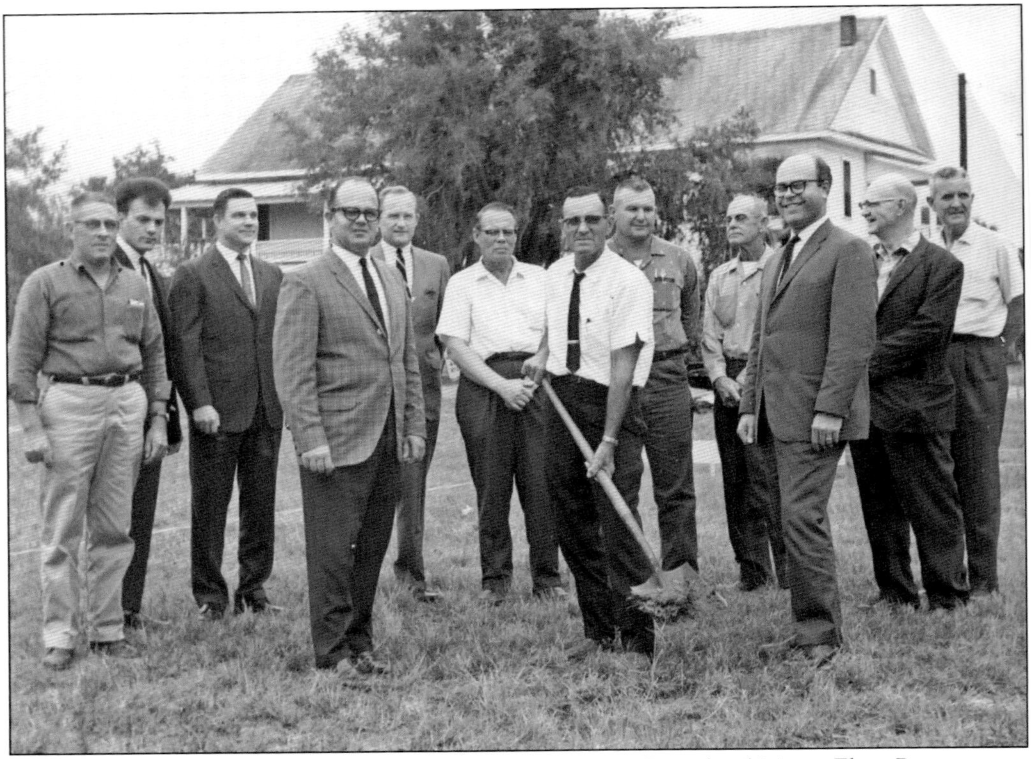

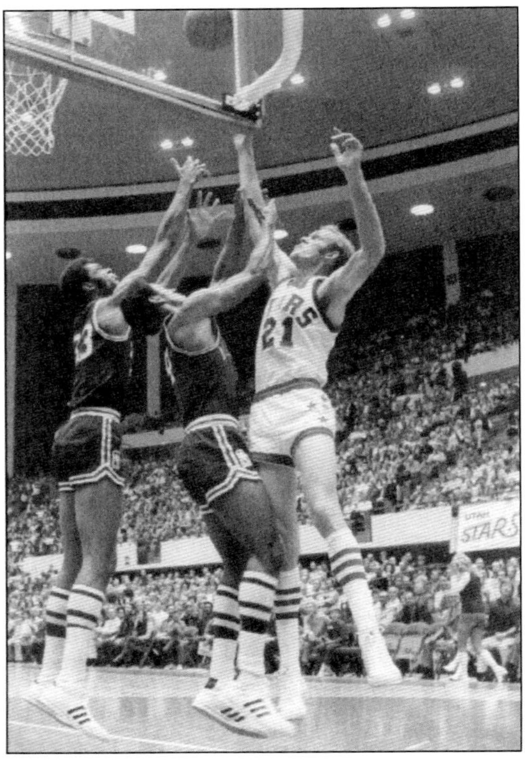

Former Groveland Mayor Elma Puryear (center with shovel), who served as mayor for 25 years, is shown with city council members and other dignitaries during the ground-breaking ceremony of the new community building completed in 1962 and named after him in 1981. Puryear, a retired building contractor and citrus broker, also spearheaded construction of a new city hall and was active in church and charitable work. (Courtesy of Gwen Puryear.)

Austin "Red" Robbins (right) was a record-setting Groveland High School basketball player who became an All-American at the University of Tennessee before joining the pros. Robbins led the Utah Stars to the American Basketball Association championship in 1971. He also played with the San Diego Conquistadors, New Orleans Bucs, Virginia Squires, and Kentucky Colonels. His scrapbook collection and Tennessee jersey are displayed at the Groveland Historical Museum. (Courtesy of Austin Robbins.)

Julian "Soup" Rowe (left) is a Groveland native and historian who volunteered for decades as the high school's athletic trainer. His service was recognized by having the field house named after him. The U.S. postmaster general presented Rowe with an award honoring his 50 years with the Groveland Post Office. Rowe also was honored with the Irwin Barwick Award for being an outstanding Groveland High School alumnus. (Courtesy of Julian Rowe.)

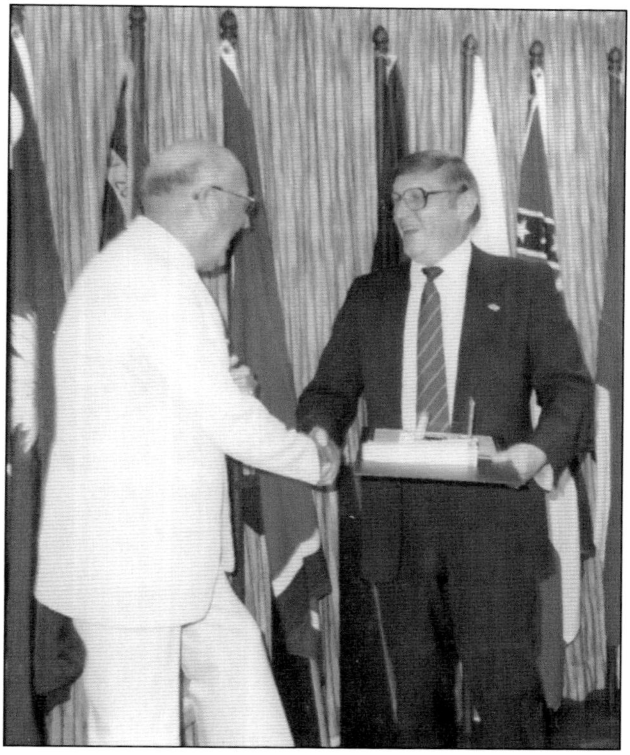

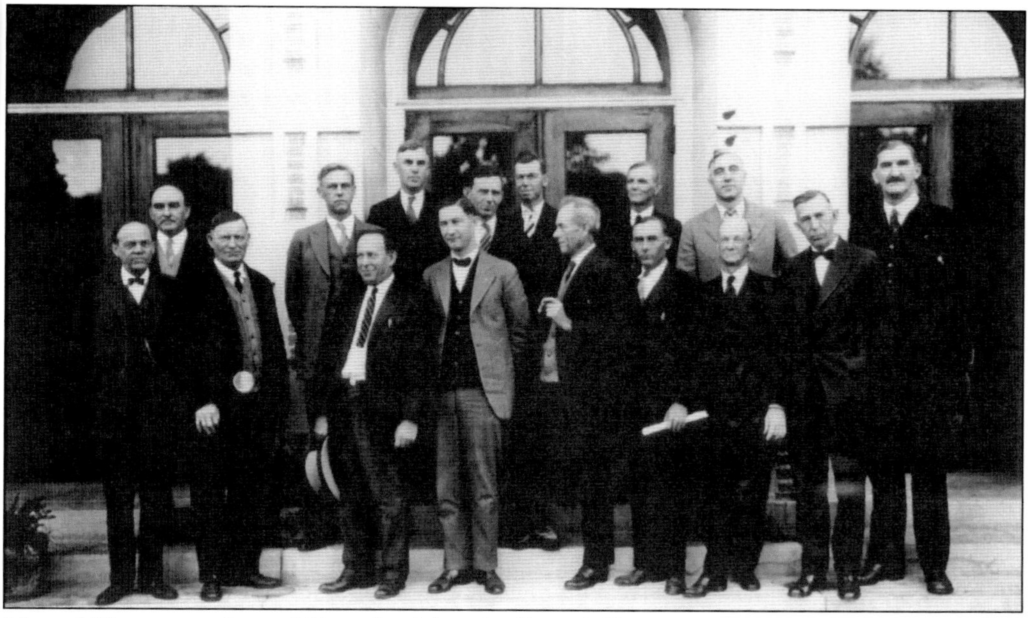

Manuel Sloan, grandson of Groveland founder Daniel Sloan, was born in 1894. He served on the Board of County Commissioners beginning in 1926. Pictured in the first row, sixth from left, Sloan is holding in his hands the plans for the Howey Bridge that spans Little Lake Harris. Sloan was well liked and remembered for his willingness to help his neighbors. He was a lifelong farmer and cattle rancher. (Courtesy of Peggy Parrish Sloan.)

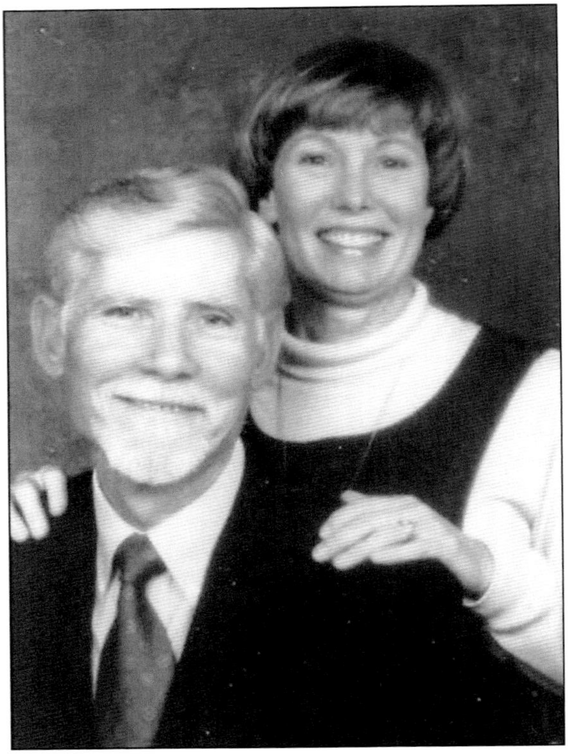

Marilyn Gammon Smith (right) built and maintained the Groveland High School Alumni Web site that promoted a tightly knit network for hundreds of graduates. Her efforts to start a historical museum were cut short when she died of cancer in 2007. Her husband, Kemp (left), donated money to start the Groveland Historical Museum, which was dedicated to his wife. (Courtesy of Kemp Smith.)

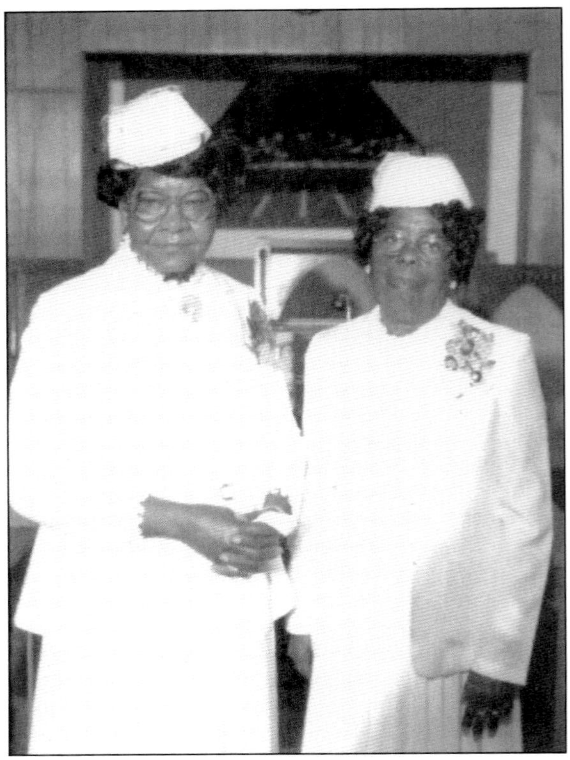

Elease Tomlin (right) has seen more of Groveland's history than any other human. At 104, she is Groveland's oldest living resident. Tomlin's family was one of the earliest settlers who came with E. E. Edge's logging and turpentine crews. She is known by many, such as Alberta Taylor (left), as a great cook who made snow cones for children. (Courtesy of Emma Sullivan.)

Brig. Gen. Jimmy Watson (right), a Tuscanooga native and graduate of Groveland High School, oversaw the largest ever deployment of the Florida National Guard to Iraq. Until retirement, he supervised the operations and allocation of more than 10,700 members of the National Guard. He is seen in this 1998 photograph talking to a helicopter crew fighting wildfires. (Courtesy of the Florida National Guard.)

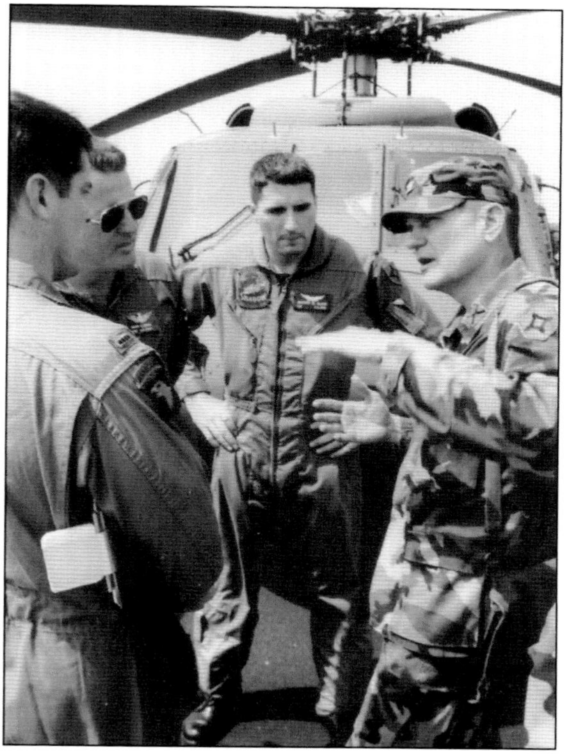

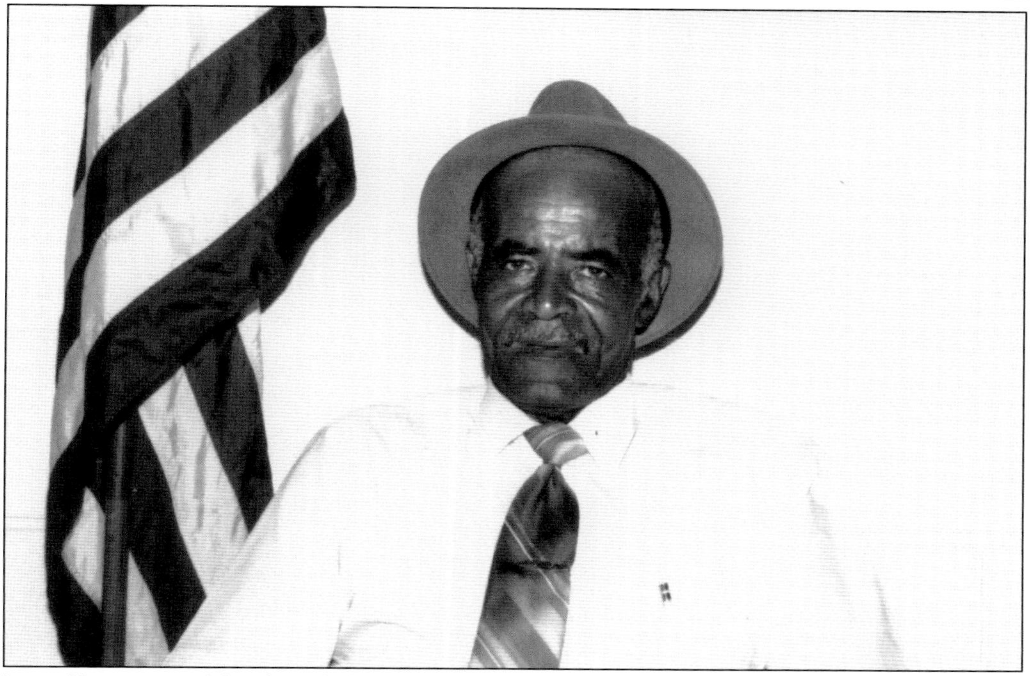

Lewis Hart is one of the elected officials who are honored for making history by virtue of being first to break new cultural ground. Hart was Groveland's first elected African American city council member. He was elected in 1972 and served for 28 years. (Courtesy of City of Groveland.)

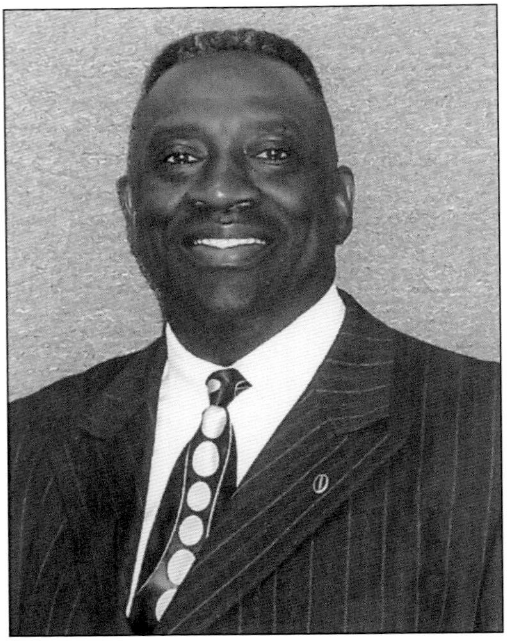

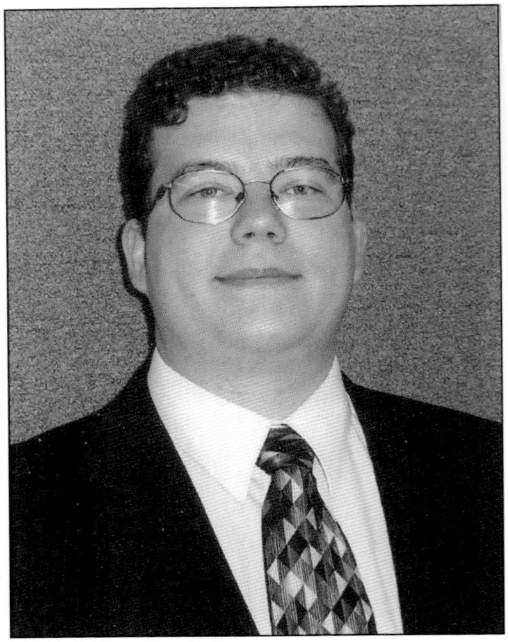

James Smith (left) was Groveland's first African American mayor. He served from 2004 to 2006 and was recently reelected to the city council. Matthew Baumann is the youngest mayor in Groveland's history. He was 25 when he was sworn into office in 2007. (Both courtesy of the Groveland Historical Museum.)

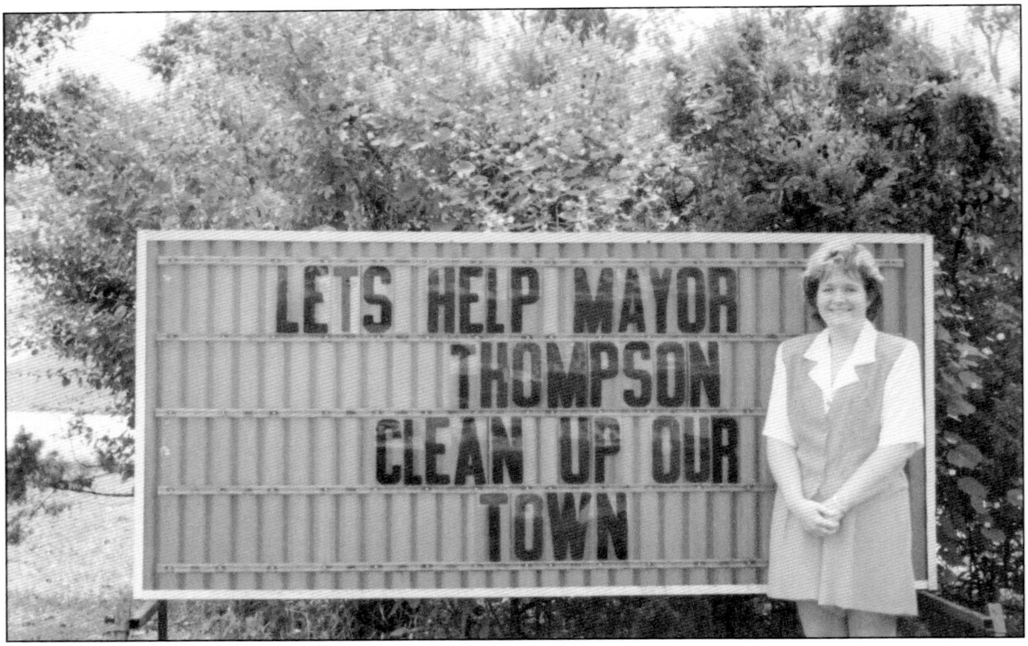

Doris Thompson Davis's election marked another milestone in the city's history when she became Groveland's first female mayor in 1994. At the time, she also was the youngest person ever elected to the office. (Courtesy of City of Groveland.)

Eight

NEIGHBORS
MASCOTTE, CLERMONT, STUCKEY, MINNEOLA, AND MONTVERDE

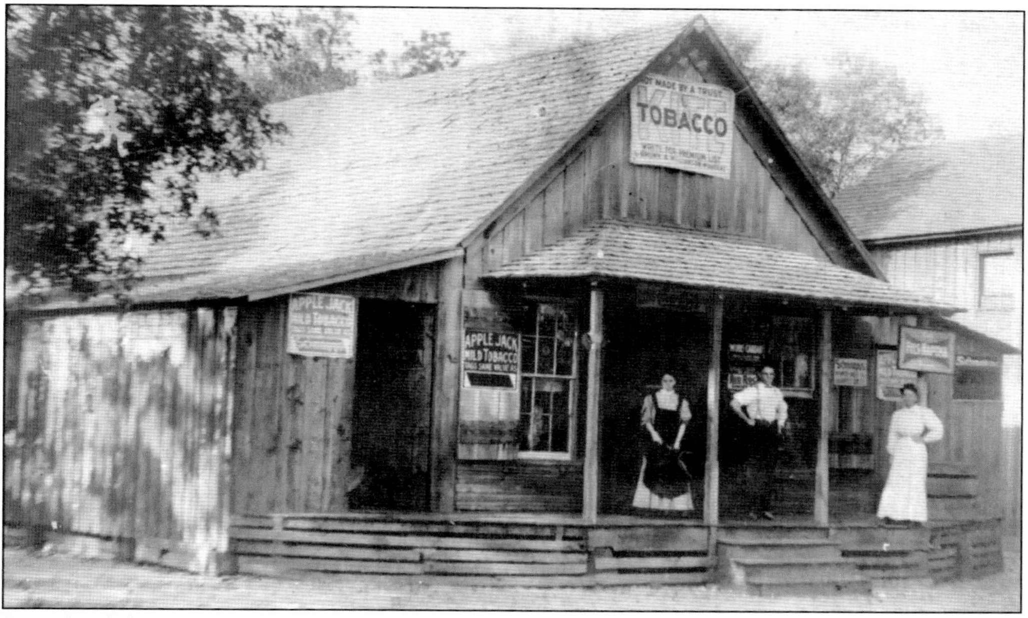

Groveland's history would be incomplete without mentioning its neighbors. Mascotte and Groveland families shared similar histories and relatives. Mascotte children historically went to Groveland's schools beginning in the seventh grade. Theodore Ruff was the town's first postmaster and owned the first store. A schoolhouse was built around 1900. Dr. Herman Watson, founder of Lakeland's renowned Watson Clinic, started his first practice in Mascotte in 1919. Mascotte's first mayor was George Myers, who later became Groveland police chief. In the 1920s, Mascotte was home to three fruit and vegetable packinghouses. Pictured at an early store from left to right are Annie Watson, James Alan Pate, and his second wife, Willie Pate. (Courtesy of Imogene Weir Tallant.)

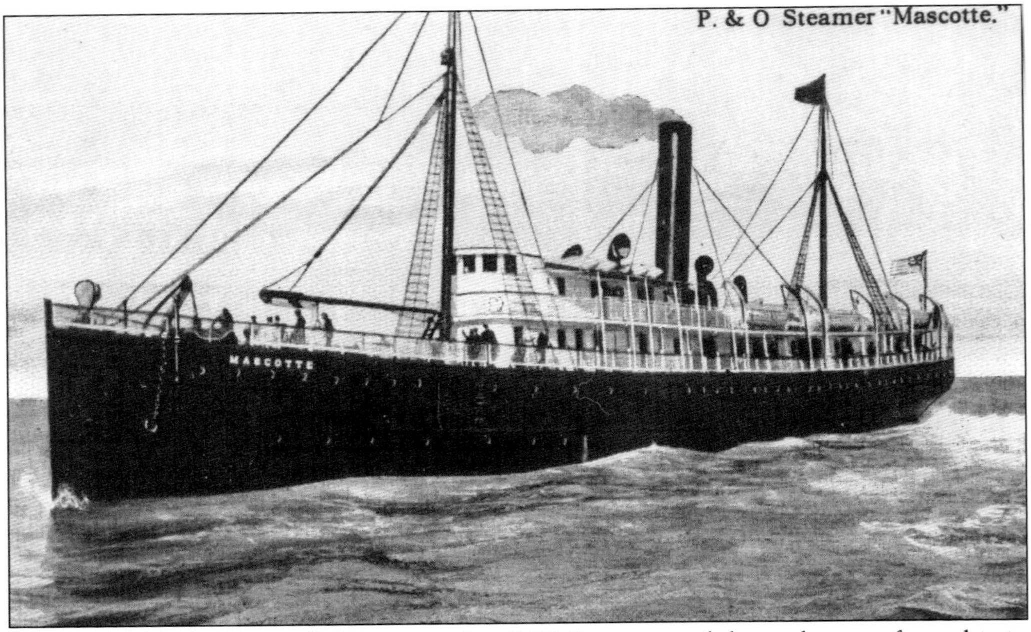

Tradition holds that former Baltimore resident J. W. Payne named the settlement after a ship in which he had an interest. The SS *Mascotte*, pictured here, was built in 1885 for the Peninsular and Oriental Steam Navigation Company. It ran between Tampa, Havana, Boston, and Maine. In 1898, it rescued more than 700 Americans after the explosion of the USS *Maine*. (Courtesy of the State Archives of Florida.)

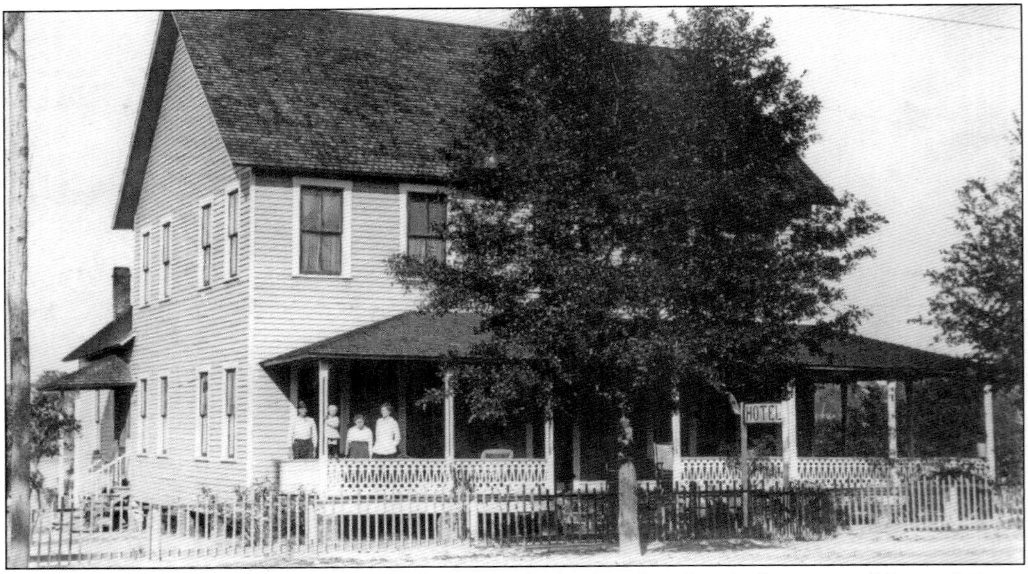

From 1919 to 1928, the Mascotte Hotel was run by husband and wife George and Susan Myers. George became Mascotte's first mayor in 1925. The street on which the hotel was located is the present-day Highway 50, which was named Myers Boulevard to honor its first mayor. The hotel was a popular destination for Northerners who came to the area to hunt. (Courtesy of Carol Murray Tomlinson.)

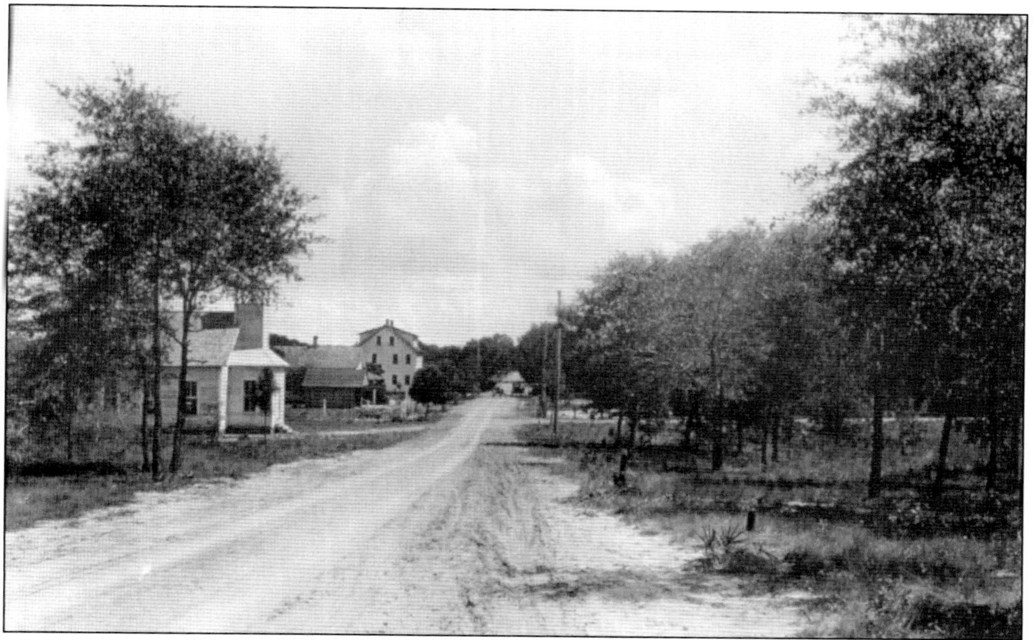

This eastbound view shows Mascotte in 1923. The dirt road became Highway 50. From left to right are the Methodist church, McConathy family garage and home, and the Mascotte Hotel. First United Methodist Church of Mascotte remains today and is one of the city's oldest surviving structures. (Courtesy of Peggy Parrish Sloan.)

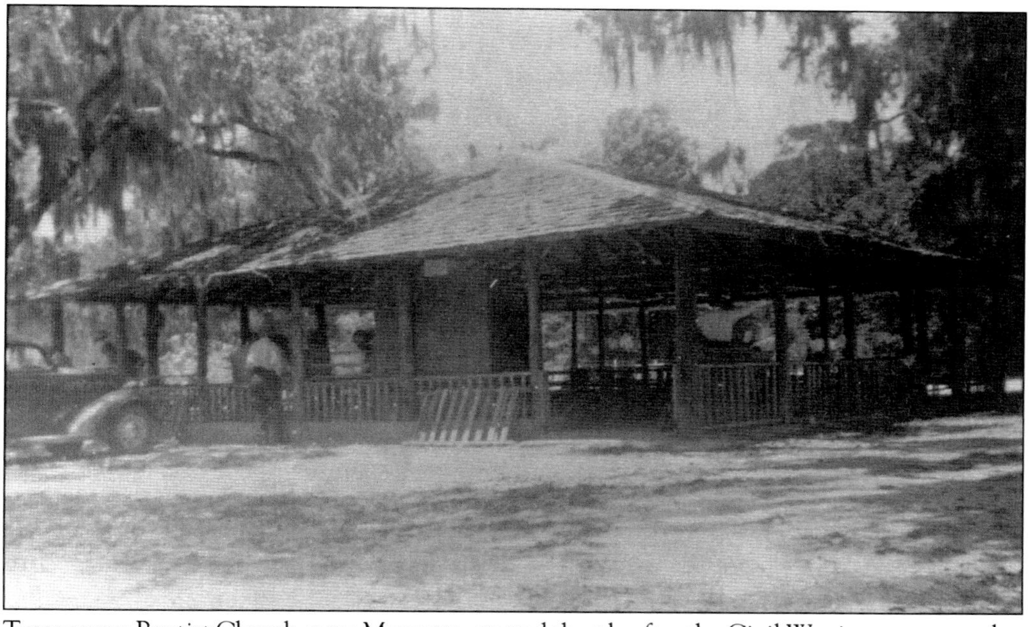

Tuscanooga Baptist Church, near Mascotte, started shortly after the Civil War in a one-room log cabin. Groveland pioneer Daniel Sloan preached here. A frame church built in 1897 was destroyed by a 1919 hurricane that killed more than 600 people in Florida and Texas. The congregation reorganized and built this open-air "Tabernacle" in 1933. Today the church has a modern facility and large, active membership. (Courtesy of Mary Helen Myers.)

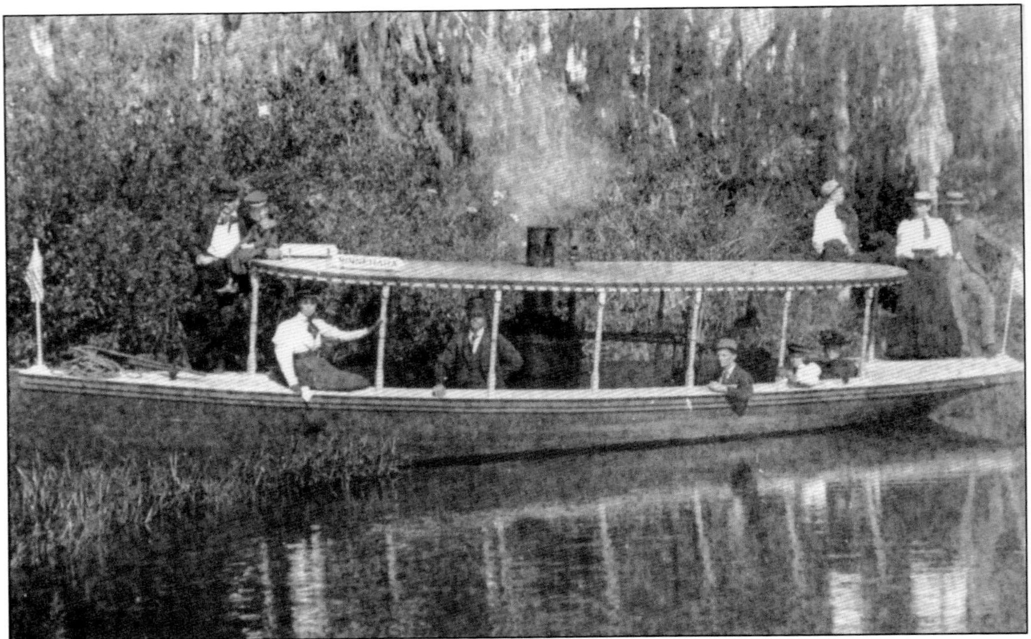

This 1902 photograph shows early Clermont settlers enjoying a steamboat ride on Lake Minnehaha. Steamboats, such as the one pictured here, were a popular means of transportation among the major trading areas of Lake County that included Clermont, Leesburg, and Groveland's Palalakaha Creek. (Courtesy of the State Archives of Florida.)

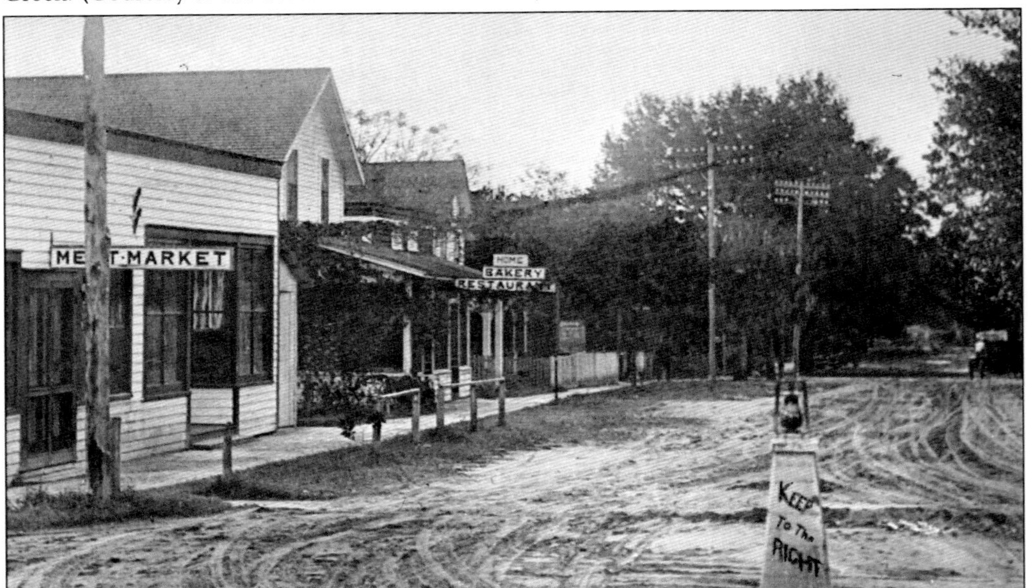

A sign of early Clermont's growth is this traffic signal at the intersection of Montrose Street and Seventh Street photographed looking west in 1908. The signal warns drivers to "Keep to the right." Clermont was mostly a truck-farming community with a few citrus groves at this time. Most shopping was done at Kern's General Merchandise Store on Montrose Street. (Courtesy of the State Archives of Florida.)

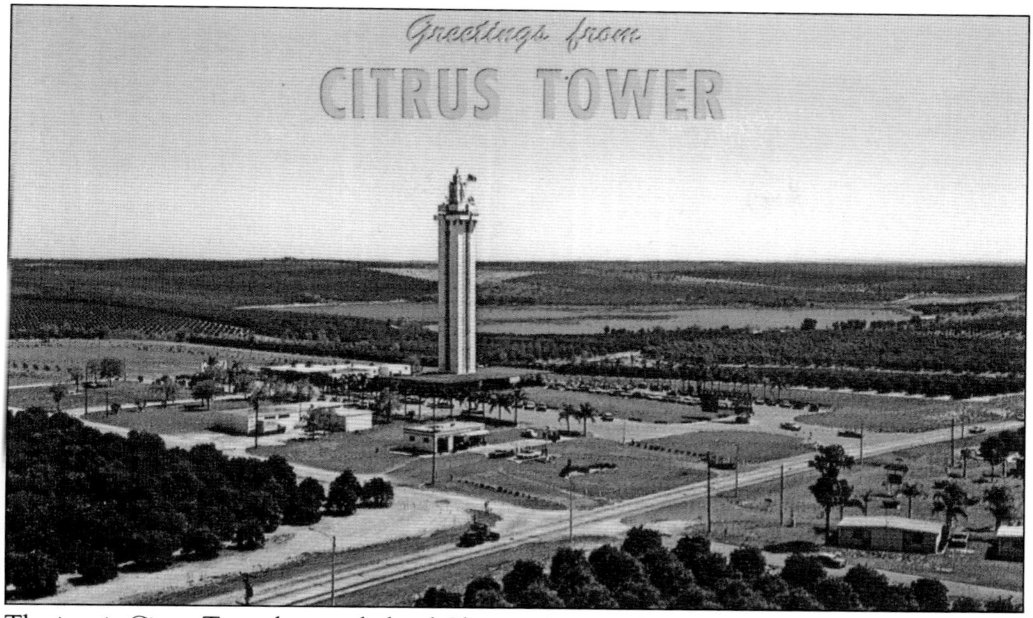

The iconic Citrus Tower has symbolized Clermont's scenic beauty since it opened in 1956. The 226-foot-high tower, constructed of steel and concrete on U.S. Highway 27, offered a spectacular view of thousands of acre of citrus groves, rolling hills, and lakes. A series of devastating freezes in the 1980s wiped out the groves, which were replaced by subdivisions. (Courtesy of the State Archives of Florida.)

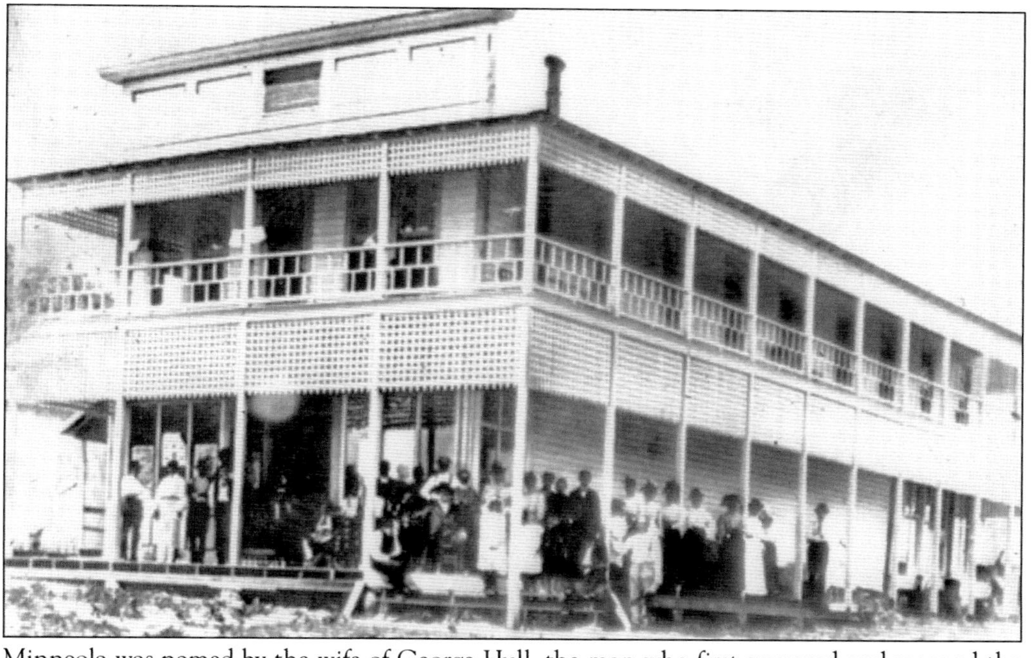

Minneola was named by the wife of George Hull, the man who first surveyed and mapped the community on the east side of Lake Minneola, formerly called Cow House Lake. Around 1890, W. G. Hanson built the store shown in this 1910 photograph. The store was owned by Duncan Campbell until it burned in 1945. (Courtesy of the State Archives of Florida.)

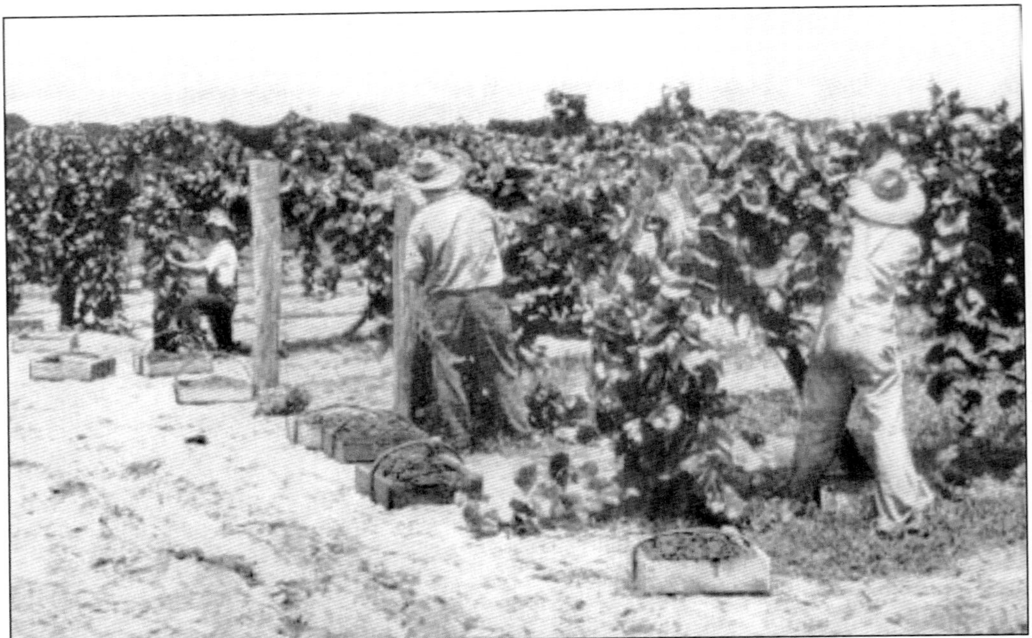

Before it gained a reputation for its internationally known Montverde Academy, the community was known for its grapes and vegetables. The rich muck soil bordering the west side of Lake Apopka made it an ideal place for growing grapes, shown being harvested in this 1920s postcard. Montverde was incorporated in 1924. (Courtesy of the State Archives of Florida.)

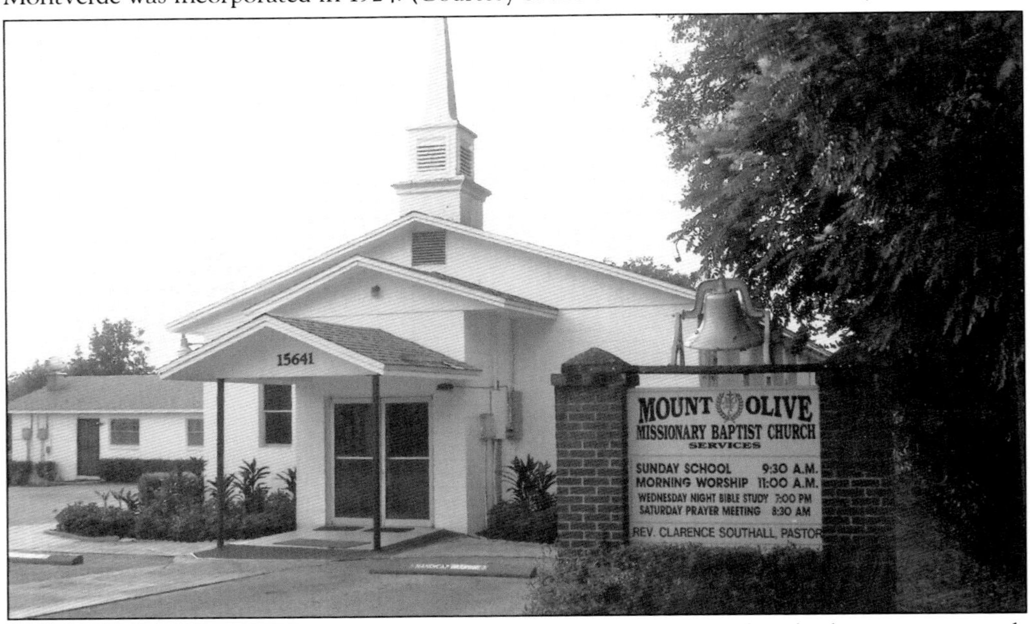

The Stuckey community, home to Mount Olive Missionary Baptist Church, shares its start with Groveland. Both were picked as turpentine still locations by brothers C. C. and B. M. Taylor. The close-knit Stuckey residents celebrate at the annual Stuckey Homecoming Celebration. Many of its earliest settlers were part of the logging crews that followed Groveland pioneer E. E. Edge. (Courtesy of the Groveland Historical Museum.)

About the Organization

The Groveland Historical Society is a 501(c)(3) nonprofit organization whose mission is to preserve the significant history of Groveland, Florida, for the education and enjoyment of the public. The Groveland Historical Museum is run under a cooperative partnership of the Groveland Historical Society and the City of Groveland. The museum is dedicated to the memory of Marilyn Gammon Smith, whose love of the community and its people inspired a movement to gather and share information, photographs, and memorabilia connected to the city's past. As Marilyn said shortly before her death, "You can't forget where you started." (Courtesy of the Groveland Historical Society.)

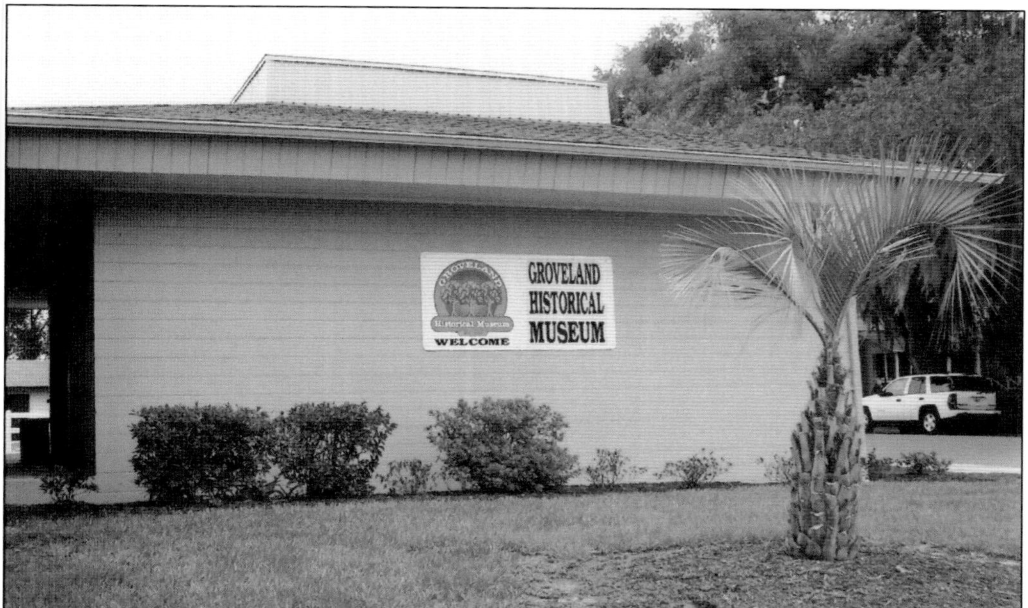

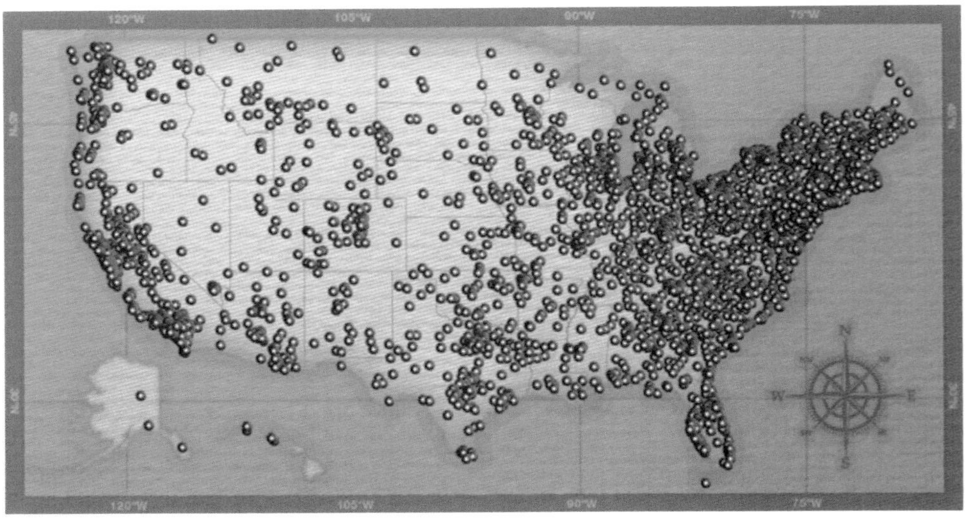